I0458939

A
MOUNTAIN
WITHIN

SPECIAL EDITION

RICK VASQUEZ

ISBN 978-1-969820-00-7 (paperback)

ISBN 978-1-969820-01-4 (hardcover)

ISBN 978-1-969820-02-1 (digital)

Copyright © 2025 by Rick Vasquez

Printed in the United States of America

From the Author

————————

Thank you for reading my novel. Before we begin, I would like to mention that I wrote this novel in 1976. I was twenty-three years old. I was born in the early 1950s and raised in the era of peace and love. In the early 1960s, it was a revolution of music, political rebellion, and uproar against parents, teachers, the police, and religion - anything that we were forced to believe as truth. This enlightenment from the young marked the beginning of a free-minded era. "Love the one you are with," generation. And guess what? Parents were too drunk, addicted to alcohol, their own generation's social dysfunction lost in their own lies. Trying to figure out what the truth really was.

By the time the Vietnam War came, the draft started in 1969, and was being used to conscript our young American boys into the Army. I was 15 years old at the time, and I saw the war as my final destination. Emerging myself in drugs and alcohol, trying to experience a lifetime of dreams, I too betrayed myself with drugs, free-minded philosophy, believing in the me concept. "You have to love yourself." Unfortunately, I had no idea who I was.

Please love the Lore family. A typical American family caught in the deception of the American Dream. I love the sisters. Mainly because they were given the gift of love from their Father, and understand the need in life for them to overcome their daily mountains.

Love you, Rick Vasquez

Dedication

I dedicate this book of love to all of us who have searched and wandered and found the true meaning of who our creator is:

Our Father, Our God,
who loves us and wants to be in each of our lives.

"Choose God."

RICK BB
P R O D U C T I O N S

Chapter 1

The Gathering of the Lore Sisters

2004, Medford, Tennessee

The small twin-sized bed filled the entire emergency recovery room of the hospital. The life support machines snuggled in tight at the head of the bed. The odor of death and disinfectant from the last patient hung heavy in the room. In the corner, dangling on a chair, was a small bundle of bloody towels that resembled human tissues or an excised organ from the last patient. Susan Lore, one of the middle sisters, thought it was ironic that the folds of the towels took on the face of Jesus. She didn't mention it to the others, mostly because she thought the timing wasn't appropriate, considering the last patient wasn't as fortunate as Dorine Honeycutt Lore.

The five Lore sisters surrounded the bed, staring at their mother. She was lying, recovering from a heart operation that was considered life-threatening. The surgeries had been complicated, and were it not for the machine's huffing and puffing, Dorine's life battle would be over.

At this moment, it was only a matter of time before she would recover. The Lore sisters thought it was severe enough for them to travel across the country to be by their mother's side.

Lana, the oldest sister, a 56-year-old, stood stoically at the foot of the bed. Her eyes glazed with a look of reminiscence, not allowing a smile or a frown. She just stared at the woman she had known as her mother. "I hate her." In an instant, silence filled the room. "I hate her. It's that simple. I don't hate this old woman lying in this bed. I hate the woman that she was our mother."

Kathy, the youngest of the sisters, stood up and put her arms around Lana. Lana continued. "I don't even want to be here. It doesn't matter to me if she lives or dies."

For many years, Lana and her mother had never resolved their bickering. Too many words had been left unspoken.

"John made me come." Lana was speaking about her husband, "He told me that I need to make things right before she dies. You know all those horrible things she did to us as a family. It all must be left behind. It all dies with her. When I see this old lady fighting for her life, it makes me mad.

Where was the effort to fight for our family? It makes me hate her more because, once again, it's all about her."

2

Chapter 2

Because We Are Lore Sisters

2004 Medford General Hospital

The small community hospital is in the middle of Medford, Tennessee. Throughout the years, buildings clustered around the hospital. A large circular driveway allowed temporary drop-offs, but visitors who did not want to pay the hourly parking fees thought parking was okay for free during the daytime.

A small sidewalk running the length of the building led the weary to the emergency entrance. A double door with aluminum siding dented by many hurried gurneys separated the healthy and the ill-hearted.

To the Lore sisters, all emergency room entrances seemed alike. It was the side door of mental terror. This hospital was no different as they exited, leaving their mother behind.

You could hear the buzz from the overused electrical wires above the hospital's roof.

The air was thick, still waiting for the promised breeze of the early morning. The moon peeked through clusters of clouds, not allowing one to enter or escape without being noticed.

The doors automatically opened inward, sucking in all the warm, humid air. The heaviness of God's sweat and the hospital's stale odor gave off a scent of misery. The five sisters, leaving the hospital, approached the emergency door. Lana lifted her head as if she were finishing a race. Diane and Kathy held each other's arms and followed their sister with the confidence that she knew where she was going. Alice and Susan staggered behind, feeling the fatigue of the long day that had passed.

Alice exploded, "This is Bullshit! Bullshit! Bullshit!"

Susan grabbed her and pulled her aside. "You can't say bullshit so loud!" Looking around to see if anybody had heard her sister.

The youngest sister, Kathy, stopped Diane in motion and turned to Alice. "The doctor said that she is going to be okay. At least she'll be alive."

Lana turned and responded to Kathy. "No way, not even the devil can take that woman so easily."

Diane pulled away from Kathy and flopped down on the cement curb. "I'm so sick and tired of all we have been through." She paused, hoping this was the right time to vent their past.

She raised her hand in the air, pushing away hate, misery, pain, and sorrow. A tear glistened in her eye and rolled down her cheek. "It's not fair that we are damned to such sorrows and tragedies. Do we have to die ourselves before we can have peace in our lives?"

Alice, the second oldest by 18 months, always ready to give a hug, rushed to Diane's side, struggling to sit next to her on the curb.

Susan, the beautiful peach with a bruised dark side, was the middle child, already insecure with life's lessons. She leaned her body against a pole and covered her mouth with the horrible thought of death to end all pain.

It was Kathy who gathered her strength from her faith in God. "You'll see, we can endure this; Jesus will see us through."

Susan gathered herself and reminded her sister. "We're the Lore Sisters. We can make it through anything if we have each other." Susan said with confidence instilled in her by her father.

Diane raised her hand to the sky. "My Sisters, my family."

Lana, still pretty from the soft life that her husband provided for her, quietly added, "Daddy would be proud of us that we are here right now together."

Diane nodded her head. "No matter what she did to us, he would have wanted us to give her all our support."

Kathy grabbed a pole supporting the entrance of the emergency building. "We just need to trust Jesus that she'll be okay."

Alice shied out," That's a lot of shit to put on Jesus," Not saying shit too loud.

Kathy, not ready to accept a life of doom, pleaded with her sisters. "Let's go home. I'm hungry."

Alice, the fixer of all, scrambled up from the curb. "Let's go to Diane's house. I'll make us a big breakfast."

"Make mine a Bloody Mary," Diane said, extending her hand for Alice to pull her up.

As she always has been, Susan, being thin, agreed with her baby sister. "I'm starved. I didn't even stop to eat on the way from the airport."

Alice nudged Diane. "Hum, right, like she'll take two bites and be full."

Diane laughed and added. "Then, she'll have the nerve to ask us, do you all think I'm getting fat?" Diane bent over, laughing at her sister.

Susan struck back at Alice, "Just because I didn't win a pie-eating contest doesn't mean I should be considered different."

Alice snapped back, "I was ten years old, and Daddy made me. It wasn't as though I had to eat several pies. It was who could eat one pie the fastest." Alice explained.

The girls all laughed, loving every moment that they shared. Resenting that, it seemed only the hard times had brought them together again.

Chapter 3

Breakfast at Diane's

2004: Medford, Tennessee, Diane's house

One by one, the sisters were starting to awake from the previous night. Diane was sitting on her couch, smoking a cigarette, which she had never done before noon, especially inside the house. Diane had lost her husband to a massive heart attack not more than six months ago, and breaking her house rules seemed petty in comparison to what she had been through the last two years.

Kathy had a positive relationship with her mother and had risen early to visit Dorine at the hospital. Dorine never woke up during the visit. It made Kathy feel better that somebody was there with her, just in case she was to wake up. Kathy prayed to God on behalf of her mother. It was a time of peace without hearing Lana complaining about what a terrible mother she was. After her visit, she went to the grocery store with a long list from Alice.

Alice, the family cook, was in her robe and started cooking breakfast for everyone.

Susan walked into the kitchen from the guest bedroom wearing a Jersey Cow pajama bottom and a football T-shirt cut to fit her midriff.

Lana was on the telephone, talking to her husband, John. "I don't know when I'm coming home. We'll find out what condition she will be in today," Lana explained.

"Good morning, girls," Susan gave a tired smile.
Diane came back with a cheery "Good morning, Sis. Coffee is on the counter." She announced to Susan.

Susan redirected herself to the kitchen, giving Diane the okay sign. Alice was flipping eggs and placing the bacon on the opposite side of the skillet. "Sugar, can you eat some breakfast?" Alice asked.

Susan sighed, "I'm still full from last night."

Alice snickered, which made Susan smile.

Kathy entered the side door that led to the garage. She had two bags of groceries ready to spill out and a six-pack of water huddled to her chest. "I can't believe they can charge so much for bottled water." She said, setting the water on the table.

"Did you get to see Mama?" Diane asked from the living room, genuinely concerned.

"She was still asleep. The nurse told me to tell you *all* not to come by until after 11:00 am. They're hoping that Mama will sleep throughout the morning," Kathy reported, sitting in the living room with Diane.

Lana hung up the beige telephone, kissing her husband through the receiver. She listened to her sisters talking about their mother and had to ask. "Hey, I want to know when we started to call her Mama. Was it when she demanded that Daddy move you, Southern Belles, to Texas?"

Alice, unable to stay out of it, said, "We called her mama occasionally, too, Lana."

Lana turned to Alice. "I guess she wasn't around enough for me to remember what I called her. Most of the time, I called her names that were a lot worse than Mama."

Diane started to giggle, knowing her sister Lana's humor. "Listen. We have to talk about what we are going to do when she gets out of the hospital."

Silence came over the room. Kathy was the first one to respond. "My life is so hectic. We just opened up another new branch, and I am so busy training new people for the office. Larry is hardly home; frankly, I don't know how to tell him. You know Mama and Larry have never been able to get along."

"Who the hell does get along with her?" Lana took a glass of orange juice and sat next to Diane.

"I can't," Diane whispered, barely loud enough to be heard. "I just buried my husband and spent the last two years taking care of him. I'm drained. I would have no patience for her."

Alice responded from the kitchen. "You know what's sad? If Daddy had been in this position, we would have taken him in a minute."

"That's because he was a good Dad, the only one who was always there for us," Lana said sternly.

"I was kind of afraid of him." Kathy carefully said. "Maybe it was because he spent so much time and energy on Steven, you know, him being the youngest and a boy. Daddy seemed to care about him more, and I just felt like he didn't have the time for me."

"What the hell are you talking about? He loved each of us so much. Daddy worked so hard to give us a normal life." Lana said defensively.

Kathy looked for help from her sisters, "Come on, Diane, Susan, you guys know. When we got to Texas, Mama started her games with Daddy, and he started drinking a lot. Sometimes, when he came home, he was scary to me."

"You know, Lana, you weren't there when we got to Texas. Don't get me wrong, Daddy was still emotionally there for us, but nobody gave a thought about how difficult it was for us to be in a new place with parents who loved and hated each other." Susan said, defending Kathy.

Diane stepped in. "We *all* were falling apart. You and Alice were in Minnesota. Susan, you wanted nothing to do with me, Kathy, or Steven. And Kathy, you were always so sad because we were different and poor, and it bothered you."

"Of course, it bothered me! We had nothing. We talked funny, and yes, I was embarrassed because we were so poor." Kathy said as her face turned red. "It was as though we lost our whole family when we left Minnesota," Diane said

"I think Daddy should have just let her go. He could have found a new wife in Minnesota." Lana said, bowing her head in defense of her father.

"But, we younger ones found ourselves lost and alone in Texas," Susan reflected. Alice blurted out to Susan, "I remember you weren't so alone for too long."

"Susan blurted back, "Hell no, I wasn't about to put up with Mama or Daddy's games of it's over, no, we're back together bullshit. Besides, nobody was there to tell us if we were doing right or wrong."

Now, it was Diane who was crying.

"I'm not Daddy's child."

All the sisters looked at Diane for an explanation. When Tom, Diane's husband, had his first heart attack. Dorine came out to console her. She got drunk and told Diane that she had a different father."

Year 2000:

Diane and her mother were in the living room. It was late evening, and Dorine had been drinking all night. Tom was in the hospital and had his first heart attack, and nobody knew how serious it was at the time. Diane was crying over her husband, scared of losing the love of her life. Her mother was sitting next to her, belting down the whiskey. "Sugar, sometimes life isn't what we expect it to be." Dorine's eyes were wandering, and her speech slurred. "Your Daddy and I were on one of our off periods, you know, well, I found company with another man. You would think, after all, you kids, I would know better, but I found myself pregnant. The man ran like a scared coyote, and I had nowhere to go. So, your Daddy took me back." Dorine laughed as if she were telling a funny story.

Diane had a living room pillow in her arms, and she squeezed it so hard she nearly punctured it. She could not believe the stranger sitting next to her was her mother, a woman who had just admitted that she had gotten pregnant by a stranger.

Diane was disgusted. She screamed at her mother. "I'm losing my husband, and you think this is a good time to tell me that the man I have loved as my father was not really my father?" Diane got up, threw the pillow onto the couch, and left the room. She wanted to keep screaming at her mother, but instead, she slammed the bedroom door, collapsed onto her bed, and cried.

14

2004, Medford, Tennessee

"What the hell kind of consoling was that? How could she do that?" Diane cried, not able to look at her sisters.

Alice raced to her sister's side. "You know how much he loved you, like we all." Alice tried to comfort her. "Besides, look at me. I look nothing like the rest of you. But to tell you the truth, Michael Lore will always be my Daddy, no matter what Mama would tell me."

Diane closed her eyes and nodded her head.

"That drunken bitch!" Lana exclaimed, "I hate her even more now."

"Hell, we *all* are probably not from Daddy. Susan interjected. "But no matter what she says, my Daddy is my Daddy, who was there when nobody was around to hear my cries. Susan got up, knelt next to Diane, and hugged her legs. "Mama was such a fool; she had the best, which wasn't good enough for her."

Kathy rubbed her stomach, trying to soothe the acid boiling inside, thinking about how she would break it to her husband that her mother was coming to live with them. "Okay, now *who's* going to care for her?"

Silence came upon the room; the sisters looked at Kathy and laughed. Susan was the first to speak. "What part of these last few minutes didn't you hear? She can burn in hell as far as I'm concerned."

Alice chuckled, "If we keep thinking of our past relationships with Mama, we should try to find the compassion to care for her in her last days. We may as well lock her up and throw away the key," Alice said.

Even Lana had to smile at that comment.

Chapter 4

Dorine Honeycutt Lore The Sister's Mother

1929 Middletown, Kentucky.

Dorine Honeycutt, the sister's mother, was born in 1929 in the blue hills of Goldenville, Kentucky. Dorine, a young teenager, loved her mother but couldn't understand why her mother tolerated the verbal disrespect and physical abuse she received from her husband and siblings.

The males viewed women as objects to serve their needs. They treated Dorine, her sister, and her mother without respect for their self-worth. Her mother kept the family together with all her hard work and diligence.

The house was a rotted wooden structure with knot holes as big as baseballs. The windows, covered with a screening material, kept giant insects from venturing on each of them. On the backside of the house, far behind the trees, was the moonshine still.

Dorine's Grandpa established the still back in the days when alcohol was legal, and it is now used by her family, bringing them an income. Unfortunately for her family, their business was illegal due to prohibition, which caused all sales to be conducted underground. There seemed to be a lot of private sales used for medicinal purposes only. Now, her father used the distillery as their only source of income. Most of the time, her father and brothers would return drunk from the testing of the quality of the alcohol they produced, treating the girls as if they were their servants.

"Damn it, Dorine, get these boots off my feet." Dorine's father would command.

Dorine would run over and unlace his shoes as if relieving him of his discomfort was an honor. While Dorine was pulling off his boots, her sister Peggy would run a large glass of water she had brought to the house from the cool stream earlier in the day.

Susie, Dorine's mother, would be in the kitchen trying to make the meal a success to please her husband and sons.

The boys disturbed Dorine. "Mama, Dorine won't cut my toenails." Said her brother, too drunk to bend over and cut them himself.

Susie ran over, picked up the clippers, and pushed Dorine out of the way. "It's only the big toe that needs it. You don't want them to be too short, or else they'll get stuck in the sides." Susie told her son.

Dorine was the fourth of nine children. She had three older brothers, herself, and a sister who was barely a year younger than she. Maybe it would have been different for her and her sister if she had been the oldest, but having older brothers was the worst. Nothing was beautiful about being a girl or a woman in this family. And there was no knowledge other than a gut feeling that her family's behavior wasn't normal.

The five older kids shared one of the bedrooms, while the younger kids, consisting of three girls and one boy, slept in their parents' room.

Dorine hated her life at home. With all the abuse, there was no peace in her life. The boys were always helping their father, and Dorine expected to be the second mother in the house, cleaning, making dinners out of scraps, and milking a dried-up old cow. These were Dorine's daily chores. At night starting, when Dorine was nine years old, she had to put up with the molestation and subsequent rape from her brothers.

One afternoon, a cloudy, humid, sultry day, when Dorine was twelve. She and her mother were sitting on the porch shucking peas that grew wildly over by the south side of the stream.

"Mama," Dorine hesitantly began to speak her peace. "The boys are touching me."

Dorine's mother didn't stop her stride. "That's life, Dorine. It was life for me and will be life for you and your children."

Dorine grabbed her mother's hand to make her stop. "It's my body. You have to stop them. Tell them it's wrong." Angry tears welled up in Dorine's eyes.

Dorine's mother pulled away from her grip, ready to slap her. "You don't be making trouble for your brothers. I'm telling you, it's just the way it is."

Dorine's mother continued her peeling. She threw the empty pods on the floor between her and Dorine. "You best better start thinking about learning how to serve your man, or else no man is going to want you."

"Mama, I want a man who loves me. A man who will take care of me, and not because I let him touch me."

"No man just wants a woman for company. God gave us the ability to please a man, and we must like it because that's life. And you should learn now how to please a man. Not just with your body, but what a man really needs. A good touch that only a woman can give him."

Dorine asked her mother. "Shouldn't this touch be only for one special person, like you and Daddy?"

"That touch is what keeps a woman alive. It's not there for your pleasure but for his pleasure. It makes him work hard to bring you food and a house to live in. Now, don't you be thinking all these foolish things. You just be ready to serve your brothers, and then you will learn how to be a proper woman. Any man will see you know how to please a man, and then he'll marry you."

"Mama, that's horrible. I want to please my husband, but did you have to please your brothers?"
"Yes, and my Mama had to please her brothers. It's what we women do. That's what God made us for."

"Mama, why do you let Daddy always yell at you? He calls you names, and sometimes you'll let him hit you. Why? Is he always right?"

"If I want to eat, he is. Oh, don't look so surprised if I complained every time your father was wrong; well, I don't know where this family would be."

Dorine cried out, "I want to be happy. I'm trying to be a good girl, but sometimes it doesn't seem right. To them, I'm no better than that pig in the pen. That can't be right." Dorine sobbed to her mother.

"Your brothers need to learn how to respect a woman. I guess that's my fault for letting them have their way, but they don't mean any harm. Your brothers love you."

Dorine couldn't help feeling dirty as a person, as a woman. It wasn't the physical act of sex that bothered her. It was how she felt empty, like somebody had taken a piece of her soul, leaving only enough for her to survive.

Chapter 5

The Great Escape

1944 Middleton Kentucky

Dorine was fifteen years old and knew she had to leave the house. For too many years, she dreamed about going, hoping to find a world that made sense. A world where a woman was more than an object of men's unfulfilled fantasies, and Dorine needed life with real meaning and freedom from within to be happy. All of which she never felt at home. If she was going to give her body, it was going to be her choice, her terms, her profit.

It was the day after her 15th birthday. They were sitting around the table, preparing for dinner. Dorine served her father and brothers, ensuring they had enough food, and then she and her sisters and mother were allowed to eat. The girls all sat, and Dorine's father led a prayer. After the boys said Amen, everybody started to eat.

Intimidated by her father, Dorine had decided today was the day she would ask permission to leave. For extra strength, Dorine took an extra gulp of her hooch for courage. "Daddy, I want to move to the city."

Dorine's father looked up from his plate. "You live here. This mountain is your home."

"I want to leave home and start a life in the city where I'll have an opportunity to meet a husband." Dorine knew the opportunity to meet a husband would pique her father's ears.

"How are you going to care for yourself?" Her father asked.

"I have my birthday money since I was ten years old, and every penny that has come my way." Dorine took pride in her hidden treasure.

Dorine's father wasn't about to decide right there at dinner. Dorine realized that, but knew she had to put it on the table.

Marvin, Dorine's Father, was silent; out of nowhere, he pushed his plate of food all over the table. "Damn it, Sue, I work all day. I won't put up with Dorine or any of your girl 'desires' in life. "Your only desire is to make us men happy. Do you understand, little girl?" Marvin was talking directly to Dorine, ready to give her a good slap.

Susie quickly left her plate of food and rushed to her husband's side. She started rubbing his neck and whispering in his ear.

Feeling scared and sick, Dorine got up and took her plate to the kitchen sink. She knew she was close to a beating and needed to get out of her Daddy's sight.

"It's okay, honey." Susie whispered to Marvin, "I've been talking to her about pleasing a man."

Marvin grabbed his crotch. "Maybe she needs a lesson from me."

Susie kissed him on the neck. "She needs a lesson from somebody. She thinks life is a free ride."

Marvin put his arm around his wife's head. "You're a good woman."

"Just for you... Just for you, sweetheart." Susie continued to flatter and dote on her husband.

The boys finished their meal and left the table to head outside. The oldest boy stopped and pulled Peggy's hair. "Fetch me some water for a bath. Make that Dorine help you." He released her, and she almost dropped her plate and cup. She shifted both right and left until they were once again stable. Peggy quickly went into the kitchen and put the dishes in the sink. She went to the porch, picked up the water bucket, and ran to the pump by the side of the house.

Dorine stuck her head out the window and whispered to Peggy, "I'm sorry."

Not another word was spoken about Dorine leaving until a month later. Dorine had pretty much given up the hope of leaving the house with her Daddy's blessing. To make peace in the family, Dorine submitted to her brothers as a wife would to her husband. No love, no compassion, just trying to get through the night. Her dreams faded each day, not allowing them to surface. She knew that thinking such foolish thoughts would only cause her to run away or end her life. In the past, her mother would tell each of the kids horror stories about living off the mountain. Dorine was sure that she wouldn't make it in life away from home. For sure, no man would ever love her. She would live life alone, having to beg for food and shelter.

It wasn't until her cousin Lana came to live with the family. Lana was a rebellious child in the eyes of her parents. Lana was an only child, and her father thought she was spoiled and figured maybe her male cousins could show her how a woman should act.

Lana was a thin wisp of a fifteen-year-old girl. She had recently had a child, and when her father forced her to give the child up, she ran away. Lana made it to Goldenville but had no money and no way of supporting herself. She was away for one month. It was the best month of her life. When all hope of survival was gone, Lana returned to her family's little mountain and begged her Father to forgive her and allow her to come home.

Daddy, please, I'll never leave again." Lana pleaded with her father.

"It's just not that easy. I'm going to get a hold of my sister, and I think you need to stay with them for a while. When you can appreciate all that your Mama and I have given you, you can come home."

The following day, Dorine's Uncle Darrell came to visit. Dorine's father and brothers had just arrived from the still for a quick lunch when a cart and horse appeared at the bottom of the hill. The cart pulled into the yard, and the boys and Dorine's Father surrounded both Darrell and Lana. Dorine, her mother, and other sisters stopped their work and waited on the porch, allowing the men to find out who the visitor was.

"Susie!" Marvin yelled from the cart. "Get over here, woman. It's your brother who's a coming to visit."

Susie ran from the porch with the girls following. "Well, I'll be, Darrel? It's been a long while since you have come this way."

Susie said, raising her hands to the sky in excitement.

Susie's brother looked between the boys and smiled when he saw his sister. "The road has two directions on it, missy, and I would have loved to see you all."

They both grinned as Susie jumped in the air for her brother to catch her. Darrel embraced his sister and swung her in circles. They both laughed as the rest of the family shouted excitedly about the reunion.

Looking through the cracks between her brothers, Dorine noticed a young girl with long, light brown hair hanging in her face. Dorine caught staring as the girl directed a smile at her. Dorine smiled back, only to lose it when she noticed the girl's face was bruised and swollen.

"Everybody, this here is my daughter, Lana." Lana bowed her head with a weak smile. "Don't you be a shy girl; this here is family." Lana raised her head and gave a bigger smile. Nobody mentioned the obvious, and each cousin smiled back, welcoming her to their family.

Darrel was embarrassed but asked Marvin if his daughter could stay with them for a while. Of course, Marvin would never turn down Susie's brother, having been taken in himself by Susie's family. Dorine thought to herself. "Is he nuts? He's leaving his only daughter with the boys from hell."

Lana moved her things into the bedroom, and Dorine gave up her bed to her cousin. Dorine reached out and touched her cousin's eye. "Are you okay?" she whispered. Lana looked around and nodded.

That night, while they were supposed to be asleep, Lana whispered the story of how she received the bruises.

"It was my own fault. When I returned from Goldenville, I knew I would get the licking of my life. At first, Daddy was calm, happy that I had returned. He started a little quiet, still not accepting that I left our home. However, he gave me a swift hug, and it seemed that all was going to blow over. But after dinner, while we were still sitting at the table, he just reached over and socked me. I flew from the table, and by the time I could think of what had happened, he was all over me. Crying, slapping, yelling, it was horrible. My Mama was just watching, knowing she couldn't interfere. "He finally let me go, and I ran to my bedroom. He woke me up this morning, and we headed over here."

Dorine felt sorry for her cousin. She undoubtedly understood the discipline process of their parents and believed they were right to punish them physically. Her father would say. "It's for your own good. Nobody can go through life without remembering where all the bumps in the road are. And if the punishment is light, then who's to know if you won't try it again."

That was the sincere belief of the mountains, at least their family mountain. Punish them so they will never try it again.

It didn't take long before her brothers were all over Lana. Dorine would pretend to be asleep, but she could hear every muffled scream that Lana let escape.

When her brothers and father were away during the day, Dorine drained Lana of any information about city life. She knew there was more to life than what she had at home. She allowed Lana's stories to fill her soul with hope. "Why did you come back?" Dorine asked Lana while they were separating good beans from bad.

"You have to have either a man or your own money." Looking around to see that nobody else could hear, "And I had neither. I couldn't find a job and had no place to stay. I was living on the streets, but every night, I had to worry about being arrested by the police. I just wanted to make a living and not have to come home. But living on the street was hard, trying to stay clean and keeping my few clothes together in order. Well, nobody wanted to give me a job. I think I looked as though I was going to steal or rob them, plus not having a place to live didn't help matters." Lana looked to the end of the yard, knowing there must be a way to make it. There was so much fear that Lana had no other choice but to come home. She gave up the dream and resolved herself to her father's punishment. A smile came upon Lana's face, "You should have seen all the beautiful men, all dressed up, and their hair all slicked back. Next time I'll be ready. I'll have money, and I'll find a job, and I'll live in a house with pretty flowers surrounding the front yard, and I'll meet somebody and get married." Staying on Lana's dream, Dorine shook her head; she felt sad for Lana because she had failed and returned home.

It was a few months after Dorine's birthday. The summer evenings lingered as the sun dropped into the Kentucky Mountains. Dorine's father was enjoying the sunset, sitting in his chair, watching the last ray of light disappear. Bored with the day, Dorine sat on the porch steps and regretted the thought of the nighttime rituals to come.

"You know, your mama and I didn't have you kids so that you could run off and live outside of our lives." Her father stared out to the horizon. "We are family, and family sticks together. But you have always been different, always asking them damn questions. And now you want to leave, thinking it's better out there. I'm telling you now: home is the only place a girl needs to be. Until God brings the right man, and then she should marry. But going out and finding a man is like telling God he doesn't know what he's doing."

Dorine's mother was listening by the doorway. Dorine kept her eye on her father, showing him her respect. "But, as much as it will break my heart, I'm going to let you go."

Dorine smiled, stood up from the porch steps, and hugged her Father. "Thank ya, Daddy. I'll make you proud of me." "Just be a happy child. And make me lots of grandchildren."

Dorine's mother came out of the house and hugged her eldest daughter. She knew once Dorine had permission from her father, she would be gone. It was incomprehensible to her to think that life was more than they could provide. To Susie, life was her family. Nothing going on in the world was essential to her. She had her husband, her children, and their humble home. That was her life. She was unhappy with her husband's decision, but she figured Dorine would see all the horrors of the city and be back in no time.

Dorine turned to her mother and smiled. "Don't you go worrying about me; I'll be okay." Dorine's mother hugged her and didn't allow a tear to flow.

The following morning, before the sun had a chance to rise, Dorine put on her best-patched dress and second-hand shoes that her father bought her for Christmas. Everyone was still asleep except Lana, who helped Dorine arrange her bundle of clothes and personal necessities. She wouldn't allow herself to stop and think of her loss. Lana desperately wanted to go with Dorine but couldn't betray her aunt and uncle, who were responsible for her. So, the best she could do was make sure Dorine successfully escaped the life of the mountains. Dorine announced before breakfast, which was risky in itself, that she was ready to leave. Her father started to protest, especially since he had just awakened and had nothing in his stomach. But he just blew out some air and waved his hand as if pushing her away. Her mother pulled Dorine aside, not wanting to upset her husband. "Now you just wait one minute; if you're going, you will say a proper goodbye, and nobody is ready for that before breakfast."

It wasn't as though breakfast was the main meal in the house. Some of her brothers often skipped it. Marvin would have his usual two pieces of bread heated up on the stove and a cup of coffee. He would drink plain water if there were no coffee in the house. Her brothers were not big breakfast eaters, trading breakfast for an extra hour of sleep. So Dorine sighed and made a face that her mother didn't appreciate. "No, you know what, just take your bag and head on out of here if you are in such a hurry to be gone." Dorine didn't want to fight with her mother and conceded to delay her departure until after breakfast.

Her brothers were waiting for their father on the porch. He came out partially dressed, ready to head for work. Dorine stepped out and bid her brothers goodbye. Each of them, from the eldest to the youngest, kissed their sister goodbye. Her sister Peggy cried, feeling abandoned by her, and the younger ones attached themselves to her legs, showing their love for their sister. Lana refused to shed any tears. Dorine's leaving the mountain was a glorious occasion, Dorine's first day of true freedom.

Dorine gave a last wave when she reached the bottom of the mountain, but her family had already continued with their daily chores. Several times in Dorine's life, she had made it to the bottom of the hill, but this time would be different. One more bend on the dirt road and the mountain will no longer be her home. Dorine heard a single shot fired into the air. A hillbilly's sign, a family has left the mountain.

Chapter 6

Friends Forever

1920s: Rutterfield, Tennessee

Michael Lore, the sisters' father, was raised in the small town of Rutterfield. His parents married in Germany and migrated to the United States in the early '20s. When they arrived in New York, the immigration department changed his name from Lorenzo to Lore. Michael's father didn't know enough English to protest, and their papers made it final. They decided to move on and venture through the country. By the time they got to Tennessee, they were disheartened by the lack of jobs and the attitudes they faced because they could only speak a limited amount of English. Michael's father, Arne Lore, heard that there was work for all and a German community in the town of Rutterfield. Arne was a quiet man, never having much to say. His lack of facial expressions made it seem that life was never good to him, but rather a matter of mere existence.

Arne was married to Michael's mother, Erica. Their families had arranged their marriage. The only bond they shared was their desire to work and work hard.

Rutterfield, in the early '20s, was a main street with a handful of houses scattered behind the stores. Several farms were on the west side of town, and on the east side, along the railroad tracks, shanties were built for the transients. Michael's father rented one of these huts. He did not realize that they were typically reserved for the black folk migrating with the farming seasons. Arne's logic was that the shack was empty, and the owner, a businessman from town, was happy to rent it to a white family, even though they didn't speak much English.

Arne got two jobs, one working on a farm on the west side and the other at the general store, stocking shelves nightly. It wasn't long before they moved closer into town. The Lores bought a small two-bedroom house next door to three other German families. The small town was growing, providing new opportunities for ambitious people. Michael's father quit his farming job to become the general store manager. Even though he chose his career, Arne hated it. He hated people. He was a loner who didn't see the need for friends, but for some reason, maybe it was Michael's mother, they decided to have a child.

Erica was a strong-boned German woman. She had no idea that people of her day had style, and she wore an outfit until it was reduced to rags. Then, she would purchase more second-hand clothes until they became unusable. In the morning, she would tie a scarf over her head, and at night, she would take it off before going to bed. There was nothing attractive about her. She was born to be a worker. She would leave the house each morning before the sun rose and work on a farm, milking cows, churning butter, and cleaning stables. When the sun settled on the horizon, it was time for her to go home. Even during her pregnancy, she continued this rigid work schedule. There was no choice; they needed the money to survive, and having a baby was a luxury, not a necessity.

Michael was born on February 9, 1926, one month earlier than expected, and, of course, there was little medical help available in those days. To Michael's parents, it became clear that there was a good chance Michael might not survive. The family next door heard the screams from Michael's mother and rushed over and helped her. Michael was stuck facing the wrong way. The German neighbor physically reached in, turned Michael around, and pulled him out. The crisis was over, and Michael survived.

In 1931, several bible organizations had made Rutterfield their home. These people and their money started the westward movement from downtown Rutterfield.

Even though their churches reached high on the west side, they would invariably seek out the people on the east side to save. A person pounding a drum or clanging a symbol, anything that would attract attention, would be used to get people to listen to their message.   A genuine revival began to brew when the East Side residents started to feel separate from their town. The people of the West used their smiles and good intentions to build new buildings. Their new leadership dominated the politics that ruled the town's growth. To Michael's parents, it didn't make a difference. They just wanted to work and raise their son. They didn't care what went on over on the west side.

Michael's mother didn't know how to be a mother. She was demanding, overstressed, and always riding Michael for something. She didn't know how to express love to her son. To her, love was providing a roof and food on the table. When he was young, his mother would bundle him up and carry him to work. When he was three years old, they sought their neighbor's help, paying for these services with her hard-earned money. With his parents always working, Michael learned to care for himself. He felt unwanted and knew he was a burden to his parents. Most of the time, Michael kept to himself in his bedroom, trying not to disturb his parents. Like any child, there were times that Michael would reach out to life and sometimes act out. His mother took his father's belt and became the family's disciplinarian.

At the age of five, Michael started Kindergarten. The neighbor children walked him to school on the first day and dropped him off near his classroom. Michael's birth-given name was Michel. The kids giggled and laughed when he introduced himself to the class, saying he had a girl's name. The teacher explained that the name Michel is a boy's name in some countries. One boy stood up and said, "Maybe Michel is short for Michael." The kids all knew that name, and the explanation was accepted. From that day on, Michel was Michael.

The kids in his class tried to talk and play with him, but Michael didn't know how to play or react to them. Soon, the kids ignored him. Feeling the alienation, Michael sat in his seat, waiting for the day to end.

Jimmy Parker, the boy who stood up for Michael's name in front of the class, was the exact opposite of Michael. Jimmy was loud, overactive, and had difficulty keeping his hands to himself. Before long, the classmates began to avoid Jimmy. Jimmy was the kind of kid who would ask other boys to ask their mothers if he could come over and play. If they refused, he would twist their arms, pull their hair, or just scream in their ears. Most mothers saw through this and would come up with excuses. "Not today, maybe someday next week. Jimmy can come over after school." Next week never came.

Even though Michael was quiet and Jimmy was reckless, Jimmy approached Michael, reached out, and took his hand. "Hey, friends, forever." Jimmy smiled at Michael. Michael looked at Jimmy and silently nodded his head and eyes in agreement. Jimmy lived on the east side of town, a few streets past Michael's house. He would come to Michael's bedroom window daily to pick him up for school. On weekends, Jimmy would come over early and play with Michael until it was time for him to return home. They would play hard together and always had a great time together. Michael loved Jimmy and found many opportunities to laugh and enjoy life with his best friend.

In sixth grade, they lay deep in the grass under William's weeping willow tree. A summer storm was about to hit. The clouds massed over the boys, yet the humidity made them sweat. Jimmy was talking as usual, and Michael listened intently to what he was saying. Jimmy was upset because his parents had been fighting, and he heard his mother say they were moving from Rutterfield. "I'm going to run away, and you're coming with me," Jimmy told Michael. The air was thick, and several insects flew over both. "We can ride the trains and go to California."

The boys drifted, thinking of their new lives. Jimmy got up and ran across the street, where he found an empty bottle on the side of the road. He picked it up and slammed it to the ground. The noise from the broken glass caused a group of women to turn, giving Jimmy a disgusting look. Jimmy grabbed the glass and ran back to Michael.

"To our friendship," Jimmy cut himself on the arm, and tears welled up in his eyes.

Michael grabbed the same piece of glass, clasped his lips together, and cut his arm in the same place Jimmy did. "To my friend, my brother," Michael whispered to Jimmy. They both rubbed their arms together and mixed the blood.

"We have to take care of each other forever," Jimmy said.

Michael rolled over, lying on the grass, thinking this was the first time he felt wanted. Jimmy was his friend and family.

Jimmy joined him, lying on his back, kicking his feet in the air.

"Do you think your parents would come after us?" Jimmyasked Michael.

Michael answered, "No."

"We'll leave tomorrow morning. I'll come to your house, and we'll start our trip."

Michael nodded with a smile, excited to start his new life away from his parent, apart from this town.

That night, Michael tried to stay awake, but by early morning, he had drifted off to sleep. When the sun shone through his window and woke him up, he realized their plan had gone wrong.

Michael got up, put on his pants, and went outside in the front yard with his bare feet. He looked down the street, looking for his friend. He wanted to go. It was his time. He trusted his friend; after all, they would care for each other, brothers forever. Michael returned to the house and lay on his bed, trying to make sense of what had happened.

Jimmy showed up at the window. "Hey, are you there?" Jimmy poked his head into the screenless window.

"Come in. My parents are still asleep."

"Hey, sorry, I'm late. My dad left late last night, and my mom came into my room and talked to me all night long. She cried and said she hated my dad. She said that we're going to stay in town." Jimmy said, his eyes twitching, as he tried to understand what was happening with his parents.

Michael told him to come into the room. "We're not going to California?"

"We can't. My Mom needs me around." Jimmy wasn't shy and gave Michael a hug.

Hey, we're still blood brothers." Jimmy headed to the window. "I have to go now, but I'll see you later." Jimmy left.

**

Life for Jimmy was hard; not having a father around made the town suspicious of his every move. No one was friendly to him. Nobody wanted to allow Jimmy to prove who he was. His mother tried to be a good mother. And in the daytime, she was great when she wasn't sleeping. She missed the touch of a man, and at night, she sought out men to satisfy her nocturnal whims. By the time the boys graduated from middle school, they were truly alone in life.

When Michael was 14 years old, he worked a few hours at the drugstore, cleaning windows and stocking shelves. It was the last summer he would be considered a child. The following school year, he and Jimmy, because they were white, would be attending a high school on the west side of town.

A tropical flu hit the town of Rutterfield. People blamed mosquitoes for carrying the disease. Michael's mother started getting sick during the second week of June. She became weak and was unable to go to work. After a couple of weeks, she lost her job on the farm and spent the days in bed, unable to get out of bed on her own. At night, Michael and his Father would take turns caring for her, but the room was silent. Michael had nothing to share with his mother. On August 17, 1940, Michael's mother passed away. His father decided to bury his wife at the cemetery. Nobody came to the funeral, but the neighbors next door, who helped deliver Michael, laid flowers next to the front door.

Michael's father was devastated by the loss of his wife. Even though they never had a real relationship, his wife was the only person who truly understood him.

Arne coped with his loss by taking on more work, leaving his son to find his way to deal with the death of his mother.

Jimmy and Michael were teenagers. Not even Jimmy could figure out how to make it better for Michael. He knew that Michael's parents were different and that Michael loved or at least respected them. However, numbness was the feeling that Michael felt at the loss of his mother.

It was late at night. Michael had long since gone to bed. The moonlight shone into the bedroom, exposing the mosquitoes flying above his body. The window was open, trying to suck in any air given from the warm summer night. Jimmy whispered through the window to his friend. "Michael, are you awake? Michael, wake up!" Jimmy stepped through the window one leg at a time.

Michael sat up smiling when he realized it was his friend. "Jimmy, what are you doing?"

Jimmy stood next to his bed. "We're going to drink this whole bottle right now, you and me." Jimmy pulled out a bottle of liquor from a paper bag.

Ever since prohibition was over, getting alcohol on the East Side was child's play. "Come on, put on your clothes," Jimmy commanded.

Michael jumped out of bed and put on his pants. "Where're we going?"

"You'll see," Jimmy said, heading to the window.

Michael joined him and jumped outside.

"What time is it?"

Jimmy started to sprint, leaving Michael only one choice to follow. They crossed the street and turned north on McClay Ave. Michael caught up to Jimmy. "Jimmy, where are we going?"

Jimmy stopped and turned to his friend. "We're going to toast goodbye to your mother."

Michael grabbed the bottle from Jimmy's hand, making a face like Jimmy was crazy.

"It's time you said goodbye to her." Jimmy snatched back the bottle and opened it up.

"I've said my goodbyes," Michael said.

Jimmy took a large swig from the bottle and almost choked from the aftershock of the liquor. He handed the bottle to Michael. Michael looked at his friend and took a large gulp.

They continued to walk to the cemetery. Michael's mother's plot was empty of a headstone. The necessity of identifying who she was didn't rank with his father as a priority. The graves next to Michael's mother had large stones that Michael and Jimmy sat on while they drank.

The boys were quiet as they drank from the bottle. The alcohol slapped Michael hard as he revealed to his mother's grave all the years of rejection that he had experienced.

He started to sob, unable to hold back the tears. "You weren't a good Mom, but I don't think you knew how to be a good mom." Michael softly spoke out loud. He felt the freedom to speak his heart as he cursed the life his mother gave him. "Thank you for giving me life. But I can't say you gave me much more." Michael started to cry again.

"Was I that bad of a kid, Mom? Was I too much like somebody you hated in the past? I don't know, Mom. Why did you treat me as if I were the worst kid in the world? Were you so sure I was going to be bad? I loved you, Mom. I know you were a hard worker. And I know life was a chore for you. I'm sorry you had such a bad life. And I'm sorry if I made your life harder." Jimmy got up and put his arm around his friend. Michael continued crying. "Rest in peace, Mom. I hope eternity is a better place for you." Michael raised the bottle in the air. "No more, no more hate, Mom. I'm sorry that I brought you so much unhappiness." Michael took the final zip of the bottle. "I don't feel alone because you were never there." The silence was chilling. Even Jimmy couldn't find any words to say.

Michael got up and started walking home. When he reached the front gates of the cemetery, he threw up all the years of grief mixed with alcohol. Jimmy stood next to him and started to laugh. "Are you okay?"

Michael wiped his mouth and smiled at his friend.

"I guess I told her, huh? It's kind of scary, like I expected her to come out of the grave and grab my father's belt and give me a good whipping. At least for once, she'd have a reason."

Jimmy held on to his friend. "Let's get out of here."

Jimmy helped Michael through the bedroom window when they got to Michael's house. They were loud and giggling as they entered the room.

Jimmy, still concerned for Michael, asked one last time.

"Are you okay?"

"Thanks for going with me,"

Michael said, falling onto his bed.

"Don't worry. I'll always be here for you." Jimmy sat on Michael's bed. "Hey, do you remember George Whitt from the sixth grade?   You know, Whitt the Twit, when he attacked you? I don't even know why he was going to fight you. I remember coming around the corner and seeing him ready to punch you. Fire came into my eyes, and I just jumped at him. He fell to the ground and skidded on his elbows. I saw red and went crazy, and I just started punching him. Old Mrs. White pulled me off of him. I looked up at you, and you looked mad as hell."

Michael turned to his friend. "I was scared, but I wanted to punch him. He said my parents were German spies. I didn't know what he meant, but I knew he was offending them."

Jimmy continued, "I got in so much trouble from the principal.

He brought out this huge paddle, and I was scared shitless. He kept asking me why I attacked him. I knew nothing other than I hated George, so I kept quiet. He paddled my ass so hard it lifted my body three feet off the ground."

Michael started laughing. "I remember your ass bruised for a week."

"I kind of felt the same tonight. Watching you say goodbye to your Mom. It was like somebody taking a paddle to my heart." Jimmy sniffed and rubbed his eyes.

Michael smiled at his good friend. "My heart has been bruised for years. I don't remember it not ever being broken."

Jimmy lay on the bed next to Michael. "Oh boy, everything is starting to spin." Jimmy was silent for a moment. "I guess I'll be your mother and father."

Michael whispered back, "And brother."

The boys both fell asleep.

Chapter 7

Sending in the Angels

Dorine Honeycutt walked to the outskirts of Goldenville, Kentucky, where she slept by the side of a small, perky stream. The area was full of trees, creating a cool shade for her tired body. She had a blanket in her bag, laid it flat on the ground, and fell asleep. In the middle of the night, she awoke in the dark forest.

The night animals were all out, howling, crying, and scaring poor Dorine. She bathed in the stream at sunrise and prepared to hit the city. She was determined to find an opportunity to support herself.

When she got on the main road, an older man in his forties stopped his truck to see if she needed help. Dorine asked him for a ride into town. He pushed open her door and invited her into the truck. "Where is a pretty girl like you going?" The older man said with a big smile.

Dorine replied. "Just to the next town, sir," Dorine batted her eyes, smiling and talking fast. The man patted the seat next to him. She slid over almost next to him, cautious of being in a truck. The only vehicle she ever rode in was an old cart pulled by a workhorse that her Daddy used to transport the hooch.

"Well, this must be my lucky day, finding a pretty, young girl like you to keep me company. But tell me, what is a young lady like you doing walking on this old dusty road?"

"I'm starting a new life in Goldenville," Dorine said with pride.

"Does your new life have to start in Goldenville?" The man said, trying to figure out if there was any way he could help her.

"Not really. I hoped to find a cheap room, but tomorrow, I'll have to look for a job."

The man removed his hat and scratched his head. "How about you come with me? I'm going to Nashville. I'll give you a ride and a place to stay until you see a town you may want to stay in."

Dorine smiled and turned her body to her new friend. "My name is Dorine Honeycutt." Dorine put out her hand.

The stranger replied and put his hand out to shake Dorine's hand.

"My name is Hank. It's a pleasure to meet such an inspiring young woman."

Dorine could only smile, not understanding what inspiring meant. She just kept hearing her mother's voice reminding her of all the horrible things that could happen to her. At this point, Dorine had no choice but to trust this fellow. She knew sleeping next to the creek was not an option.

The trip was pleasant. Hank was a clever, funny man. They both laughed their way out of the hills of Kentucky. Dorine was explaining her family to Hank. He listened, smiling, almost laughing at some of the stories.

"Each of us girls only had one dress. When that dress gets dirty, we wear the previous dress and wash the new dress. By the time Christmas came, the dress would almost be worthless."

Hank came from a poor family, but nothing like what Dorine explained.

"I guess the same thing with shoes. Except most of the time, my sisters and I would be barefoot. So, by the time Daddy could buy us girls shoes, they weren't as needed as a dress was."

Dorine didn't have the insight to realize that they were extremely poor. She didn't know about the better things in life. Dorine honestly didn't realize that her life on the mountain was not a normal childhood for most kids in America.

Her sacrifices and the concessions she made to her brothers didn't feel right, but Dorine thought it was the same for all girls as they transitioned into women. She sensed something was wrong with the living situation, but believed her mother and her frightening stories about life off the mountain.

After listening to her cousin Lana and her tales of living in a city, Dorine couldn't imagine what Lana told her: a store full of dresses, real furniture, and soft cushions. They only had furniture that her father and brothers had made for them, which was hard and lacked softness. It was unbelievable to Dorine to think that families had houses where girls could sleep in one room and boys in the other. And now, with her new friend Hank, she could see these things with her own eyes.

"Don't you a worry, pretty girl. Someday, you'll find a good man, and he'll give you all the life you deserve." Hank wished her.

Dorine smiled at Hank, not quite understanding his motives but appreciating his kindness.

Hank genuinely wanted to help Dorine. Listening to her stories, he could see a child in a candy store for the first time, not knowing which candy to try first. Hank felt a particular obligation to help Dorine. He realized this girl would be sent home within a month if nobody gave her a helping hand.

They got to the next city, but Hank stopped and asked

Dorine to wait in the car. When he returned, he had purchased a dark blue skirt with a white blouse, a pretty cotton floral dress, and a woman's pair of shoes.

Dorine screamed with delight. Then her eyes filled up with tears, not knowing how she would be able to accept these clothes. "Hank, you're tickling my heart; you know I can't pay you for these beautiful things." Dorine held up the cotton dress, taking a closer look at the flower print. "This dress is so beautiful. "It's too kind of you. I may as well be a stranger, and you are so nice to me."

Hank smiled. "I was a young boy who lived up in the Tennessee Mountains. My Mama and Daddy had eight kids. When I was fifteen, I left home. I had three little sisters, just like you, who had nothing. Helping you is just my way of giving back." He scratched his head, feeling very humble.

Dorine grabbed Hank's arm, reached up, and kissed him on the cheek while driving. "Hank, you're a good man."

They stopped in a small hotel at the border of Kentucky and Tennessee. The hotel manager gave Dorine a hard look. He was trying to figure out if Dorine was Hank's daughter. Dorine tried not to look at the man, not wanting any trouble to come their way.

After Hank filled out all the papers, the desk clerk gave Hank the keys.

"There is freshwater outside at the well. Just one pitcher worth at a time." The clerk yelled behind them.

Hank raised the key in the air, acknowledging that he understood the rules.

Dorine was apprehensive about entering the room, knowing it was her time to pay for Hank's generosity, but she kept telling herself that she had no other choice. At least Hank was friendly and kind.

Hank said with a genuine smile. "Come on into our home for the night."

Dorine could tell that Hank was also feeling awkward as she entered the room with her bundle of life wrapped up in a sheet from home.

The room had one bed and two side tables, with a lamp on one of them. The floor was made of gray tile, with a throw rug at the entrance to the front door.

"I think tomorrow we should get close to Nashville," Hank said, trying to make conversation.

Dorine sat in the only chair in the room, still holding her belongings. "I know a small town called Rutterfield. It might just be the perfect place for you." Hank tried to reassure Dorine that he would keep to his promise. Hank pulled a large T-shirt out of his bag and gave it to Dorine.

"I don't know if you have any pajamas in that bundle, but you can use my T-shirt to sleep in."

Dorine smiled, took the plain white T-shirt, and pointed to the door. "Where is the toilet?"

Hank walked to the front door and looked down the hall. The hallway was dimly lit, illuminated by a couple of small glass sconces. "It's down there at the end of the hall."

Dorine walked under Hank's arm as he held the door open.

The hotel seemed to be empty. Dorine did not believe that the toilet could be inside. She made a face, thinking how dirty that would be. Not hearing a sound, she felt her way to the end of the hall.

Dorine took the T-shirt to the bathroom to wash up and put it under her patched dress. When she returned, Hank was already in bed. On the side table, he had a bottle of liquor and two glasses. Dorine stepped to her side of the bed and removed her dress, leaving on the T-shirt.

"Would you like a drink?" Hank asked Dorine, raising the bottle and ready to pour Dorine a stiff one.

Dorine nodded yes, "My father was a moonshiner. I was raised with alcohol in the house."

Hank smiled, handed her the drink, and poured one for himself. Dorine put a pillow between her and the wall and sat up.

Hank did the same. He lifted his glass to her and gave a silent toast.

"You probably think I'm some kind of crazy girl. You know, getting into a car with a stranger staying with him in a hotel room." Dorine started to laugh. Hank looked at her curiously.

Dorine kept talking, trying to hide her nerves. "This is the first time I have ever been in a hotel room. I have never left my Daddy's house before."

Hank smiled, understanding her innocence. "Why such a need to get away?"

Dorine took a big swallow of liquor, "Let's just say I wanted more than a brother for a husband."

Dorine turned her head and pleaded for another drink. Hank reached over, got the bottle, and filled her glass.

"You're a nice man, Hank." Dorine sincerely said. I should be scared as hell, but for some reason, I'm not."

Hank said with a sincere, calming voice, "I want you to relax. I'm only here to help you." Hank smiled at Dorine. "Besides, I enjoy your company, and I do wish the best for you."

Dorine set her glass on her table, turned to Hank's side, and kissed him. "Thank you. You're a wonderful man." She lay herself down on her side. Hank lowered his glass, rolled over, and turned off the light. They both fell asleep. In the middle of the night, Dorine woke up to the humming of Hank's snoring. She just lay there and listened, remembering her father and how he used to snore. She remembered the odor of alcohol on his breath as he would sneak into Dorine's bed. In the early morning, without Dorine realizing it, he would manage to escape before the sun rose. Dorine didn't know how to hate her father. Her parents always presented the girls of the family as personal property. It was nice to be next to a gentleman. Without sex, Dorine felt she had no way to repay Hank. Being here with Hank was the first time she viewed herself as a person, not an object. She felt the clean sheets of the bed and imagined someday she would have a real husband with a bed made exclusively just for them.

Chapter 8

In the Service Now

December 1941Rutterfield, Tennessee

The year was 1941. Even though war was rampant in Europe, Americans felt safe and never thought the Japanese would attack our soldiers stationed in Hawaii. People in Rutterfield were frantic; any adult males who weren't already in the service joined to defend our country.

Michael and Jimmy were in the 9th grade. While waiting for Jimmy to appear at the window, Michael was ready to leave for school. The December air was cold, so Michael had his window shut. Jimmy didn't knock; he pried open the window and jumped right in. "We're going to join the service today!" Jimmy said, out of breath from the excitement of his new idea.

"How? We're not old enough to join the service." Michael continued to gather his schoolbooks.

"You only have to be fifteen years old and have a signed letter from your parents." Jimmy pulled out a folded piece of paper that his mother had signed.

Michael stopped, turned, and looked at Jimmy, realizing he was serious. "Are we going into the Army?"

"No, right now, they need men in the Navy, especially after the Japs bombed Pearl Harbor."

Jimmy rushed around the room to convince his friend that they had to join. "They have a buddy system, and they'll let us join together."

Michael hated school, especially since they had to go to school on the west side. "My dad is already at work. We'll have to stop there and get his permission."

Michael figured this idea would vanish as quickly as their trip to California did.

He and Jimmy left through Michael's bedroom window. They had less than two weeks left before Christmas vacation, an event that Michael planned to use to get extra work.

The clouds were motionless, frozen by the cold air. People wrapped in heavy coats, determined to reach their final destinations. The car's exhaust from the morning rush to the westside polluted the air for one man's gain, darkening the already gray clouds to a soft black. The nip of Jack Frost covered the neighborhood windows, sealing in people from the busy Monday morning.

The front doors were locked when the boys arrived at the general store. Jimmy pounded on the window, shaking the glass doors, hoping to get his father's attention. "Are you sure he's here? Maybe he's over at the widow Nelson's house pounding a fresh one in the morning."

Michael made a disgusting face at his friend.

The door jiggled, and Michael's father opened the door.

"Dad, I want to join the Navy." Michael boldly told his father.

Michael's father made an annoyed face. "You're too young, go to school."

"They'll let me join if you give me permission." Michael pleaded.

Arne looked at Jimmy and knew it was his idea. "Hum, if you stay, you'll get in trouble. Maybe the service would teach you a thing or two." He walked to the cash register and pulled a paper and a pen from the drawer. He wrote a sentence and signed his name. "It's your life." He handed the paper to his son.

Michael felt sad but didn't know how to act on it. His father walked to the front door, unlocked it, and held it open for him. "Don't get killed." He reached out for his son but only managed to touch his shoulder and give it a gentle squeeze. Michael nodded, listening to his father's advice.

"Yes, sir," Michael pulled away and walked out the door.

Jimmy followed Michael out of the store. He was jumping around, Michael, excited to start their adventure. "That was almost a moment. I think those are the most words I have ever heard your dad say to you."

Michael smiled, happy to have his friend by his side. "When he reached for my shoulder, I thought he was going to slap me." Michael started to laugh.

Jimmy joined in with a good chuckle. "You, I thought he was going to hit me when you asked if you could join, as if I have control of your life."

Even Michael was starting to feel the excitement, thinking about seeing the world, serving his country, leaving his hometown, and finding his place in life. He let out a loud hoot when all was silent, and Jimmy provided the holler.

***

The recruitment office was filled with men eager to serve their country. The officer in charge didn't have time to answer any specific questions. He smiled and gave each of them the necessary paperwork.

Both boys received their packages and sat with the other boys, ready to serve their country, while they hated the paperwork and answered all the questions.

When it came to questions they didn't understand,

Michael and Jimmy lied, writing down the answers they thought the government wanted to read.

Jimmy, tired of filling out questionnaires, jumped out of his seat and screamed out loud, letting out all that was bottled up inside of him. The entire room became silent, everybody looking at Jimmy and Michael, and then the room returned to the cluttered list of unanswered questions.

"Hey!" Michael dragged Jimmy back to his seat. "I don't see any place where they said we could stay together." Michael searched through the pages.

"I talked to a soldier yesterday, and he said they have a buddy system, and we can ask to be assigned together." Jimmy looked over Michael's shoulder, looking through the completed paperwork.

Michael, fifteen years old, believed Jimmy. After all, Jimmy was told by a serviceman who already knew the system. It took a couple of days for both boys to arrive in San Diego, California, at boot camp.

San Diego was beautiful. Even though it was late December, the sun shone brightly in the blue sky as if it were the middle of summer. The blue water drifted calmly up Mission Bay, and the palm trees that lined the shore slightly waved from the provided breeze of winter.

The Navy started as a mistake. On the first day, Jimmy found himself inside a headlock on the floor, defending Michael from some hecklers. They detected an accent and accused Michael of being a German spy. Michael stayed silent as Jimmy took on the whole barracks. On the floor in pain, he pleaded with his attacker, "He's French. His parents came over from France." The revelation stopped the fight. It was Jimmy's words that got Michael off the hook. From that day on, everybody called Michael by his new name, Frenchie.

The training was rigid. Michael had to use muscles that he didn't even know he had. After a few weeks of training, they became actual soldiers.

After the initial training, both Michael and Jimmy received their assignments. Michael, stationed in Hawaii, and Jimmy, assigned to another Pacific island. It was Jimmy who went to the officer in charge. "Sir, with all due respect, I think that a mistake has been made."

The officer commanded Jimmy to stand at ease. "What's the problem, soldier?"

"Sir, my buddy and I joined together with the request, sir, that we would be assigned to the same place of service."

"Soldier, we are at war. We place soldiers where they are needed. Are you trying to tell me that you want me to tell my commanding officer that the United States Government made a mistake?"

Jimmy realized there was no use pushing the issue: "No, sir, sorry, sir."

The officer continued his work. Jimmy left the room with a frown. He and Michael would be separated for the first time since Kindergarten. Jimmy felt horrible because it was his idea to make them join the service. When he entered the barracks, the guys started to heckle, but when they saw Jimmy's face, they backed off and kept silent. Jimmy went up to Michael's bunk and sat on the bed below. "I tried to get us reassigned, but it didn't work."

Michael saw that Jimmy was upset. "We'll be okay."

Jimmy smiled at his friend. "It's going to be a long war."

Michael was assigned to work with a few guys he already knew. They accepted Michael as a friend, and Michael enjoyed Hawaii, its beauty, culture, and exotic food.

Jimmy wrote Michael regularly. When Michael got to shore, he collected his mail, which consisted of all the letters from Jimmy. He would find an empty spot on the beach and enjoy whatever his friend wrote.

Jimmy couldn't stop himself from getting into fights. He lasted six months on his assignment. The Navy gave him a choice. Leave the Navy or spend the rest of his life in the brig. Jimmy decided that Rutterfield was better than a life in prison.

Dear Michael, or should I call you Frenchie? Life is a bore here in Rutterfield. Nobody is around. I guess that should help my odds when it comes to women. However, you know this town, it's natural hatred for me.

Mr. Peterson gave me your old job at the pharmacy. He has me doing all the sweeping and cleaning, the boring tasks.

I have been digging it at the Blue Lantern. It's a colored bar, but they treat me as one of their own. It's funny; they're so afraid of us, and we all are so fearful of them. Why can't people see that we're all the same? Even the bible thumpers are afraid. It seems when they're on the west side, the Lord loves everybody, but when a colored person tries to worship in their church, everybody whispers and makes the person feel unloved. I guess that's Tennessee.

Hey, I met a girl the other day. All I can say is she is beautiful and wild.

I have to go now, but I have so many stories to tell you about this girl. Her name is Dorine. Man, she makes me Doll dizzy.
I miss you, buddy; please come home soon.

Jimmy

Chapter 9

A Blossom of Love

1945 Rutterfield, Tennessee

The next morning, Hank took Dorine to the town of Rutterfield. They found the boarding house, and Hank paid for Dorine to live there for one month.

Dorine walked him to his car. "I don't know how to thank you." Dorine was embarrassed by her loss for words.

Hank got into his car and smiled. "Make it all happen with a bundle of happiness. Just think of me as your angel."

Dorine smiled at Hank through the window.

He touched her hand, started up the car, and pulled away.

The next evening, after Hank dropped Dorine off in Rutterfield, Tennessee, Dorine took her first walk before the sun was to set. The blue sky supported several clouds, trying to cluster into a summer storm. The sun lost its will to stay astride, allowing the sweetness of a Tennessee night to emerge. Keeping the boarding house in sight, Dorine noticed a boy down by the corner hopping over a fence.

It looked as though he was going to cross the street when he saw Dorine, but he changed his direction. He was a tall, thin young man. His hair was cut short like a soldier's. He was walking fast as if he had somewhere to go. When he approached Dorine, he slowed his pace, giving Dorine a nod and a broad smile. She stayed focused on the sidewalk until the last moment, then she turned and looked up at him and smiled.

The boy took the smile as an invitation to begin a conversation. Walking backward, keeping up with Dorine's stride, "Are you new around here? I've lived here all my life, and I have never seen such a pretty girl like you around here."

Dorine blushed and nodded her head yes. "I just moved here yesterday."

"Where do you live?" The boy asked.

Dorine pointed to the women's boarding house. "I rent a room at the boarding house."

"Don't you have a mama and daddy?"

Dorine smiled, "Yes. They live in Kentucky."

"I'm sorry, where's my manners? My name is Jimmy. Jimmy Parker."

"It's nice to meet you, Mr. Parker. My name is Dorine, Dorine Honeycutt."

"Don't you be calling me Mr. I must be close to your age?"

Dorine gave a fake giggle. "Where I come from, everybody

is Mr. This and Mr. That."

"Well, you just call me Jimmy." Jimmy put his hand out to shake Dorine's. And Dorine took his hand gently into hers.

"Dorine, could I interest you in a soda at the corner drugstore?" Jimmy asked with confidence.

Dorine smiled. "Jimmy. I would love to have a soda with you."

Jimmy tried not to dominate the conversation on the way to the drugstore, but he had so many questions that they never lacked communication.

Jimmy and Dorine sat at the drugstore and immediately hit it off. Jimmy wanted to tell her his whole life story, but he stopped and allowed her to contribute a few sentences of her own.

"Hey, do you have a job?" Jimmy changed the subject. Dorine's smile was replaced with a look of concern. "No, I need one badly. I was actually going to start looking tomorrow."

Jimmy almost jumped out of his seat. "You can have my job!"
Dorine looked confused.

"Well, my job was my best friend Michael's job, but he went into the service. Now it's my job, but I hate it because there's a lot of cleaning and not really talking with people. That's what I like to do, talk to people."

"What would you do without your job?" Dorine said, still not believing what she was hearing.

"Oh, I can find a job anytime, with all the farms around here. I'll probably be working by the end of the week."

Dorine spoke with a sweet voice. "Jimmy. I don't know how to thank you. Being new in town, I was already starting to feel lonely."

Jimmy smiled, "With me here in town, I guarantee you, you'll never be lonely."

The new friends finished their drinks, laughing and talking until, finally, the owner had to escort them out.

Jimmy walked Dorine home, the moonlight fresh and bright. "I have to work tomorrow at 10:00 am. If you could meet me here, I'll take you over, and maybe Mr. Peterson will let you start work right away."

Dorine got all excited and reached up and kissed Jimmy on the cheek. Jimmy got all embarrassed. No girl has ever been so sweet to him as Dorine was. The morning came early. Dorine got up and ironed her blue skirt and white blouse. She brushed her hair and smiled in the mirror. She had never had a job before. The only responsibility Dorine ever had was her daily chores and servicing her brothers. The thought of working in a real store thrilled Dorine. She couldn't wait to meet Jimmy so that she could begin her new life.

A place to live, a job, and maybe a boyfriend; this was almost too much excitement for Dorine. She looked outside her window and saw Jimmy coming down the street. She ran out of the house and met him on the front steps.

Mr. Peterson loved Dorine and was all for hiring her. He liked Jimmy, but having Jimmy around was like having a trapped animal in a cage. The work was boring and beneath Jimmy's actual abilities. Mr. Peterson had daily pep talks with Jimmy, trying to motivate him to accomplish the most menial tasks. Now Jimmy was set free, and Dorine could start her life.

The work at the pharmacy was easy for Dorine. She cleaned and cleaned, and she loved that Mr. Peterson was thrilled with her.

"Boy, God gave me an angel when he brought you here to work," Mr. Peterson said with a big smile.

"Thank you, Mr. Peterson. Please tell me, sir, if I'm doing anything wrong. I really enjoy working here."

"You're doing just fine. The only thing you could do wrong is quit."

Chapter 10

The Facts of Life, According to Dorine

1945 Rutterfield, Tennessee

Dorine didn't know she lived in a whore house. When Hank brought her to the boarding house, they were only responding to the sign on the door, "Room for Rent."

Dorine was in her room, hanging up her dress for the next day. A knock at the door startled her.

"Miss Dorine?" A soft-spoken voice with an accent was heard.

Dorine walked to the door and opened it to see the landlady standing in the hallway.

"Yes, ma'am, how can I help you?"

The short German woman entered Dorine's room and closed the door behind her. "It seems that a young gentleman from a very good family is on his way here, and none of my girls are available to spend time with him."

Dorine didn't understand what she was saying, but knew she needed her help. "I'll be happy to meet this man."

The madam smiled, "Now you know what I really need for you to do. Just be nice and comforting to him."

Dorine nodded her head, thinking she understood.

When the young man arrived, the madam called for Dorine to join them. Dorine was wearing her floral print dress. She went down the stairs, wishing it was Jimmy that she was meeting, not someone new.

The madam displayed her product, and the young man shook her hand in agreement.

He went up to Dorine and kissed her on the lips. Dorine, surprised by the kiss, backed away. He stiffened up, and Dorine looked to the madam for an explanation. When the madam only smiled, Dorine understood what was being offered. The young man approached her again, and Dorine responded that she had done so for her brothers and father many times in her life.

After the young man left and Dorine cleaned herself up, the madam knocked on her door. Dorine opened the door, and the madam handed her more money than Dorine had ever seen. "This evening will be our little secret." The madam said as she handed Dorine her share of the money. Dorine took her share and felt a sense of worth that her services weren't given for free.

Chapter 11

Going Home

1946 San Diego, California

Jimmy's letters helped Michael make it through the insanity of the war. Michael was assigned to Pearl Harbor. The effect of the enemy scorned the beauty of the harbor. The fear that ruled the city, not knowing if another attack was in the making, haunted the islanders with their nightmares of exploding bombs. The security of hosting the American military was challenged, as Hawaii received punishment on behalf of our nation. Feeling betrayed by the Japanese Hawaiian community, the natives were victims of the world's insanity.

The clean-up was horrifying, with whole mangled bodies drifting onshore, the debris from the downed airplanes, fragments of bombs, and the waves of echoes of many who gave their lives for our country. Michael wanted to go home. He wanted to hang out with his friend, his brother, Jimmy.

The end of the war finally came, as did Michael's term with the Navy. His trip home was endless. All he could think about was the freedom to make his own choices. Michael boarded the train in San Diego, California, with a duffle bag over his shoulder and a select bundle of letters from Jimmy. Watching the Desert Mountains roll by kept Michael occupied as the hot sun burned on the bare glass of the train. Despite the desert's beauty, Michael couldn't help but miss the beautiful green scenery of Tennessee.

The train roared through the canyons of Arizona, the painted cliffs of the home of the native Indians. Michael reached into his duffle bag and pulled out a piece of fruit. He set the bundle of letters on a table in front of him. He untied the only communication from home he received throughout the years in the service. All the letters were from Jimmy. The bundle consisted of Michael's favorites, but a few of them were new from Jimmy that Michael hadn't had the chance to read.

December 17, 1945
Dear Michael,

It's late at night. I just finished taking Dorine home. She lives at that woman's boarding house. You know, the house with all the beautiful honeys where Dr. Reynolds used to live.

Dorine came over to meet my mom for the first time. Michael, she is something. I would be so lost here in this town without her being here. We have been going out every night. She seems to have the energy of a whole town right in one person. She never gets tired. You wouldn't believe what happened tonight. As I said, my mom asked her over for dinner so that they could meet. Dorine wore the new beige dress she bought. It was beautiful against her blond hair and blue eyes.

My mom made a roast with potatoes and carrots on the side. Having Dorine there almost made it feel like we were a family. I can't believe her. She was talking with my mom across the table, and she would be rubbing my leg with her foot. Boy, I'm so crazy for her. After dinner, we decided we were going to play hide and seek. Mom went to her bedroom, and we played in the rest of the house. Dorine was the one to hide, and I was the seeker. I counted to a hundred and started looking for her. I swear I checked every place.

At first, I thought she tricked me and went home. But then I heard a slight rumble in the kitchen closet. There she was, wrapped between the broom and mop. Michael, I swear she pulled me into the closet and took me right there. I was breathing all hard and everything. At first, I thought that my mom was going to catch us. But Michael, it felt great. I mean, I know we talked about it all our lives, but this girl knows how to do it. Oh. I'd better quit now, or else I'm going to be up all night. Hey, I wish you were here. I miss you, my friend. I have told Dorine everything about you. I know she already loves you. Only a few months are left. Hey, it's almost Christmas. Do you have any

plans? I hope to spend it with Dorine. She has no family here in town, so maybe Mom will let her come over for the day. I think I'm going to tell her tomorrow that I love her. Can you believe that? She hasn't told me yet, but I can see it in her eyes. She loves me, too.

Take care, my friend.
Jimmy.

Michael smiled, thinking about this new girl in Jimmy's life. He was happy that his friend was happy. Jimmy deserved all the happiness in the world.

April 2, 1945
Dear Michael

I can't believe it is time for you to come home. I know the first thing we are going to do is get a bottle of whiskey and go to William's weeping willow, and we're just going to talk about all you missed. Michael, I'm a little confused today. I sure wish you were here now. Dorine told me last night that she's pregnant. Can you imagine me as a father? I love Dorine; you are the only thing missing in our relationship. Michael, I know you are going to love her too. She has such a spirit that lights up every room that she enters. Of course, the folks around here talk and gossip about her, mostly because she's with me. But she loves life and looks it right in the eye and goes for whatever she wants. I'm scared, Michael, because being a father, I mean a good father, is what I want for my child. I don't want this child to have a shit father like mine. I made this baby and want the best for it for the rest of its life. Oh my God, I just thought about the fact that it might be a girl. Come home, Michael, quick! It's going to be a real ride this time.

Love you, brother.
Jimmy.

It was late, and Michael had drifted asleep to the train's motion. When he woke up, he found Jimmy's letter on the floor. Michael bent down to pick up the letter and felt a wave of nausea. He couldn't stop thinking about Jimmy. For some reason, a fear came over him. Maybe it was that nothing would ever be the same. Jimmy and Dorine would marry and could even leave town, leaving him alone without his friend. It was the thought of being alone again in life that scared him the most. Michael thought about his mother, how she abandoned him on the day of his birth, and how his parents' lack of love was mean and damaging. It was Jimmy who showed Michael what love was. His real family and friends. He picked up the letter and set his head against the window. Home was right around the corner, yet it seemed miles and miles away.

The morning sun peeked through the Tennessee horizon. The blue-green hills welcomed one of their own back home. Michael's father was right. The service made a new man out of him. Michael learned the appreciation and value of being a man. He was ready to take the necessary steps to find completion. Life was going to be completely different from this point forward. His life would have purpose and direction, and he was determined to fill it with love.

The train station on the Westside of Rutterfield was full of unfamiliar faces. Michael threw his duffel bag over his shoulder, smacking himself in the rear. He stepped off the train and looked for Jimmy, but he was nowhere to be seen. Everyone was waving, calling, and whistling, looking for someone else's attention. Michael figured that Jimmy would have been there. He hoped his lifelong buddy would be anxious to see him, but there was no sign of Jimmy.

The pathway to the main entrance of the train station was a long way. Michael thought to himself that it was good that he was in good shape because this walk would have killed him in the past, carrying his life on his shoulders.

Nobody was waiting for Michael at the front drive of the station. He decided to start walking home. He wasn't very far when a car with two boys pulled over to the curb. "Hey, soldier, do you want a ride?"

Michael turned and smiled at the boys, wiping the sweat from his face. "Sure, thank you." Michael threw his duffel bag in the back of the car and joined the boys in the front seat. The boys took Michael all the way home, asking questions about the war. When he got out of the car, the boys thanked him for serving their country. Michael gave them a salute as they drove away.

It had been four years since Michael had been home. Even when the opportunity came for Michael to go home on leave, he passed them up and stayed on base, spending time with Jimmy.

The house looked as though no one cared for it throughout his term of service. Michael wanted to go in through his bedroom window, but instead, he used the front door. He was sure there would be a bunch of people in his living room ready to yell surprise and welcome him home. He thought to himself that Jimmy had better not have invited Whit the Twit. Michael was still mad at him for calling his parents spies.

Michael set his duffel bag on the porch and opened the front door. The front room was empty. The only noise was an annoying fly chasing after a couple of mosquitoes. "Dad? Jimmy? Nobody answered. Michael walked to his room and opened the door. The bedroom was still in the exact shape it was four years ago. Michael spoke softly to himself. "Thank God I made my bed." On his bed, leaning against his pillow, was an envelope. Michael picked it up and broke the seal. He sat on the old, familiar bed and read the letter.

Chapter 12

No Way, I Lost My Brother, My Friend?

2004, Medford, Tennessee

Dear Michael;

I'm sorry to be the one to tell you, but Jimmy was killed earlier this week. He was on his way to California to meet you in San Diego and had a train accident. His remains were sent home yesterday. His mother is having a service on Friday at noon.

Dorine.

Michael had to read the letter several times before any understanding came over him. He set the note on the bed and walked to the window. A scream, like that of a wild animal, came out of his soul. His eyes started to tear as he fell to his knees and sobbed. He crawled back to his bed and lay his face on the green bedspread. He cried, muffling his anger, fears, and sorrow for his brother.

Michael cried himself to sleep. When he awoke, it was dark. His heart ached, knowing that Jimmy was dead. He went to his window, opened it up, and stepped outside. Michael ran out of his yard, crossed the street, and flopped under William's willow tree. He sobbed for his friend, his brother, and wished it wasn't true.

Michael was moaning, face down in the grass, when a voice startled him. It was his father. "I thought I'd find you here."

Michael quickly turned, feeling violated; this was his and Jimmy's place. "Jimmy's dead."

"I know." Michael's father barely whispered.

"He was my only friend." Michael tried to say.

Michael's father sat down, leaning against the base of the tree.

"Nobody liked him. Everybody always thought he was nothing but trouble." Michael cried.

Michael's father didn't reply.

Michael sat up, facing his father. "How did you know to find me here?" Michael wiped his nose.

"Just watching you boys over the years." Michael's father said.

Michael appreciated his father there, knowing how hard this must have been for him.

"You can't go with him," Arne said. "Love who he was, but live on."

Michael was silent, trying to understand what his father was trying to say. Arne got up from the tree. "It's going to take time to heal. Say goodbye to your friend."

He stepped over the tall grass and walked away, leaving Michael alone.

Michael moved to the base of the tree and spent the rest of the night remembering his dear friend, feeling his presence in their special place.

The morning dew woke Michael up as he lay under the weeping willow. Two birds were squealing and tugging over a piece of string. They fought diligently, reminding him of his own personal Pearl Harbor. Michael walked home and entered through the front door. He went to the bathroom, looked in the mirror, and saw a crushed boy in a man's body.

Michael went to the kitchen and found some coffee. He continued trying to figure out how he would tell his buddy goodbye.

It was 11:50 a.m. when Michael arrived at the cemetery. A wooden casket was set on the ground next to a deep hole. Rows of empty seats lined up at the foot of the container, and one chair was beside the coffin, and that was where Jimmy's mother was sitting. A girl sitting on the last chair in a row of empty chairs was staring into space. She was not crying, just staring into the sky as if she could see Jimmy looking down upon her.

Michael sat on the opposite side of the girl and waited for the clergyman to start the service. He had a hard time believing that Jimmy was in the box. As much as he tried to listen, he could only hear the screams within his own head. His heart was broken, and there was no fixing it. Michael tried to hold back the sobs, but they burst out of him. Dorine turned her head towards him but made no move to comfort him. Jimmy's mother, dressed all in black, couldn't allow herself to take her eyes off her son.

"At this time, in the service, I invite anyone who wishes to share a story about James." The clergyman bellowed to the three of them.

"Jimmy. His name is Jimmy. And he was my best friend." Michael choked the words out.

Silence came upon them. The clergyman didn't know whether to wait a moment longer or end the service.

"I would like to say a word." Dorine broke the silence.

The clergyman motioned her over.

"If you don't mind, sir, I'll just say my peace from right here. As you can see, not too many people are here. That's because not too many people gave Jimmy a chance. But those of us who did will always be inspired by him. He was a man who knew how to love. He knew how to show love. He wasn't afraid to express love. I thank God that I got to be loved by

Jimmy. Jimmy was life and knew how to live life. He was fun and energetic, but always concerned about the ones he loved. Jimmy, you will never be forgotten." Dorine boldly wiped her nose and sat down.

The service ended after Dorine's speech. Michael approached Jimmy's mother and placed his hand on her shoulder. Words were too challenging to come by. Michael just let his tears explain the pain he was feeling. He walked away from the gravesite and went home.

Chapter 13

Saying Goodbye to My Friend

The same evening they buried Jimmy, Michael decided to return to the cemetery. The air was heavy, not giving up an extra breath to anybody. The streets seemed empty, and everybody was shut up in their homes, waiting for tomorrow's call. Michael stopped at an ABC store and bought a bottle of liquor. With the courage in a paper bag, Michael entered the gates of the dark graveyard. He walked past the tall headstones that reached out to the sky. He could hear the souls begging to be taken up. Jimmy's gravesite was bare, covered with dark, rich Tennessee soil.

Michael sat on the grass next to the freshly turned earth. "No more tears, my friend." Michael opened the bottle of liquor. "Here's to your next adventure. I just wish I could go with you. But I guess it's like the service. It's hard to say that somebody made a mistake." Michael took another swig.

"Thank you for being there for me. I'm sorry for all the times you had to protect me. Even if it meant getting beat up, you were the best friend anybody could have asked for."

Michael quickly drank down another gulp. "I just hope you knew how much I loved you."

"He did know." A voice from the dark interjected. Michael, startled, turned to see who was there. "Michael, he loved you more than life itself. Every chance, every moment, he would always say, Michael, my brother, or Michael, my best friend. You see, Jimmy knew that nobody liked him. He didn't understand why, but because you loved him, that meant more to him than if everyone in town had liked him."

Michael didn't know if he should stand up or what. Dorine motioned for him to stay seated. She walked over to him and sat next to him. "Got any room in that bottle for me?"

Michael smiled and handed her the bottle. "He loved you, too. He loved your spirit, beauty, and sense of freedom." Michael softly said.

Dorine smiled. "I know. We were going to get married. We were just waiting for you to get home because there was no way he was going to get married without you being there." Dorine set her head on his shoulder. "Michael Lore, I know a lot about you. I know about the first day you and Jimmy met in Kindergarten, and nobody wanted to be your friend, how he went over and took your hand and said friends forever. How in the third grade, you peed your pants, and Jimmy ran home, climbed through the window, and brought you clean clothes while you hid in the bathroom. And you know what, the most important part of that story was that I was the first person he ever told." Dorine continued. "He told me how you were ready to run away with him because his parents would split up and move away from town. You were a big part of Jimmy, and I do understand why you're sad."

The silence was deafening. Michael had to ask. "Do you know how it happened?"

Dorine took a deep breath. "He was halfway to California and was out between the passenger's cars. The conductor said he saw somebody hanging over the side with his arms spread out as if he could fly. By the time he could get to Jimmy, the train took a curve and threw Jimmy off, only to suck him under the train."

Michael was quiet; then, he began to laugh. That sounds like Jimmy. You know darn well he was bored. He was sitting there, watching the scenery. I'm sure he had to get up and walk around. Michael rolled onto his stomach and lay over Jimmy. "I miss him already. Damn it, it hurts."

Dorine stretched over and lay in Michael's arms. "Michael, he wouldn't want this to be so hard. He wouldn't want us to hurt so badly."

"When my mom died, Jimmy was right there with me. He told me his heart felt like it had just gotten a good paddling.

I didn't understand what he meant at the time, but now my heart is broken into pieces, and I'm too sad to put it back together."

"Stop it, Michael. You're tearing me apart." Dorine started to cry.

Silence once again came upon them. The stars above were peeking through the clouds, giving each of them a sense of one. The noise of the city was hushed, allowing this special moment for Michael, Dorine, and Jimmy.

"You really are beautiful. Jimmy wrote and told me how beautiful you are. He said you have a mole just south of your belly button." Michael lifted his head, hoping that Dorine would show him. Dorine slapped him and laughed.

"It feels good being here with you. It's as though I have known you forever, and being here with you just feels right." Dorine said, snuggling deep into Michael's arm.

"It's kind of different. I mean, I know about hide and seek."

Dorine screamed. "NO!"

Michael smiled, "And the Willian's willow tree, behind the Westside Baptist Church, and in my bedroom! He just loved you. He was happy."

"I can feel him right here with us. He's smiling with us." Dorine said.

Michael and Dorine spent the night with Jimmy, lying

under the stars, telling happy Jimmy stories throughout the night. It wasn't awkward that they could share such intimate details of each other's lives; Jimmy was there, laughing, crying, and sharing with them.

Morning came and took the freshness of the night away with the morning dew. Michael was the first to wake up. He rolled from under Dorine, lifted his head, and stared. He was confused about what had happened last night. It felt as if Jimmy was right there with them, but this morning, he felt selfish, as if he was trying to take Jimmy's girl away from him. Michael started laughing and thinking. "Like I can take a girl away. I have never had a girlfriend."

When Dorine awoke, she saw Michael's face looking frightened. She smiled. "Last night, it really was beautiful," Dorine tried to understand what Michael was experiencing. "Michael, Jimmy, is only gone from us physically, but his spirit will always be with us. She sat up and kissed Michael on the cheek. Last night was one of the most precious nights I have ever experienced. We said a lot of things. I'll let you go home and think about what we said. If you want to see me tonight, meet me at the corner drugstore at seven, and we can talk."

Dorine stood up and brushed off her cotton dress. She reached for Michael's hand as he stood up and walked her out of the cemetery.

"Should I be feeling guilty?" Michael turned to Dorine.

"Let's just think about the beauty of the night and let it happen if it's right."

Michael smiled at the logic of Dorine's answer. "I did have the best night of my life. Was it me, or was it Jimmy within me?" Michael asked Dorine.

"I know it was you that I was with last night. I know Jimmy would have wanted this to happen. He'd want the two people he loved most to be together." Dorine said, staring into Michael's eyes. "I have to think about it." Michael let go of her hand.

Dorine started to walk toward the boarding house.

"Maybe I'll see you at the Drug store?"

Michael smiled. "Yeah, you will."

Michael went home, bathed, and lounged around the house. His father was at work. He was alone in the haunts of the previous night. Half the day, he mourned his friend; the other half, he couldn't stop thinking of Dorine. It was six o'clock, and Michael opened his closet and realized he had nothing to wear. He still had the clothes from when he was fifteen years old. It is something when you can see how pathetic you must have been. The only special thing about him is that he is Jimmy's friend. Michael stopped and gave one last tribute to his friend. After several moments of shedding tears, he still hadn't figured out how to turn this situation around, but in his mind, he knew it was all right with Jimmy. For the first time in his life, Michael wished that his father were here to give him advice. Of course, he already knew what his father would say. "Give it some time." Michael's father didn't realize Dorine was pregnant, and they had no time to spare.

The evening air was still. The afternoon breeze ceased, trying to cool the town down, leaving it open for bugs and mosquitoes to become rampant. The sun was resting on the low surrounding Tennessee hills. Still high from the previous night, Michael left his house through the front door and walked to the drug store to meet Dorine. He was scared, not knowing what to expect from Dorine, but was more curious to find out how she felt about him. Michael dressed up in his service clothes. He had no choice but to wear his Navy blues.

Dorine was waiting at the drugstore when Michael walked in. She was sitting at a booth in the corner with two soft drinks on the table, confident that Michael would show up. If Jimmy told her the truth about Michael, she knew that Michael wouldn't let her down. "I hope I am doing the right thing by being here," Michael said, sitting opposite Dorine.

"You can't just put this all on me. Either you are here because you are interested in seeing where this will lead, or you need to get up and say your goodbyes." Dorine gave him the option.

Michael looked up from the table. "I think you're wonderful. I know a lot about you through Jimmy's eyes, but I want to get to know you through my heart." Michael reached for her hand.

Dorine smiled. "It was me who you spent the night with last night. And it is me who is sitting here in front of you right now."

Michael looked out the window. "Why? You are beautiful, loving, and giving. Why would you waste your time on me?"

Dorine lost her smile. "You really don't know who you are, do you? Sure, I had Jimmy's stories to get to know you, but you have rare qualities in men today. I feel safe with you. I know that I can be myself with you, and you would accept me as I am."

Michael confesses his heart to Dorine, "I've never had a girlfriend. How am I supposed to know what is right or wrong?" Michael looked away from Dorine's eyes, embarrassed that he had admitted that he was a virgin.

"That's what's special about you. Your feelings are genuine and innocent." Dorine smiled.

Michael and Dorine continued questioning each other throughout the night. On the way home, Michael asked her if she would go on an official date the following night. Dorine kissed him on the cheek and said. "Yes, I would love to go out with you."

The next day, Michael went shopping for clothes. He was determined to get it all together: the loss of a friend and the beginning of a relationship. Michael was nervous thinking about his date with Dorine. He had no idea what to expect. What he knew was that Dorine made things happen. That excited him, but why must she be Jimmy's girl?

Michael picked up Dorine at the boarding house. He knocked at the front door and was greeted by the woman who ran the place. Michael entered the foyer and saw Dorine coming down the stairs, wearing a dark blue skirt and a white blouse. Her red-painted lips and penciled-in eyebrows made her look simply beautiful. Michael's heart jumped with excitement at her smile.

They walked to an Italian restaurant that had been in Rutterfield for years. Michael had never eaten there, but everybody said it had the best food on the east side.

The restaurant was dimly lit, its ambiance enhanced by glowing candles on each table. A man played the violin softly, allowing the music to mesh with the flavors of Italy. Michael couldn't help staring into Dorine's eyes. With the flicker of the candles, her eyes invited him into her soul. Dorine was impressed with the restaurant. She started to get misty; this was the first time anybody had taken her to a fine restaurant. Engulfed by the moment and enjoying each other's company, Michael and Dorine began a new chapter in their lives together.

After dinner, they proceeded to the Rainbow Room. The streets are lined with people seeking a place to spend the night. Dorine and Michael held hands, allowing each other to gaze into each other's eyes. It was a Sunday, and the dance club was almost empty; the usual patriots lined up at the bar. The dance floor was bare. The band was on a break. The bartender put on a record as Michael asked Dorine to dance. The song was a slow country-western type of song. Michael put his arm around Dorine, grabbing for her lead hand. Dorine smiled and put both of her arms around his neck. Michael put his arms around her waist and stared at Dorine's creamy lips as he wanted badly to kiss them. Dorine could see Michael's intent, bringing her lips close to his, allowing him to connect. They continued to dance, swaying to the music. Michael softly laid his lips on hers. Dorine received a kiss and pushed hard against his lips, letting him know he did well.

Michael was lost in pleasure; the music and the sensation almost made him faint. He had to stop and refocus. Dorine opened her eyes, smiled, and kissed him again. Michael felt the love. He knew, dancing with Dorine in his arms, that he wanted her to be his wife. When the song ended, and they walked back to the table, Michael asked Dorine to marry him.

Chapter 14

Loving You Forever

Spring 1946, Rutterfield, Tennessee

The morning was bright, not tainted by the usual afternoon clouds. It was spring in Rutterfield. America was back in business after the shock of war had subsided. Most of the servicemen had returned to their previous jobs, and for those who were jobless, the government had programs to help them get re-established.

Rutterfield was an old town, much smaller than Nashville. Over the years, it expanded westward and evolved into a progressive city. Unfortunately, the progression benefited only the wealthy, leaving the poor and the unwanted on the east side of town. Many old buildings were abandoned for the unfortunate, who sought shelter at night. Most townsfolk blamed the influx of crime, fearful of the crazies on the east side. However, it was a mixture of people who stayed on the east side of town, loyal to the good folk of the east side.

The Chapel of Serenity, once located on the west side, doubled as a wedding chapel and funeral home before the migration. The large brick building, in need of maintenance, stood defeated next to the Rainbow Room. The Rainbow Room, a worn-out bar that was once a classy dance hall, was a place that attracted those free-spirited, the Beat Generation, and the poor. On the other side of the chapel was a woman's boarding house managed by a strict German lady who allowed her girls to provide sexual services to the special men of the west side. The blue and white two-story wooden boarding house was once owned by Doctor Reynolds, who sold his home to move to the prosperous haven of the fortunate.

On April 14, 1946, Michael Lore married his pride and joy, Dorine Honeycutt. The time was 9:00 a.m. Michael was standing on the steps, waiting for the chapel to open. He was wearing an ill-fitted gray suit that he borrowed from his Father, much too big for him. Early in the morning, Michael searched his Father's closet for the perfect tie, hoping to impress his future bride. The decision to wed was sudden, and there had been no time to invite guests. Michael and Dorine would be the only attendees of the morning.

When Dorine arrived from the boarding house next door to the chapel, she smiled at her fiancé, waiting nervously on the church steps. She wore a loose beige dress with lace sleeves that she had sewn on the previous night. Her hair was loosely curled, with a small doily resting on her head.

The streets were empty, except for the transients who had been unable to find shelter the previous night. Michael and Dorine stood hand in hand, waiting for the chapel to open. "You ain't having cold feet, are you?" Dorine said to break the silence.

"I wouldn't be here if I did," Michael said confidently.

Dorine smiled, "I thought these places were supposed to be open all day and night?"

Michael asked his bride-to-be, "Are you sure you don't want to wait until your parents can come to the wedding?"

"I'm afraid that time would never come. Mama and Daddy don't travel much with eight kids at home, especially from Kentucky to Tennessee."

Michael squeezed her hand, unable to think of anything else to say. His mind was racing, wondering how they got to this point. Michael had never been intimate with a woman, but Dorine made it seem so natural, so inhibited. When he was in the Navy, the guys bought him a prostitute, but he was so scared that they only lay together and talked throughout the night.

The chapel door opened. A young man with a giant smile on his face greeted the couple. "I hope you two haven't been waiting all night." The clergyman said, propping the door wide open.

"Are you both ready to commit for a lifetime?" His smile got more prominent as he invited them into his place of business. His wife came running out from the back room, still patting her hair down as she beamed beside her husband. "Oh, such a lovely couple. Young Lady, where are your Mama and daddy?" The pastor's wife questioned Dorine.

"My parents live in Kentucky and send blessings in this telegram." Dorine had a letter just in case she was to get married.

The Pastor's wife read the note:
Happy if you are Happy (space), *We give you*
Our permission (space) *to marry.* (space).
They ended the telegram with
love, mom, and pa.

The wife handed back the letter to Dorine. "Miss Dorine, how old are you?"
Dorine had to think before she answered.
"I'm 16 years old."
"That's young! But you do have a letter from your parents." The pastor's wife scrutinized.
The pastor was preparing for the service. "Do you want music? Emily, my wife, can sing a beautiful Amazing Grace."
Dorine put on a fake smile. "Please, can we get on with the ceremony?"

The pastor's wife put on an extra-large smile. "Look at you two, all young and ready to move on with your lives." As if she knew them forever.

"Harry, let's not delay these young folks any longer." Harry approached the front of the pews where Dorine and Michael were sitting. "Marriage is a big step in life." He said, hoping they realized what they were doing. Michael nodded his head, hoping to expedite the ceremony.

"Okay, Missy, you stand over here." Harry got up and went to where he wanted Dorine to stand. "And Michael, stand right here. Did we decide if we want music first?"

Dorine rolled her eyes so that Michael could only see. However, Michael wrinkled his nose at the pastor before he could say no. Dorine answered. "Since it's just us, we can start without music."

The pastor's wife quietly began to play the organ, but the pastor shook his head, causing her to come to a squeaking halt.

"Usually, Emily sings the last verse, and then the wedding march begins."

"Sir, no disrespect, but we both are already here," Dorine said impatiently.

Michael reached out and touched Dorine's hand.

Emily slid off the organ bench and rushed to the side of Dorine. "I hope you don't mind me being your maid of honor. I mean, since nobody will be standing next to you."

The pastor looked at his wife as though she had just given her last crumb to the poor. "We are here today to join together this man and woman."

Michael turned towards Dorine, looking straight into her eyes.

The pastor continued. "Do you, Michael Steven Lore, take this woman to be your wedded wife?"

The clergyman had to ask Michael again. "Michael, do you take Dorine Honeycutt to be your wedded wife? Michael smiled at Dorine and said, "Yes, I take Dorine Honeycutt to be my wedded wife." As the clergyman turned and directed Dorine, the baby inside Dorine's womb kicked and startled Dorine. Dorine made a slight noise, stiffening up her body in surprise. Scared to reveal her condition, she shrieked out a yes.

Chapter 15

My Love, My Wife Forever

1946 Rutterfield, Tennessee

After Michael and Dorine married, they hired a cab to take them to Triggers, a restaurant set right on a shooting range, patronized mainly by the folks from the west side. But today, in celebration, Michael and Dorine each ordered a deluxe breakfast. They were relieved that the ceremony was over, and they were officially married. Dorine sat next to Michael on the same side of the booth. She couldn't help telling everybody around, including the guys sitting at the breakfast bar, that they were newlyweds. Michael would smile, knowing that Dorine was way out of his league. She was beautiful, caring, and a lot of fun. The most crucial aspect of Dorine was caring. No matter what she put Michael through during their marriage, she never stopped caring for him. Of course, she hurt Michael numerous times in their lives, but it was never her personally trying to harm him. She could not be content, always thinking there was more to life than what she was living.

Michael's love for Dorine never ends; his arms are always open when she is ready to get it right.

The first night they spent together in bed, Dorine realized that Michael was inexperienced, and since she wasn't, she was determined to make the night special for him. While they were lying next to each other, the night's silence made it too clear for Dorine that she would have to tell Michael that she was already pregnant with Jimmy's baby.

With her head on his chest, she said, "You know that Jimmy and I were going to be married just as soon as you were to get home."

"Um, do we have to talk about Jimmy right now?" Michael didn't want to bring Jimmy into the most intimate night of his life.

"I think we need to talk about it. Jimmy and I were going to get married quickly because I'm pregnant. Jimmy and I were going to have a baby." Dorine closed her eyes tightly, waiting for the explosion to happen.

"I know you're pregnant. I told you, Jimmy told me everything." Michael whispered back to her.

Dorine couldn't help herself, and she just started to cry. "Michael Lore, you mean to tell me you knew I was pregnant and still wanted to marry me?"

Michael kissed Dorine's head. "It is my best friend's baby, too. I can't think of anyone on earth with whom I would want to raise my child other than Jimmy. And I think Jimmy felt the same way about me."

"That's the only reason why you married me?" Dorine sounded a little disappointed.

"No. I married you because you swept me off my feet with your beauty and kindness. Of course, I fell in love." Michael squeezed Dorine tighter.

"Michael, you're a wonderful man. I can't believe I was lucky enough to become your wife. You're handsome, generous, and a loving person. God gave me a wonderful husband. And now you are going to be a daddy." Dorine looked up to see the reaction on Michael's face. He was smiling, happy to be the daddy of Dorine's and Jimmy's child.

Chapter 16

When Love is Not Enough

1950, St. Paul, Minnesota

Dorine and Michael had been married for four years. They had Jimmy, and Lana was a baby. They had recently moved to Minnesota, and Michael was working two jobs. One was a janitor at a local school during the daytime, and at night, he tended a neighborhood bar down the street from their home. Dorine was a stay-at-home mom, complaining she was bored and hated feeling trapped. When Michael came home in the middle of the day, he needed to sleep before leaving for his second job. He understood Dorine's feelings but was exhausted trying to make ends meet.

He was at work when a teacher friend told him he had seen Dorine while running errands.

"I know this is none of my business, but you are such a nice guy." The teacher said, taking a big sigh. "I think your wife is fooling around on you. I saw her and a gentleman entering the St. Francis Hotel. She had your kids with her."

"Are you sure it was my wife?" Michael asked, swallowing down hard all that was trying to escape.

"Yeah, I'm sure. Dorine didn't see me, mostly because she was all over the guy."

Michael was silent. He grabbed his coat and left the school.

The afternoon was still cold as Michael walked to the St Francis Hotel. The hotel was located in the middle of St. Paul. It was one of the oldest hotels in town, now home to many transients who needed shelter from the winter cold. The thought that his wife was cheating on him wasn't the only factor that drove Michael crazy; it was the fact that she took the children with her. It wasn't the first time that Michael suspected that Dorine was cheating, but he wouldn't allow his kids to be subjected to Dorine's behavior. When he arrived at the hotel's front desk, there was a man as grungy as the hotel itself. Michael assured the man that he would not cause a problem, but he just wanted to get his children and leave. The man felt sorry for Michael and gave him a key. She's on the 2nd floor. Michael took the key and silently nodded, thanking the man. When he reached the room, he placed his ear to the door and could hear his wife in the midst of having sex. He used the key and opened the door. Dorine was on top of the man as she turned and saw her husband enter the room. The kids were placed in the closet, Lana was asleep, and Jimmy was sitting in the dark, playing with one of his toys.

Michael could barely contain himself. His vision was blurred, and he heard himself yelling at Dorine in his head, "Where are the kids?" but nothing came out. Dorine got off the man and pointed to the closet. Michael turned and went to the closet, bringing Jimmy and Lana. He took a deep breath and replaced his tears with a smile for Jimmy.

"Come on, son, let's go home." Michael reached out and grabbed Jimmy's hand. Lana was still asleep as he rolled her out of the room. Michael didn't want to explode in front of Jimmy, and he just continued to walk out of the room. Michael told Jimmy to wait for a moment. He went back into the room. In tears and shaking, Michael pulled a nickel from his pocket and tossed it onto the bed. "This one is on me."

"Stop it, Michael," Dorine yelled at him.

"No, you stop it," Michael said to Dorine. "How dare you bring our kids to such filth. What kind of person are you? What kind of wife are you?" Michael turned around and left the room, and took his children home.

The walk home seemed endless as Michael reflected on his wife with another man. He didn't know what he should do. Michael considered taking the kids away and leaving Dorine, but upon returning home, he decided to stay and have Dorine leave the house. He fed the kids dinner and put them to bed.

It was close to 8 pm when the front door opened. It was Dorine. She came into the house, ready for war. Tears were running down her face. "I've been walking around this block since this afternoon. I didn't do it to hurt you. We needed the money, and I thought I could help." Dorine tried to explain, showing Michael a handful of money.

"You whored yourself out to help us?" Michael sarcastically said.

"I love you, Michael; I'm sorry; it's just that I'm always here alone, and we need the money."

"Listen, I'll provide for my family," Michael said, not buying Dorine's story.

Dorine took a cigarette out of her purse. "Making love to you is special because I love you. When I'm with another, it means nothing to me. I know how to separate the feelings. Dorine tried to explain. "Michael, it's not about us. It's about who I am."

"Oh, you're a whore!" Michael said, shaking his head.

"I'm a survivor, and if it means selling my body, then they can have it," Dorine said, looking Michael in the eye.

"And I have nothing to say about who screws you or not?" Michael turned away from Dorine.

"I think you should leave," Michael said, crying at the thought of losing his wife.

"Michael, you are my husband, the most important person in my life. But I'm different from most girls, you know."
"I guess you forgot that you were my first girl. I don't know what most girls do." Michael yelled back at Dorine.

Dorine came back strong. "You knew that I had been with Jimmy, and you lived in Rutterfield your whole life, and you had to know that the boarding house that I lived at was a whore house."

Michael turned and looked at Dorine. "You were a whore when you were with Jimmy?"

"Michael, sex means nothing to me. I was raped nightly by my father and brothers. When I'm with another man, it's a job. It's a way I earn money; it has nothing to do with love or feelings. It pays the bills that you can't."

Michael sat on the couch, not believing what he was hearing. "What am I supposed to say? It's okay, dear. Thank you for loving us so much and giving your body to a stranger so we can pay bills."

Dorine stood up. "I guess we can't be together. If you can't understand me, then I can't be married to you." Dorine cried. "Michael, try to understand. If I'm not moving forward, I'm no better than being trapped back on that mountain. And yes, I'll be a whore before I ever find myself living the life I led before. Sex is not about you and me.

I fell in love with you, but even your love isn't enough for me to give up my dreams, my life."

Michael put his hands over his eyes. "I love you, Dorine. I can't stand the idea of us being apart. But you're right; I could never understand how you could give yourself like that." Michael wiped his tears away. "What do we do now?"

"I'll never do it again," Dorine whispered. "Please forgive me."

Michael looked at Dorine and saw a desperate girl lying to his face. "I think you should leave. I'll take care of the kids."

"And who will care for the kids when you're working two jobs?" Dorine asked.

"Dorine, taking the kids to a hotel while you service some man is not taking care of the kids," Michael said.

"I already told you that I'd never do that again." Dorine started to cry. "It's my life, Michael, and this is the person you married. But I promise I'll never put our children in a situation like today." "Please, forgive me. Please."

Michael stood up and put his arms around his wife. "I do forgive you. It hurts, but without you, I would be lost."

Dorine put her arms around Michael and began to cry. "Michael, no matter what happens in our lives. You are my only love, forever.

***

St. Paul 1965

It was 1965. Dorine had left her family and was living in Texas for the past year and a half. Her relationship with her boyfriend went sour. Desperate, she begged Michael to move the children to Texas so they could be a family again. Dorine's running away and making a mistake was not the first time she had left, but it was the first time she had done so over a man, calling off her marriage and giving up her children. In the past, Dorine would get bored with the children and her home life. She would become unstable, irritable, and just hard to handle. She would move to the other side of town, sometimes just down the street. Dorine needed to feel her independence, and of course, Michael knew that meant other men in her life.

Throughout their marriage, Michael put up with Dorine's unfaithfulness, mostly because he realized he couldn't satisfy his wife. It wasn't him; personally, it was because Dorine didn't view sex as a pleasure but as a means of security. Dorine knew that Michael had always tried his best. But she needed more out of life than God gave her through Michael.

Michael loved his wife and was always there for her. When she was ready to come home, she was greeted with a smile and a hug from her husband. Everybody knew that Michael loved Dorine, and his soul would light up when she entered a room. During her leaves of absence, you could tell that something was missing in Michael's life, like the spark just couldn't make fire.

Chapter 17

Splitting of the Family

St. Paul Minnesota

It was in the evening, late June 1965. The time had already changed, so the Minnesota sun didn't set until 9:00 p.m. The younger kids, Susan, Diane, Kathy, and Steven, played outside in the front yard. Alice was cooking dinner at fifteen, and Lana was painting her fingernails. Jimmy arrived home, hoping to be in time for dinner. Michael exited his bedroom and joined his older children in the kitchen.

"I got a letter from your mother today," Michael said, waiting for their attention. Jimmy took a seat next to Lana. Lana finished her nails and was shaking her hands in the air furiously. Michael continued, "She wants us to move down to Texas to be a family again." Michael said it matter-of-factly.

Alice almost dropped a pan of hot water on the floor, but tossed it into the sink instead.

"Now that's typical of her." Lana tried to hold back her thoughts.

Michael continued, "I want to move. She needs us; we're her family, and we need to support her."

"I don't want to move," Lana said, getting upset. "I'm going to be a senior this year. All my friends are here. I don't want to start a new high school."

Alice stopped cooking and pleaded with her father. "Daddy, please don't make us go. Why can't she just move back home?"

"She's not in a good mental state. She needs us."

"Dad, don't go," Jimmy said. "She'll be fine for a while, and then she'll start up again and leave you down there. It's not going to bring the family together. It's going to split us up." Jimmy gave his point of view.

"I understand, but she's my wife, and I have a responsibility to her. When we married, I promised to be her husband through the better and the worse."

Lana was outraged, "I can't believe what I'm hearing. She left us! She didn't care about her responsibility to you or us." Lana said. "She's only going to use you; when she gets bored, she'll leave us again."

Knowing his children were right, Michael was silent, but he also needed his wife. He had already decided to move before he approached them. He grabbed his whiskey bottle from the middle of the table. Alice saw that her father needed a drink and hurried a glass to him.

Michael poured himself a stiff one. He was having a hard time thinking that he may have to leave his older children. His children were his life. To think that they would be apart and that he would miss that part of their life was unimaginable to him.

Michael took a deep breath and allowed tears to well up in his eyes. "When each of you was a baby. I held you in my arms and promised never to leave you." Michael tore up from trying to make the right decision.

Alice went to her father, knelt on the floor, and put her head on his lap. "You will always be with us. We know our father, you are kind, hardworking, and your heart is made of gold." Alice said, smiling at her father.

Lana tried again, "Daddy, she doesn't deserve you. Let her go! Find somebody in Minnesota to love and allow somebody to love you, somebody who will stay with you." Lana pleaded with her father.

Michael started to get upset. "Don't you think I've tried? I can't get past the fact that I still love your mother. I have no desire to love somebody else. So, I'll wait until she wants to love me."

Jimmy listened to his father and sisters. He didn't truly understand how somebody could love so unconditionally, but that was who his father was. "Dad, take the younger kids with you. Love them as you loved us. Leave Lana and Alice with me. Try again with our mom and bring our family back together. I'll take care of Lana and Alice here in Minnesota."

Michael had no words to oppose Jimmy's plan. He didn't want to split the family; the idea of leaving the older children behind did cross his mind.

The decision was made. Jimmy, Lana, and Alice would stay in Minnesota, and Susan, Diane, Kathy, and Steven would move to Texas with their father.

The older children found a two-bedroom apartment. They moved a significant amount of the family's furniture to their new home. The furniture they couldn't fit, they sold or gave away.

It was the last day before the rest of the family moved. None of the younger children were happy about the move. They were sad to leave the only house they knew as home. They didn't want to move to Texas to reunite with a mother they barely knew. Leaving their brother and sisters behind made the move unbearable for the younger ones.

Lana came into the empty girl's bedroom, looking for Diane. "It's hard to believe this room is so big," Lana said, walking on the wooden floors, making a hollow clicking noise with her shoes. She sat down next to Diane, who was now eleven years old. "Do you remember the plastic tea set that Daddy bought you for Christmas a few years ago? Between his hectic days, how he made you that small table, and the two little chairs. Remember how you and Kathy would pretend you were two Queens having tea together as your countries carried on. And if Alice or I ever interrupted 'tea,' then the two of you would get so mad."

Diane smiled at the thought of her tea set. "I remember Jimmy playing with me one day. I was the Queen, and he was the King. There was a jester in our presence who just wasn't funny. And after several attempts to make us laugh, Jimmy had him beheaded." Diane started to laugh.

"Sweetie, we'll always be in your life. I'll always be your big sister." Lana put her arm around Diane. "And don't worry, just because you are there. And I am here; you'll always be my special sister." Lana whispered so the others would not hear her say she was her favorite.

Diane started to cry. "You know, Susan is so beautiful. What if everybody loves her, and nobody will love me?"

Lana smiled. "Now don't worry about that, you're a Lore, and everybody loves the Lore's. Besides, Daddy will be there with you. And if you feel unloved, you just hug him, and you'll see all the fears and pain will disappear." Now Lana was tearing up. "I know I'm going to miss those big daddy hugs."

***

The apartment felt unbearably empty, even though all the furniture was familiar. Lana missed her father, sisters, and baby brother Steven, who was only eight years old. She hated her mother even more, blaming her for their separation.

Jimmy was very busy. He was working at the Minneapolis/ St. Paul airport for Northwest Airlines. He had a great job, many hours, and excellent benefits, and brought home a good weekly paycheck. Jimmy tried to spend time with his sisters, between work and his girlfriend, but they never seemed to have enough time to enjoy each other. No matter where Jimmy was, he would call home at least once a day just to check in and chat. Sometimes, he would bring over his girlfriend, but it wasn't the same as when they got together. Lana and Alice didn't want to embarrass their brother, so they were always on their best behavior when she was around.

Lana and Alice seldom had friends over. Even though it was no longer imposed, the girls still followed Michael's rule of no friends unless an adult was present.

Jimmy would sometimes bring his friend John over. Having people in the apartment would make the place come alive. John was great, and he was Jimmy's best friend forever. John doesn't like Jimmy's girlfriend and feels she isn't good enough for him. She was always complaining and demanding all of Jimmy's extra time. *"Jimmy, you're always working and never have time for me."* Jimmy would listen to his girlfriend and would try to accommodate her demands, but Jimmy's attitude was that best friends were forever. A girlfriend could be gone tomorrow.

Jimmy was popular during his high school years. He was the quarterback on the football team, and everybody loved him. The fans, his fellow teammates, and all the cheerleaders always wanted a piece of his time. Jimmy's life was good. Even though Lana and Alice were no trouble for him, Jimmy took his responsibility for his sisters seriously. He never complained; the transition from boy to man was not taken lightly.

His love for his sisters was evident, as he always protected them and ensured they had everything they needed.

The kids had been living alone for a month when Alice came home, all excited. Lana and Jimmy were in the kitchen when she burst through the door. "I got a job!" She entered the kitchen and pulled a chair from under the table. "I got a job taking care of Mrs. Volker's mother. She's about 110 years old and needs somebody to cook for her and ensure she is okay."

Jimmy jumped up and congratulated his sister. "That's great!" he said, feeling like things were starting to look up.

"They're going to pay me fifty dollars a week," Alice said with a giant smile. "And the best news is," facing Lana. "They want you to work with me. They'll pay you fifty dollars a week, too."

Lana's eyes got huge. "What do I have to do?"

Alice was eager to explain the job. "We can trade off shifts. I can start in the morning before school, make breakfast, and get her ready to go. Then, when you leave school, you can stop by, make sure she's okay, and make her dinner. Then, at about 8:00 at night, we can both go to make sure she goes to bed safely. And that's it!"

Lana smiled and said, "Yes! When do we start?"

"Tomorrow, if you want," Alice answered.

The three of them enjoyed each other, thinking of all they could do with an extra $100.00 a week. Jimmy was proud of them working as a team. They all missed their family, but being able to provide for themselves gave each of them a sense of pride.

The girls started working a few days before school started. They realized that they had nothing special to wear to school. It seemed that Michael, their father, had a hard time providing clothes for the last year, so the clothes they wore were almost two years old. Jimmy went to the old bar where his father had once worked. He picked up some extra hours to help his sisters out. With Jimmy's money, he bought a couple of dresses, pants, and a few blouses for his sisters to share.

A large package came in the mail on the day before school started. Michael had sent a box full of new clothes for all three kids. Michael never forgot his babies and always came through for them when they least expected it. On top of the dresses was a simple note. "Love from your Dad."

Lana and Alice traded and switched dresses back and forth with each other. They giggled and loved their father for remembering them. They sat down and wrote him a long letter telling him how much they loved him and that he was the best father in the world.

It didn't take long for the news to spread around the school that the Lore sisters had their place. For some reason, this made both girls very popular.

A boy in Lana's science class asked if he could sit beside her. The boy was so handsome; you could tell by how he dressed that his family was well off. Lana was nervous but boldly looked the boy straight in his eyes and said, "Yes, please."

The two of them talked whenever the teacher wasn't looking. The boy was charming, and Lana couldn't help but fall in love.

The months passed. The kids had their first Christmas to endure alone. Jimmy bought a tree, and the three of them used the family decorations to spruce up the apartment. Even though they all missed their family, there was a healthy love between them. Jimmy's girlfriend came over on Christmas Day and opened their gifts together.

There was still one large box left under the tree with a note that read. *"Do not open until Christmas."*

How many days did each of them consider opening the box? "They'll never know if we waited or not," said Lana,

"I can't believe how close I came just to peek. Alice snickered. If it wasn't for Jimmy calling when I was in the middle of the act, I don't know if today would be so special."

Jimmy almost broke the trust when he came home late; his sisters were already in bed. He knew how important the box was to each of them and was determined to wait for Christmas.

Without saying a word, Jimmy pulled out the box under the tree. The girls got up and helped him rip the paper away from the giant present. They all stopped and reflected on the significance of the present. The box itself seemed more special than any gifts enclosed.

Jimmy broke the silence. "Should we wait for New Year's Eve?"

The three of them looked at each other and said, "Nah!" They all tore open the box. Inside were individually wrapped presents from each of their siblings. Along with their sisters and Steven's presents, each got a special gift from their father. It bothered Lana, not for herself, but for Alice, that their mother didn't even write a separate note wishing them a Merry Christmas. But she wasn't going to let these feelings stop her Christmas cheer.

Steven gave Jimmy a model ship he had built and told him that the ship was a replica of the battleship their Father was assigned. And for his sisters, he painted a "paint by number" picture of poodles, one for each of them. He added a note saying he hoped they could hang the paintings in their bedroom.

Kathy made each of them snowflakes out of string. She said in her note that they could be used as a coaster on the coffee table when not used as a decoration.

Diane knitted slippers for each of them. Lana's is a bright green, Alice's is red, and Jimmy's is a combo of dark brown and tan. They loved their new slippers and wore them until nothing was left of the bottoms.

Susan was more practical; her note said she got a job modeling. She bought her Christmas present with her own money. For Jimmy, Susan gave him dice for his car. Lana received an electric shaver for her legs. And for Alice, she bought a "fall" that attached to the back of her head. Alice was amazed at how closely the color of the hairpiece matched her own.

Lana was the first to get up and leave the living room. She excused herself and went to the bathroom. Alice knew darn well that Lana was in the bathroom, crying her eyes out. And she, too, was crying, missing her family, while she made Jimmy and his girlfriend some hot chocolate.

Jimmy put on some old Christmas music that belonged to their parents. Bing Crosby, Pat Boone, and Andy Williams provided nostalgia for their first Christmas alone. Lana came out of the bathroom and joined the rest of the kids. She started laughing at the music. "I can't believe we are listening to Bing Crosby. Lana smiled and told all, "This is a good Christmas!" Which made her tear up, "I guess I miss the rest of the kids, but it's great being here with you guys."

Alice brought Lana a cup of hot chocolate. "It's our first Christmas together. I should put something harder in the chocolate." She started to laugh.

Jimmy stood up and started lip-singing to Bing. Lana joined in and provided background vocals. Jimmy's girlfriend sat back, not knowing what to do, and Alice fell on the floor, laughing at her brother and sister.

Lana helped Alice with the early dinner. Alice tackled the turkey, and Lana made all the side dishes. Jimmy and his girlfriend, Judy, had made pies earlier, but they kissed and hugged in the living room as Lana and Alice stressed over the dinner. Jimmy's friends started arriving around 4:00 p.m. Lana looked at Alice and gave her a reassuring smile. "It's going to be great. Alice opened the oven door for the hundredth time, smiled at Lana, and whispered. "I hope so."

Lana offered Alice a cup of apple cider. "I'm sorry I got

so emotional this morning. I was thinking of Daddy and the kids. But what made me cry was thinking she could have written a note telling us Merry Christmas. I just can't understand her. Is her life so important that she can't take the time to say I love you? I know she has always been this way, so why would I think it would be any different now? But it still hurts."

Alice put the cider down and hugged her sister, "She is who she is. And she does love us. Besides, Daddy gives us enough love for both."

Lana smiled and pulled away from her sister. She wiped away a wandering tear and smiled. "You're right, and we have so much; we have each other."

Jimmy came walking into the kitchen. "Hey, a guy out there says he's Lana's boyfriend!"

Lana smiled and took off her apron. "Jimmy, talk to him. I'll be right in. I just want to fix my hair and makeup. Lana turned to Alice. Will you be okay with the dinner? Don't let my potatoes burn. I'll be back to help serve. Jimmy, can you set the table?"

Alice told Lana to get out of the kitchen with a quick shake of her head. Lana walked out of the kitchen and smiled at Roy Davis, her boyfriend. It was John, Jimmy's best friend, who came over and hugged her. "Merry Christmas."

Lana returned the greeting to John. "Excuse me; I have to change. I've been cooking all morning. Lana left the room and went to her bedroom.

The Righteous Brothers came out with a new Christmas Album, and John's girlfriend asked Jimmy if she could play the album on the Hi-fi. Judy, Jimmy's girlfriend, went into the kitchen and helped Alice. Roy sat on the couch; he didn't know anybody, so he just sat and waited for Lana to return.

Lana came back into the living room. She sat on the sofa next to Roy and grabbed his hand. Roy handed her a small package. The present was wrapped in blue foil with a navy-blue ribbon. Lana carefully opened the gift without tearing the paper. Inside was a little red box. Lana was excited just by the box, forgetting about what was inside. She opened the lid, and inside was a gold heart. She loved it and grabbed onto Roy's arm. She looked around and then kissed Roy on the lips. Roy settled back on the sofa, pleased with their first kiss.

John and his girlfriend slowly danced to the music while Jimmy and Judy giggled at the table. There was a knock at the front door. John turned down the music, and his girlfriend opened the door. There was a young man with a present in hand. "Merry Christmas. May I talk to Alice, please?"

Jimmy looked over from the table and yelled for Alice. "Alice, there's a boy here for you."

Alice came out of the kitchen to see who had dropped by. Lana got off the couch and escorted her sister to the door. Alice smiled when she saw Ronnie Stark at the front door. He wore tan continental pants with a light blue shirt, his black hair combed in a wave. His blue eyes made Alice melt. She had never seen Ronnie like this. He came from a small town called Penury. His family was self-employed, struggled financially, and was one of the unfortunate in the community. Usually, Ronnie wore old pants and T-shirts. He was more into cars and repairing them, so seeing him clean and dressed up made Alice appreciate him even more. She invited him into the apartment. He gave her a beautifully wrapped gift.

Lana approached Alice and whispered in her ear. "Where have you been hiding this guy?"

Alice felt ecstatic, and her Christmas was complete. Even the turkey came out golden brown and juicy. At the end of the evening, when everybody was leaving, Alice was in the kitchen with Ronnie. "Thank you for coming tonight. You really made me feel special. "I'm sorry I didn't get you a gift. Oh my God, I forgot to open your present." She took her hand from Ronnie's, hurried to the living room, and returned to the kitchen with the present.

"Can I open it now?" Alice asked Ronnie.

Ronnie smiled back and nodded his head yes.

Alice unwrapped and revealed a picture frame with a picture of Ronnie and her together at school. She put the photo to her heart. "I'll keep this next to my bed forever."

Ronnie quickly kissed her and said, "Merry Christmas, Alice."

Alice unwrapped and revealed a picture frame with a picture of Ronnie and her together at school. She put the photo to her heart. "I'll keep this next to my bed forever."

Ronnie quickly kissed her and said, "Merry Christmas, Alice."

Chapter 18

The Loss Of Your Child

1967 St. Paul, Minnesota

The New Year arrived with a slowed economy. The airline laid off over 500 people, and Jimmy was one of them. Times were hard for him. Judy, his girlfriend, waited until after Christmas and broke off their relationship. He tried to find work, but the only place to hire him was the bar where their father worked. Since Jimmy wasn't 21 years old, he wasn't allowed to serve drinks, so he was reduced to cleaning each night after the bar closed. Jimmy needed to find a job that would pay more. He received a severance package from the Airline, but with the minimum wage and severance pay running out, he would be out of money before summer. Jimmy talked to the girls about going to Texas, but Lana and Alice told him they would work more hours to help. When their father heard about Jimmy losing his job, he immediately sent money to help his kids make ends meet.

Early one winter evening, when the air was silent, you almost forgot you were in such cold. Lana and Alice were coming home from work. They were in good spirits, sharing each other's secrets concerning their boyfriends. When they walked into the apartment, all the lights turned off, and the apartment was dark. They entered the living room, flicking the switch that lit up the entire room. Jimmy was in the living room, sitting in the corner with a bottle of whiskey.

Lana was the first to ask. "Hey, I didn't see you. Are you okay?"

Jimmy nodded his head yes. "I just needed some time to think."

"I'm sure that bottle didn't help you come up with the answers." Alice scolded her brother.

"I joined the Navy today," Jimmy said.

"No, Jimmy! Come on." Lana rushed to the chair.

"I called Dad and told him I needed to do more than just clean a bar; besides, the Navy would be great. Dad was a Navy man, and look how much he always said those were the best days of his life." Jimmy explained to his sisters.

Lana answered, "Sure, they were the best days of his life; he's married to our mother, and any day would be great compared to their marriage." They all started to chuckle.

"There's nothing here for me. The Navy will give me some direction."

Both girls were in shock, "What about us?" Alice asked her brother.

"Dad said if you want, you guys can go to Texas with the rest of the family. Lana and Alice almost started to cry. "Don't worry; I didn't sell you out. You can stay, I'll send money, and Dad said he would help you both. Besides, I need a place to call home when I'm on leave."

Lana sat on the arm of the chair. "I don't care about the money; we need you. You're all that Alice and I have left. We're a family."

Alice tried not to cry but was emotional and couldn't find the right words.

"I have to leave by the end of the week. Besides the war, the government is discussing the draft. At least this way, I have a choice of what branch of service to serve." Jimmy explained, feeling up his glass with more whiskey.

"Can't you tell them you must care for us?" Alice finally found her words.

"It doesn't matter to them because you have parents."

Lana stood up. "We'd better think about moving to a smaller place."

"You don't have to move. It will all be okay, just the way it is. You'll see I'll be home on leave more often than I'm probably home now. Jimmy said, smiling at both of his sisters.

That night was sullen. Alice cooked a big dinner, but none of them had an appetite. Lana went to her room early, and Jimmy met his friends. Alice took an empty glass, slugged down two shots of whiskey, and cried herself to sleep in the living room.

It wasn't the fact that Jimmy was going into the service. All he said He was probably right. The tearing down of the family seemed to be spinning too fast for Alice and Lana. What always seemed home in Minnesota was making them question if they should be moving on. Their father, sisters, and Steven are so many miles away. It wasn't a good thing to live away from them. Now that Jimmy is leaving, maybe they should consider moving to Texas.

The roads were frozen when Lana and Alice drove Jimmy to the train station. The ride was silent except for the sniffles from Alice in the back seat. "Now, promise me you won't use my car unless it's an emergency." Jimmy directed his demands to Lana.

"I already told you I'd park it behind the apartment and cover it throughout the winter.

Jimmy's friend John was there to say goodbye when they got to the train station. Lana and Alice both hugged their brother. Lana had a hard time breaking away. John went for Jimmy's hand, but they ended up hugging each other.

Jimmy broke away and looked sternly into John's eyes. "Take care of my sisters. I'm leaving them in your hands."

John couldn't stop a tear from forming in his eyes. "I'll take care of them, I promise. You just take care of yourself."

Jimmy waved goodbye as he disappeared up one of the train ramps. Lana, Alice, and John were left alone, hoping that Jimmy would come running back. It wasn't until the train left the station that they decided it was time to go.

John put his arm around Lana and grabbed Alice's hand. The three of them left the train station and fought the bitter cold of reality.

The apartment felt empty without Jimmy. Alice and Lana each took on another old lady client, so there wasn't too much time spent at home. The extra money made up for what Jimmy couldn't provide. The winter was brutal, spreading ice throughout the streets.

"Can't we take Jimmy's car to school today? It's too cold to think of walking." Alice begged Lana.

"I promised Jimmy we would only use his car in an emergency. Just because you're cold doesn't make it an emergency." Lana said, gathering her book and bundling it up, ready to fight the cold weather. When they got to the school's front doors, Lana went her way, meeting with Roy, and Alice went another way to find Ronnie.

Lana and Roy were continually holding hands and kissing before and after class. Because she was Roy's girlfriend, Lana became a part of the 'in-crowd,' mainly because she was Roy's girlfriend. This commitment put a lot of pressure on her. She had to know how she dressed, did her hair, and how much makeup she put on her face. Old friends were significant to Lana, but being so popular so quickly was new to her, and it was hard for her to assimilate. Lana's popularity was especially difficult for Alice. Lana was always on Alice. "You're not going to wear that old dress, and can't you fix your hair differently, Lana would protest.

Alice tried to take Lana in stride, but occasionally, Lana pushed Alice too far. Alice rebelled and exploded several times at Lana's demands. She loved Lana, but her new attitude was too abrasive for her, and she felt justified in defending herself.

Roy's family lived in a wealthy neighborhood in downtown St Paul. The Davis mansion, built before the turn of the Century, boasted a driveway that circled a beautiful seasonal fountain.

The double-wide doors held a welcoming wreath that hung throughout the year. Several foreign cars honored the driveway. Full-time landscapers worked daily, keeping the estate looking like a park.

In the middle of the night, Lana would drag Alice with her and drive Jimmy's car over to Roy's parents' house, which Lana considered an emergency. They would park across the street and dream of what it would be like to live in such a place. Alice would always agree to go with Lana, but she silently didn't consider their adventures urgent.

"Someday, I'm going to be a part of that house," Lana said as if she were telling God his job.

Alice clicked her tongue, "I don't know, a big house like that, there's too much space for one to hide. I want Ronnie to be right next to me all the time." Alice said, just trying to dig into Lana's dreams.

Lana explained to Alice how the inside looked. "Oh, believe me, if you saw the house's interior. It would be goodbye, Ronnie, hello, Mr. Rich boy. Lana told Alice. "When you walk in the front doors, the ceiling reaches up forever. A double staircase leads you down from the top story into this room, which is empty of furniture, allowing the marble floor to shine elegantly. On the far side of the room are two doors, one leading to a study and the other to the main living room.

The living room is the size of our apartment complex. It had two fireplaces, one on each side of the wall. There was a full kitchen in the living room, excluding the large kitchen used by the staff. And the pictures on the wall were taller than me." Lana explained.

The house was more than Lana or Alice could imagine. To Lana, it was a real possibility that Roy and she would someday marry, and all this would be part of her life. After all, Roy had mentioned marriage several times. And they do say they love each other. It seemed that every dream of Lana would suddenly burst as the nightmare of these people meeting her family, especially her mother, made Lana very uneasy.

Lana placed her head on the steering wheel. "How will I ever explain Mom and Daddy to these people? Oh, they're married, but sometimes they go their own way, but they always end up back together."

"They're our parents. We didn't choose them, and they're all we got. How could Roy's parents ever hold that against you?" Alice said, placing a hand on Lana's shoulder. "Besides, what does it matter if Roy loves you and you love Roy? He ought to thank Mom and Dad for raising such a girl."

Lana turned her head toward Alice and peeked through her hands. She started to smile. "After all, we are Lore's," Lana said, sitting up straight and taking a deep breath.

The first time Lana had to meet Roy's parents, she borrowed Alice's lavender dress with white lace on the sleeves. She manicured every hair on her head and ensured she wasn't wearing too much eye shadow or dark lipstick. When Roy knocked at the door to pick her up, she took a deep breath, and they departed for his parents' house.

When they pulled into the gates, her whole body felt limp as Roy took her hand and helped her out of the car. When they reached the front door, and Roy invited her to enter, Lana had to command her feet to proceed. Roy's father came from the study to greet Roy's friend.

"Well, well! Hello. I'm Mr. Davis, Roy's father." Roy's father said.

"It's a pleasure, sir," Lana managed to say.

"Dad, this is Lana. Lana and I go to the same school." Roy made the introductions.

Lana was a little taken aback by the fact that Roy introduced her as a girl from school. But she smiled, and Mr. Davis invited them into the living room.

Lana went for Roy's hand to help her get through this, but Roy dropped her hand and placed his hand on her back, leading her to follow his father.

Roy's mother came in, dressed like she was going out on the town. She smiled broadly as she came in and kissed Roy on the cheek. She cocked her head and said. "So, you must be Roy's friend from his science class?"

Lana smiled back and nodded yes, even though she wanted to scream. Roy is my boyfriend, and we have shared much more than science; we want to get married. She then thought maybe this is how rich people play the game, so she replied. "Yes, we both have science together and math."

Oh," she said, acting surprised that Roy hadn't mentioned that. "And your parents, would we know them from the neighborhood?"

The question took Lana aback. How could she tell her, 'Oh, my mother is back into the family,' and most of the family lives in Texas? I live here alone with my sister Alice.

It was Roy who spoke up before Lana had to speak. "You wouldn't know her parents; they are from Texas."

"Texas! Roger?" directing her question to Roy's father, "Don't we know people from Texas? The Bushes, you know, George, and what's her name?" Roy's mother was trying to figure out who was who in Texas.

"Barbara." Roger spat back at her.

"Well, whoever. Please sit down. I'll have Alice get you some soft drinks." Roy's mother turned around to leave the room.

Lana almost died, wishing Alice could have been here to see that the maid was named after her. As much as it seemed like the longest day in Lana's life, she felt that she had made an excellent impression on Roy's parents.

One day, Lana was coming home and saw Alice and Ronnie walking home together. Lana rolled her eyes at the fact that Ronnie was always with Alice. Lana felt that Alice could do better. For Alice, Ronnie was her man, and she was ready to defend him, especially from her sister.

Lana walked up and said. "Ronnie, it's time for you to go home. Alice has to work today, and before she goes, she has to clean the house."

Alice's eyes bulged. She placed her hand on her heart and opened her mouth. "What?"

Lana continued. "You have been spending too much time with Ronnie, and I think you need to concentrate more on your studies and keeping our house."

Alice stopped and couldn't hold it in any longer. "You're an arrogant bitch. Don't you ever tell my friends or me what to do. Alice pushed Lana. Lana lost her footing on the ice and fell on her rear end. Alice stood right over her. "You think you are so high and mighty with your new friends. They're so phony, and you think they are the most important people in the world.

You better start remembering who you are, because if you think you are one of those rich, pretentious snobs, you had better come back to reality. Because when they dump you, guess who you will turn to? Me, that's who."

Lana sat there, fuming at her sister. Alice turned away, grabbed Ronnie's hand, and walked away from Lana. Lana got to her knees and pulled herself up using a picket fence beside the sidewalk to brace herself from the slippery ice.

When Lana got home, Alice was sitting alone in the living room. Lana burst through the front door, slamming it shut hard enough to shake all the neighbors. "Who the hell do you think you are to talk to me like that? Everybody in the world heard you call me a snob." Lana paused, waiting for Alice to explain. Alice was silent, and as Lana approached her, she saw that Alice was crying.

A wave of guilt fell over Lana. "What are you crying for?" Alice was still silent, and Lana knew she had gone too far. "It really hurt when you pushed me on the ground," Lana said, still mad about that, but she could tell something else was wrong, more than a fight between them. "Okay, I'm sorry. I shouldn't have come down so hard on Ronnie, but he sometimes can be so needy."

Alice handed Lana a one-page letter. Lana started to read:

Dear Lana and Alice,

My dear daughters, I wish I were there next to you as I bear this terrible news. Your brother Jimmy was killed yesterday in a motorcycle accident on base. My heart is so broken. I find it hard to explain our loss.

My son, my first son, is dead.

I don't know how any of us will survive this, but I know Jimmy would want us to be strong. But I find myself to be weak. God be with us because this trial is going to be hard to endure.

I have notified the Navy to send Jimmy home to Rutterfield, Tennessee, the town where I grew up. It would be nice if you both could meet us in Rutterfield for the burial.

I'm sorry, my lovely ones, for giving you such news. The funeral will be on Friday, the 21st. I feel helpless, not even understanding what it means to be a father if you can't keep a child from dying. My son, my son, he was such a good boy.

We're all going to miss our Jimmy.

Dad.

Lana dropped the letter, stepped backward, and sat on the couch behind her. Alice got out of the chair and picked up the letter. She reread the letter, stopped, and screamed, "This is bullshit, bullshit, bullshit." She started crying, grabbed her coat, and ran out the front door.

Alice walked and cried around the block in a daze for at least an hour. She went to Ronnie's house but decided she wanted to be alone when she got to the front door. Her face and hands were frozen, but the thoughts of her brother made her numb. She hated life at this moment. She stopped and yelled at God to return her brother, but then she ended up on an icy curb, asking God to forgive her for her foolish thoughts. The pain was unbearable, and she decided that she needed to check with Lana to make sure she was okay. When she opened the apartment door, the lights in the living room were off. The kitchen light was on, and Alice saw Lana standing by the stove. She entered the kitchen and saw a burnt piece of French bread, as black as charcoal. Holding a glass of whiskey and a cigarette, Lana looked at her sister and whispered, "I'm sorry about yelling at Ronnie. You're right. I was trying to be somebody else, not me." Lana started to cry as she sat down at the table. Through her tears, she threw back the whiskey down her throat, made a face, and poured herself another one.

Alice walked to the cupboard and got herself a glass. "I'm sorry that I pushed you down," Alice said, walking over to the table and pouring herself a glass of whiskey. Alice took a sip, then poured the liquor down, allowing the burn to hit her stomach. She sat across from Lana, wondering what they were going to do. "I can't believe he's dead." Alice barely whispered. Lana reached over and took her hand. "It can't be true. There must be a mistake?"

Alice was silent, allowing her sister to pretend, but she could feel that her brother was gone. The loss of Jimmy would be difficult for both of them, as it would be for the entire family. It was too hard to accept that someone so full of life, young, and a great son and brother could pass away so quickly. To Alice and Lana, to admit that their brother was dead would mean they would have to look at their immortality. Being alone, without their brother, knowing how hard it would be for their father, made them both consider moving to Texas.

Alice was crying. "I want to go home, but I don't know where home is."

Lana nodded her head, agreeing with Alice. "I don't feel so old right now. I think I need one of those hugs from Daddy to make it all go away."

Alice asked. "Do you think we should pack up and move to Texas?"

"I love Roy; how can I leave?" Lana stood up and ran to the bathroom. Either it was the thought of losing her brother, leaving Roy, or the Whiskey, but she found herself on the floor hugging the toilet.

Alice knocked on the door to make sure her sister was okay. "I think we need to wait to see Daddy before we decide to move to Texas," Alice told her sister through the bathroom door. Alice collapsed under the weight of her sorrow. She slid down the bathroom door and cried over her brother's thoughts.

While Alice was away from the house, Lana called Roy, but his parents would not let him come over on a school night. Then she called John, Jimmy's best friend, and told him that Jimmy was dead. Minutes later, the front door burst open, and John entered the house.

"Lana, Alice!" John called out.

Alice looked up from the floor outside the bathroom door. She was crying, shaking her head in disbelief. John saw that she was in shock. He slowly approached, sat beside her, and put his arm around her. Alice just started bawling, not able to control herself. "Jimmy's dead!" she cried.

John held her and let her use his shoulder as he tried hard not to break down himself. Lana gently opened the bathroom door and found Alice and John on the floor. She bent down and put her arms over John, wishing it was her brother instead of his best friend.

John stood up, hugged Lana, pulled Alice off the floor, and walked them to the kitchen. They all sat quietly as John had his turn to break down. "He was my best friend ever." John blurted, not able to stop himself from crying. He started to get up, but Lana was there first to settle him down. She held him and let him cry all his tears over her shoulder.

Alice got up, went to the cupboard, got three clean glasses, and returned them to the table. She poured straight whiskey into the glass and gave John one. Lana grabbed the other glass, and Alice sat back across from John.

Lana sat back down in her chair and sipped on the whiskey. "My Dad must be going crazy." Lana directed her comment to John. "He loved Jimmy so much, more than he loved himself."

Alice started to shake as she brought the glass to her lips. "I can't believe Jimmy is gone forever. I mean, it was already sad knowing he joined the Navy, but never to see my brother again." Alice broke down again this time, raising her hand to stop Lana or John from getting up to comfort her. She just took a deep breath and allowed herself to catch her breath. "Why would God take such a good person? Jimmy loved life, and life loved Jimmy." Alice said.

Lana agreed with her sister. "He had so much love for all of us. He was a great brother," allowing her voice to rise when she said, a great brother.

John gulped down the whiskey and reached for the bottle to refill his glass. "You know I got a letter from Jimmy two days ago. He was telling me about boot camp and the crap he was going through. Even though things were hard for him, he didn't complain about the difficulties. He was more concerned about me, telling me that it was a good thing I hadn't joined. He was sure it would get better, but what they had him do didn't make much sense to him." John said as he saw the letter from their father on the table. "May I read the letter?" Lana handed it to him. The three of them were silent as John read the letter to himself. After John finished reading, he set the message on the table, put his head down, put his fist over his eyes, and cried. Lana let him cry as she poured him another glass of whiskey.

John looked up and took the glass. Lana stood up, no longer wanting to be there. She got up fast and headed to the sink. All the emotion, liquor, and grief got to her and dropped her to the ground. John and Alice rushed to her side and revived her. They sat Lana up against the cupboard door. Alice got a cold rag and set it on Lana's forehead. The three of them sat quietly on the floor, thinking of their brother and their friend. "Did you know about Jimmy's real father?" John said to the ground, not asking either girl or waiting for an answer. "I remember when Jimmy came to my house the day your father told him he wasn't his real father. Jimmy was so upset.

We went into my bedroom, and he let it pour. Jimmy was angry, mad at your father for telling him. At first, he felt that your father didn't want him as his son. After we discussed it, he better understood that your father thought he was doing a good thing for Jimmy, releasing him from all the restrictions of being a Lore.

"Jimmy was such a good friend; no matter how manly we thought we were, we could still cry with each other. I'm going to miss my friend."

Chapter 19

Slumpville

John drove Lana and Alice to Rutterfield, Tennessee. They left on a cold, dreary Wednesday morning. The day after they received the letter. With the three of them driving, they figured they would arrive by the following day.

John owned a light blue two-tone 55 Chevy. All three of them sat in the front seat and put their luggage in the trunk. Alice made a bunch of sandwiches and brought along a jug of Mom's soda with three glasses. She placed them securely in the back seat, ready to satisfy their hunger or thirst.

Usually, one would leave Minnesota via Wisconsin. However, due to the weather and snow on the ground, John decided they should head south to Arkansas and then east through Memphis, Tennessee, to Nashville, arriving in Rutterfield by mid-afternoon.

After several hours, John surrendered the wheel to Lana. She moved the entire front seat closer to the steering wheel, making it uncomfortable for Alice and John, even though neither of them complained. The conversation was slow, and tears from the previous day had dried up, as Lana and Alice tried to make the drive pleasant. They decided that they would not talk about Jimmy's death, but the good things they would remember about him forever. The positive stories made each of them feel better about Jimmy. They could laugh with each other and share funny memories from their life. Lana shared how proud she was of her brother, being a quarterback, a charmer, and her big brother. She didn't allow herself to cry when she remembered how he would talk to her about girls in the middle of the night. How, as much as she loved him, he loved her.

Alice smiled to herself, trying to stick to their silent agreement, "the no more tears" agreement, but she felt cheated that she wanted more time with her brother. To see the dreams, he had become real. That he would be a part of her happiness, sharing special times in each of their lives, like seeing their parents as one again, hopefully forever; all these things were to come, and it was just too sad for Alice to think that all they had wished for would come true without her brother being there.

John shared a funny story about Jimmy getting caught dating two girls at one time. Lana or Alice had never heard this story and laughed halfway through Arkansas. John felt better, knowing he would always have his friend close to his heart. John's stories made the trip fun until one of them remembered why they were taking the trip. Then, the other two would be strong and pull the other up and out of Slumpville. That's what they called it after seeing all the "Ville's" in Arkansas. Slumpville is the sad part within yourself, like quicksand, when you emotionally get stuck and can't seem to pull yourself out.

It was Alice's turn to drive. John was in the back seat, sleeping, and Lana was changing the radio channels, trying to find a good music station. "Do you think Mom is going to be there? Alice asked.

"Oh my God, I didn't even think about that." Lana continued. "It's been a couple of years, almost three years since I have seen her. God, she was on her knees crying because she was going to Texas with some Tom, Dick or Harry." Lana smirked, thinking she didn't even know his name or cared too.

"Charles, his name was Charles," Alice said, keeping her eyes on the road.

"What was he like when you met him?"

"You know, like the others. White, redneck, drinks a lot." Alice described.

"God, could you imagine me having to introduce him to Roy's parents? I mean, what if he were to fart right there in front of everybody? I would just die."

Both Alice and Lana were laughing. "I can hear Mrs. Davis already. "Texas, are you friends with George and Babs Bush?" With a smile, a mile long.

Alice laughed with her sister, "See, you must admit they can be a bit snobbish."

"I don't think they are snobbish. They think they are normal, and all people act like them." Lana explained.

"Not everybody lives in a house like theirs, especially us. Daddy works three jobs just to keep a roof over our heads. Can you imagine a house as long as a block?" Alice tried to make her sister understand. "How can you live in such a huge house, knowing that most people worldwide are one step from living on the street?" Alice asked Lana.

"With Roy in my arms, I could live anywhere," Lana said.

"With Roy in my arms, I could live anywhere." John copied Lana's voice, making her sound sugary.

"Oh, my God. Were you listening?" Lana was embarrassed. "You better not be dating this guy just because his parents are rich," John warned Lana.

"I'm not. I loved Roy way before I found out he was rich." Lana tried to defend herself.

"Ronnie's broke, and his parents have less than we do," Alice added. "But I love him."

"Yuck! You sound like two lovesick girls." John laughed at them.

"Oh, and I suppose you're just hanging with your girlfriend. I've seen you with her, whatever you want, darling." Lana was imitating John's conversation with his girlfriend. They all started to laugh.

"I'm sure she knows where I stand. I'm not ready to settle down with one girl."

Alice started to laugh. "Yeah, right, but us girls know you're one foot at the altar and one foot on the go."

"No, I have another year of school, and then I have to get a job, and then maybe, just maybe, I'll find the perfect girl." John lingered in his thoughts, trying to hear his plan.

"Not me," Lana said. "I'm going to graduate, and the next time Roy says, let's get married, I'm going to jump on it."

Alice took her eyes from the road. "What about me?" Then Alice remembered that Jimmy was gone, and now her sister wanted to run off and get married. She started to get teary-eyed. Lana looked over, still smiling, thinking of Roy. She saw Alice starting to cry. "What's wrong?"

Alice said in a soft, blurred voice. "With Jimmy gone and you're racing to get married, where the hell am I supposed to go?"

Lana reached over and put her hand on Alice's shoulder. First, Roy has to ask me to marry him, and then he has to agree that you can come and live with us." Lana smiled at her sister. John lay his head down with a groan, reclining on the back seat, and tried to go back to sleep. Lana pushed the buttons on the radio. Alice concentrates on her driving, considering she doesn't yet have a driver's license.

It was early morning, and Alice woke up in the back seat. The sun shone in her eyes as she tried to remember the last time she saw the sun. The sky was a bright blue, with not one cloud floating by. Alice was thinking about heaven and her brother's final destination, not letting the others know she was awake. They were raised Catholic, and they did believe that Jesus died for their sins, but it had been a while since they had gone to church, at least a couple of years before their mother left them. Alice was sure Jimmy believed in God, and now Jimmy was in Paradise with Jesus.

Lana was sleeping with her head on John's lap as he drove. John kept blinking his eyes, trying to stay awake. Alice sat up and saw that John was having a hard time focusing.

"Do you want me to take over?" Alice whispered to John.

"No, just talk to me and keep me awake," John responded.

"How much further do we have to go?" Alice asked.

"I don't know; Lana is lying on the map." John laughed.

Lana heard them giggling and got up right away. She looked horrible, with her hair sticking straight up. She rubbed her eyes and stretched her back. "It seems like we have been driving for weeks."

Alice, from the back seat, said. "Hey, the sign said we are 20 miles from Nashville! Yeah!"

Lana grabbed the map from under her. "It says we need to keep going past Nashville, and we should see signs that say Rutterfield."

Alice started to get excited that they had made it, but then she remembered why they were there. She slumped back into the back seat and took a deep breath as they merged off the country road.

***

The three of them arrived in Rutterfield around 1:30 in the afternoon. They were a couple of hours earlier than John calculated. From the low-rise ridge, you enter Rutterfield on the west side. The streets were freshly paved, and the flowers were in bloom. All signs of winter were over.

"Which one of your parents lived here?" John asked.

"My dad was raised here, and my mom moved here when she was fifteen. I think she lived here for a year, and then my dad and mom married." Lana tried to brief John.

"Who lives here now?" John was looking around, thinking this was a pretty little town.

"I think my dad's cousin. After my grandfather passed away, the house became my father's, but my mom didn't want to come back to Rutterfield." Alice told John.

"I don't think my mom was around when our grandpa died," Lana added.

"Were you guys close to him?" John kept his eyes on the road.

"No, I only remember meeting him once. But I was young. Daddy used to talk about him often, and we have a picture of him and my grandmother, but that's about it." Lana said.

The kids approached Grand St., the dividing line between the west and east sides. The streets became dirty as they ventured eastward on Main Street. The buildings were old and unattractive. Even downtown St. Paul in the middle of winter didn't look as dreary as the east side of Rutterfield looked. It was as if the town was put on hold, hoping it would disappear over the years.

Lana felt threatened in this city. "I think we should have brought Jimmy back to Minnesota, to his home, instead of this God-forgotten place." Lana started to cry, thinking that she wouldn't want to be buried in this city.

Alice tried to comfort her sister. "This is where life began for Jimmy.   Maybe Daddy wanted him buried by our grandparents? At least Jimmy won't be alone.

"Right, like he really knew them." Lana ended their discussion. "I rather be alone than in this shit hole."

Looking through the window, Lana thought she was glad Roy didn't come. People were hanging out on the side of buildings, sleeping in the alleys between the stores. Kids ran barefoot, as if it were midsummer, while beat-up cars leaked tons of smoke. It would have been embarrassing to explain to Roy that her father was raised in such a town, even though Lana realized that Roy's parents would have never let him come on such a trip in the first place.

Alice started to laugh. "These people look as poor as we are."

Lana turned her head and didn't appreciate Alice's comment.

John was busy looking for the address. "Did they mention the Rainbow Club? I think that's what that sign says." They all looked at an old, damaged sign. "I just don't see any addresses. I think it will be on the left side of the street."

"What about those houses? Lana said and pointed, "Under that flock of trees."

John got in the left lane and stopped. "That's it over there, Alice pointed. See on the side of the house. It's missing the 3, but I'll bet you that's the house. John pulled into the driveway where Michael's car was hidden beneath one of the trees.

"That's Daddy's car!" Lana was excited about seeing her father. The car was a creamy yellow 1956 Ford Fairlane. Michael bought it when she was only two years old. Throughout the years, the vehicle has been faithful to keep the family moving, causing minimal problems. Seeing the vehicle bearing a Texas license plate made Lana feel betrayed as if the car didn't belong to her side of the family. It was just another reminder of the damage her mother had caused.

The driveway was covered with overgrown foliage; the surface was cracked from the roots of the trees. Diane was leaning against the side of the house, taking a break from the gloom within the home. "They're here! They're here! Diane screamed, running to the car, back to the house, and back to the car.

Lana was the first out of the car, and a big smile spread across her face when she saw her beautiful little sister. "I can't believe how pretty you've gotten." Lana smiled, loving her sister.

Diane threw her arms around her big sister. "I've missed you so much," Diane said with a strong southern dialect.

Alice jumped out of the car, and the other kids joined them. Everybody was screaming, jumping up and down, hugging and crying, and just loving each other. When things started to settle, Lana asked Susan, "How's Daddy?"

Susan made a sour face and told the group she was worried about their father. "He's been drinking more than usual, and his heart is so broken, the tears won't stop coming down. He never smiles, and sadness rules his life." Susan reported to Lana and Alice.

"Where is he now?" Lana asked.

Kathy cried out. "He left about an hour ago. He said something about finding his old haunts."

Alice tried to understand her sister. "What is that supposed to mean?"

"I think Mama was driving him crazy, and he wanted to be alone," Susan said.

Alice screamed when she saw her brother Steven. "Look at you. Oh my God, look how big you got. You look so handsome, just like Jimmy." Alice was almost able to stop herself from saying his name, but it came out, and everybody was forced to think of their brother. After a short pause, she said, "Jimmy, and that's something to really be proud of." Alice smiled without showing her teeth.

The kids all went into the house. Dorine was sitting in a chair in the corner under a floor lamp. She was donning a pair of Steven's socks. Dorine didn't bother getting up but shifted her glasses lower on her nose to get a good look at her children. Alice immediately went to her mother and hugged her while she sat in the chair.

"I'm so sorry about Jimmy, Mrs... John found himself lost, not knowing if she had changed her last name.

"It's still Lore," Dorine said, looking John in the eye. "Of course, I'm sad, but if we all just understand that we are born once, and we must die once. That's in the bible! It was just Jimmy's time. I guess God needed him more than we did."

Lana couldn't stand it any longer. She rolled her eyes and walked out the front door. Shouting to herself, "I hate her, I hate her, I... HATE HER!

John excused himself and followed Lana out the door. He put his arm around Lana and whispered to her. "Jimmy's in a better place; he is with his heavenly family now, and he is feeling love and peace, and all the pain of this world is gone for him."

Lana lay her head on his shoulder. "Even with a mother like that, Jimmy still could show love to all, even her." Lana cried to John.

John released his arm around Lana and grabbed her hand. "Let's go for a walk."

The two of them walked down the street. They passed Mr. Peterson's pharmacy, where Dorine got her first Job. The general store that Arne, Michael's father, managed, The Rainbow Club, where Michael asked Dorine to marry him, and in front of the mortuary, the same place used as a wedding chapel, where Michael and Dorine were married.

Standing in front of the mortuary, looking at the cracked open door, Lana and John could only imagine all the misery that lined the walls inside.

"I think my brother is in there," Lana told John. I don't really want him to agree.

"Do you think his body has arrived?" John asked.

"When I talked to Daddy, he said Jimmy was supposed to arrive this morning," Lana answered John.

"I'm going in. Do you want to come?" John released her hand.

"Yeah, if my brother's in there, I want to be there." Lana started to choke up again, mostly out of fear of seeing her brother.

They walked up the cracked cement stairs to the large wooden door. It was perched open, and they couldn't see inside the dark sanctuary. There was no sound, and it seemed the world had stopped as they walked inside. At the front of the chapel was a large wooden casket, which rested on a stand with a curtain hanging below. Next to the coffin was a chair with Michael sitting beside his son.

Lana released John's arm and asked him to stay behind. John took a seat in one of the pews as Lana approached the altar. Michael didn't notice his daughter because his eyes were closed, as he sent final thoughts to his son.

"Daddy?" Lana quietly said. "Daddy, are you okay?"

Michael opened his eyes and saw his daughter standing before him. His swollen eyes were almost shut as he acknowledged his daughter. He started to get up, but his knees didn't have the strength to support his will. Lana rushed to grab his hands and hug her father. Michael placed one arm free from Jimmy's casket around his daughter. Neither one of them said a word. There were no words that could express their loss. Lana felt dizzy from the pain that was piercing her heart. "Daddy, I'm sorry. Seeing you here makes me feel like I could have done something different, but I don't know what." Lana hysterically cried.

Michael put both of his arms around his daughter. "It wasn't your fault. If anything, I should have never left you all alone."

Lana, right away, interjected, "It was an accident. It didn't matter if you were in Minnesota or Texas. It just happened."

Michael closed his eyes and squeezed Lana, wanting his pain to go away. "He was my son, and I should have been there for him," Michael said. He took a deep breath, trying to catch the flood of tears rushing from his soul to his eyes. "He loved me, and he trusted me, and now he's gone."

"Daddy, we all love you, but we know you can't be responsible for a death." Lana consoled her father.

"You know, when Jimmy called me and told me he wanted to go in the Navy, I thought it would be a good thing for him.

I knew it would mean you girls would be alone, but I also knew you had each other. But Jimmy, he was always giving, and I wanted him to do something for himself." Michael laid his head on the brim of the coffin.

"He told me he loved me. To think a grown boy like him was able to say such a thing." Michael whispered to his daughter. "God, I'm not ready to give up my son. He was my heart and my soul. Did you know I never had to spank Jimmy? When he was bad, he would come to me and tell me his mistake. How could anybody punish a person who would recognize his own mistakes? And he was so smart and good and loving. I can't let him go." Michael was crying over his daughter. Lana was helpless in his arms, not knowing what to say or do. She knew she was losing her brother and a big part of her father.

"Daddy, please be strong. It's not our choice that God took Jimmy." Lana stood up and motioned for John to come to the altar.

Lana said to both, "We have to say goodbye and trust that God has Jimmy in his arms."

Lana started to feel faint. She pulled away from her father and told John that she needed air. John jumped to her side and helped Lana out of the sanctuary. Lana collapsed on a low block planter that lined the building. She put her head between her legs, trying to stabilize her mind. John ran back inside to bring Lana some water.

When he came back, Lana covered her eyes, allowing the memory of seeing her father so weak, unstable, and broken to give Lana a fear she had never experienced in her life.

John sat beside her, wrapped his arms and body around her, telling her to let it go. Don't worry; I'm here, and I'll be your strength. John placed his head on Lana's and silently prayed to God to give him His strength. Lana stopped sobbing, and the shaking of her body stopped. John kissed the top of her head. "I think we need to go back home and check on the rest of your sisters and brother, and all of us will return with dinner for your father.

When John and Lana returned to the house, Susan asked if they had seen their father.

"Daddy is at the mortuary with Jimmy. He's going to spend the night there. He doesn't want to leave Jimmy alone." Lana explained.

Susan started for the door. Lana stopped her. "Where're you going?'

"I'm going with Daddy. I don't want him to be alone."
"Let him be with his son. We can go later after dinner." Lana told her sister.

Susan stopped and listened to Lana. "He's hurting so much, and I think he needs all of us." Susan pleaded.

John answered for Lana. "Just give him some time. I think that's what all of us need."

Alice and Kathy made a big lasagna dinner. A chair was left empty for Michael. Dorine took the seat of honor, and she dressed in a blue shirt with matching pants. Her hair was loosely curled.

Dorine broke the silence, "John, would you do us the pleasure and say grace for us tonight?

John, not being overly religious, was taken by surprise. "Um..." Looking at Lana for help. Never has he had to ask God for help 2 times in one day. "Help us, Lord, in this time of need. Thank you for the food. Please take care of our Jimmy." All the girls started to cry, as did John and Steven. John looked up and apologized. "I'm sorry, Jimmy wouldn't want this. He hated sad things; he was full of happiness. And God is taking good care of Jimmy. It's only sad to us. John smiled and reached for Lana's hand on the left and Diane's on the right. They, in turn, held onto their neighbor's hand. John started again. "Thank you, Lord, for giving us each other so that when one of us is weak, the other will be strong." Everybody smiled, released their hands, and said 'amen.'

When they finished dinner and cleaned the dishes, everybody except Dorine headed out the door to be with Michael. Alice brought a plate of food, and on the way to the mortuary, John stopped to purchase a bottle of whiskey.

It was dark, and even though street lights lined the street, half of them didn't work. The kids arrived at the mortuary and joined Michael at the altar. Michael couldn't help but smile as he saw his beautiful daughters, Steven, and Jimmy's best friend. He managed to stand up, and the family hugged, respecting their brother, who will always be a part of them.

Lana smiles, "Daddy, your family is right here with you. When you cry, we're crying; when you feel pain, it's our pain too. We're one family, including Jimmy, and we will miss our brother, but in our hearts and memories, our brother will always be here, loving, helping, and protecting each of us."

Michael shook his whole body. "You're right, sweetie, together we'll make it through this. Jimmy would want us all to be as one. The sadness was over, and the celebration of Jimmy's new life began.

"Do you want to see your brother?" Michael asked.

Everybody froze. Not one person said a word. Steven stepped down from the altar, and Alice reached for his hand. "It's okay, sweetie; he's our brother."

Steven tried to understand. He was 13 years old, and seeing his big brother dead was terrifying to him, but with the strength of his family, he got back on the altar.

Michael opened the casket, and Jimmy was lying peacefully, looking as though he were asleep.

At least, that is how Kathy described it. Diane wasn't comfortable with the situation and hid behind Lana until she realized it was only Jimmy in there.

Dorine sat by herself in the back of the sanctuary, watching her family say their goodbyes to her son. She suffered her grief, not only saying goodbye to her son but to the last link to the first man she ever loved.

Morning came sooner than any of them wanted it to arrive. The front door squeaked open around 6:15 in the morning. Michael sneaked in from being in the mortuary with his son all night. John was on the floor and propped his head up. Lana was asleep on the sofa, and Alice was squashed between an overstuffed chair and the coffee table. Susan and Diane were in Michael's parents' old room, and Dorine, Kathy, and Steven were in Michael's old bedroom.

Michael went to the kitchen and started a fresh pot of coffee. Lana got up and went to the kitchen to hug her father. "Dad, take the sofa and get some sleep."

Michael smiled and loved his daughter. "I'm okay; you go back and get a couple more hours of sleep." Michael was slurring his words from a lack of sleep.

"I'll finish making the coffee. At least go and sit down." Lana commanded.

Michael took a deep breath and headed for the couch. Only moments before his head slumped forward, he was asleep.

Lana poured a cup of coffee for herself when her mother entered the kitchen. "Got any left for me?" Dorine asked.

Lana was already irritated because Dorine was so loud. "Everybody is still asleep," Lana whispered loud enough for Dorine to get the message. She poured her mother a cup of coffee and added the exact amount of milk she liked, along with ½ teaspoon of sugar. She handed the completed cup to her mother.

"What time did your father get home?"

Dorine asked Lana.

"Just a few minutes ago, he was exhausted."

Dorine went into the dining room, hoping that her daughter would follow. Lana looked for any escape but ended up joining her mother.

"I don't know what to say to you anymore." Dorine started. "It's a lot of water under the bridge. I really don't know where to begin."

Lana closed her eyes and sighed. She was right; too much water was under the bridge, and she didn't feel like getting her feet wet. "Let's just get through the day," Lana said.

"Your father and I met for the first time at a funeral. Who would have ever thought?" Dorine was reflecting.

Lana wasn't in the mood for stories this morning. "I hope Daddy is going to be okay."

"It'll take a while, but you know how much your father loves you, kids."

"And you, Mom? Do you love us kids?" Lana dug into her mother.

"I love every one of you. Yes, even you, Lana, if that is what you're implying?"

"Right now, mom, it doesn't matter, and I surely don't want to fight over it today."

Dorine crossed her legs and took another sip of her coffee. "Jimmy was my first boy, and he'll always have a special place in my heart just because he was my first."

Lana couldn't hold back. "I don't have a problem with that. Nobody has ever told you that you had to love each of us equally. But I don't know if you know how to show your love to any of us. But I'll tell you right now, Jimmy loved you, and so does Alice."

"What about you?" Dorine turned to hear Lana's answer.

"I think you have done a lot of damage to my Dad and the family. And yes, I love my family, so I guess I can't say that I don't love you, but I don't understand you. Maybe someday I will, and then maybe I can answer that question."

"You don't know how much it hurts your father, you girls up in Minnesota." Dorine tried to share the blame for the family's separation.

"That's the problem, Mom; why doesn't it hurt you?" Lana couldn't take anymore and got up, walking to the kitchen.

Dorine followed, not giving the last word to Lana. "I would say I cared, and it hurts me if I thought it would mean something."

"Mom... It's Jimmy's day. Let's not fight. Let's pretend we are a family and say goodbye to my brother."

Dorine nodded her head yes. "Let's make this a special day, a good day."

"Without my brother, no day will ever be a good day. Just a day dedicated to him."

For some reason, Dorine thought it was okay to hold Lana's hand. Lana felt awkward and pulled her hand away.

Dorine, feeling rejected, said, "Someday you'll understand, and I won't be that mean, horrible mother." Dorine said, leaving the kitchen and returning to Michael's room.

Lana took her coffee to the front porch. The sun was already up, but the morning dew was still lingering. Lana gazed over the horizon and thought about Roy. She became upset because she had somehow forgotten about Roy amid all the chaos. Lana loved Roy and couldn't wait until she and Roy married and started their own family. She promised herself in front of God and the rising sun. "I'll never be like her, never!"

Chapter 20

Saying Goodbye to My Son

The chairs were all arranged when they arrived. Mr. Peterson and his wife sat behind the kids on the single row of chairs. Michael and Dorine sat next to each other on the right side of Jimmy's coffin. Dorine was wearing a black sweater and a black skirt with black nylons. Michael was wearing his black suit, his only suit because that was what Dorine had laid out for him to wear.

A priest from Westside Catholic Church came to preside over the ceremony. The minister who married Michael and Dorine volunteered to say the last words, but Michael thought it was important that Jimmy had a proper Catholic funeral The priest was old, saying most of the service in Latin. Nobody, including Michael and Dorine, knew when to respond, so the priest continued the service without waiting for the family's participation. At the very end, after the priest blessed Jimmy, he asked if anybody had anything to share.

At first, it was silent, but then Michael stood up. "I loved my son, and I thank God for the time I had with my son, but now, Jimmy, my old friend, I give you back your son. He is yours to share eternity. Love him as you loved me, and always stay with him. And son, this is your father; he was a wonderful man like you. Love him, son, as you loved me. Michael stepped forward to the casket and placed a rose in his hand on top of the coffin.

Dorine stood up, stepped over to the casket, fell on her knees, crossed herself, said a silent goodbye, got up, put her rose on the coffin, stepped back, and sat in her chair. All the kids were crying. They held each other's hands, holding each other steady. Nobody wanted to say anything, and they had already said goodbye to their brother the night before.

Charles, the minister, and his wife sang "Amazing Grace" harmoniously. The sweetness of the notes penetrated each of their souls, confirming that Jimmy was in this peaceful place, hearing all the angels singing in perfect harmony.

Each sibling held hands and made a line to the exposed casket. They stood in a row, still holding hands, surrounding Jimmy, and in silence, each of them placed their rose on top of the casket. From their hearts and souls, each asks God to love their brother in eternity and help each of them to make it through life without their son and brother.

Chapter 21

The Mending of a Broken Heart?

When they returned to Minnesota, the girls hugged and kissed John goodbye. They begged him to stay in touch, and John promised he would; after all, he promised Jimmy to take care of his sisters.

On the first night home, Lana called Roy on the telephone. His mother answered and told Lana that she was sorry to hear about her brother. Lana thanked her for her concern, but was more anxious to hear her boyfriend's voice.

"Hello," Roy said, sounding like he just woke up.

"Hi, sweetie, I'm back." Lana waited for this moment, hearing Roy's voice, knowing he missed her as much as he missed him.

"Are you okay? I missed you." Roy was not giving Lana a chance to answer. "Can I see you tonight?"

Lana almost bursts with joy. "Yes, please, yes!"

"I'll act like I'm going to bed early and sneak out about 11:00. Is that too late?

"No, not at all. I just can't wait. It was horrible, mostly because you weren't there." Lana poured it on.

The conversation was coming to an end. Roy had to hang up because his parents disapproved of him spending too much time on the telephone. "I love you, he whispered, making it so that his parents didn't hear him.

"I love you, too," Lana said, hanging up the telephone.

Lana and Alice decided that Lana would move into Jimmy's room. It was hard, but they packed Jimmy's belongings and placed them deep into the closet. Lana put her sheets and bedspread on the bed, took down Jimmy's posters, and put up her pictures, including Steven's painting of a Poodle.

That night, Alice went to bed at about nine, knowing they had school the next day. Lana didn't want to explain to Alice that Roy was coming over and acted like she would go to bed, too. It was about a quarter to eleven when Lana dressed, waiting for Roy to arrive.

She entered the living room and sat in the dark on the sofa. When she heard Roy come up the porch, she jumped up and answered the door before he could knock. She placed her finger over her lips and smiled at Roy. "I don't want to wake up, Alice."

The two of them started kissing at the front door, then moved to the couch, and finally, Lana asked Roy if he wanted to spend the night.

Roy couldn't get enough of Lana's lips as his hands explored her body. Lana, feeling in control, showed Roy to her new bedroom. Once inside, they both giggled and kissed and made love for the first time. When early morning came, Lana was the first to wake up and look at her clock. She woke up Roy, and he hurried to dress and run home before his parents could discover he was gone. Lana rested in her bed, not wanting to face her morning routine. She couldn't stop thinking of the previous night. Roy was her first love, and he was beautiful and gentle. She loved him. There was nothing Lana did that made her ashamed. She loved Roy, and he loved her; soon, they would be getting married.

Roy snuck over each night after. Lana and Roy would spend the first part of their secret time discussing their upcoming marriage, and the other part of the night making passionate love.

It was the beginning of summer. Lana had graduated from high school, and her father sent her a beautiful pair of diamond earrings as a graduation present. The ceremony was long, each classmate's name read, the diplomas handed out, and the long-winded speeches about what Sally Fagerson thought about the future of her class. Alice and Ronnie were bored, but they made the best of it by kissing between each name called out. By the time they got to Donna Wilson, Alice's lips were sore, and her mouth was tired, but she, too, was falling in love with Ronnie.

Lana and Roy decided they would attend the community college in St. Paul. Lana had the grades to participate in a university, but her father couldn't afford the tuition. To Lana, attending a university would be a waste of money since the classes at the community college would transfer over later to a college of her choice. Besides, Roy said he would go to the community college so they could stay together.

The summer was hot and sticky. The swamp cooler in the apartment didn't help unless you were in the same room. Lana would keep her window open throughout the night, hoping to suck in any extra air. Roy would show up late at night, ready to share the night with his love.

Lana and Alice seemed to find themselves apart from each other. Alice took on another old lady for the summer and spent the time she wasn't working with Ronnie, mostly at his parents' auto shop. When she was home, she would cook, clean, and try to catch up with Lana, but the separation and Lana's secret nights kept a reasonable distance between them.

It was mid-August, and Alice was cooking fried chicken for dinner. The apartment was sweltering, and Lana exited her room, starting to yell at Alice. "Why are you cooking when it is so damn hot in here?" Lana snapped at Alice.

And quit cooking for me. Look at me. Your cooking is getting me fat." Lana pulled up her top so that Alice could see her stomach.

"Alice was just as hot as Lana and wasn't about to take crap from her. "If you don't like my cooking, then make your own dinner. What a bitch." Alice whispered, "what a bitch."

"I'm sorry, it's just hot." Lana approached Alice and wrapped her arms around her waist. "I love you, sister. And you better watch those words. You are not too big for me to wash your mouth out."

Both girls laughed. They shared a good dinner that night, enjoying each other's company. With their lives in different directions, it was good to take a moment and catch up. When all the dishes were clean and Lana was heading back to her bedroom, Alice yelled from the kitchen. "Don't think you're fooling anybody with Roy sneaking in every night." Lana didn't answer. She smiled as she closed her bedroom door.

***

As much as Lana wanted just to ignore specific symptoms she was experiencing, feeling suddenly sick, her breasts sore to the touch. She refused to believe that she was pregnant. When her period failed to come two months in a row, Lana knew that meant trouble. She made an appointment with her family doctor, but when she saw the forms she had to fill out, she left the office when the receptionist was away from her desk. Lana decided to visit the free clinic to determine if she was pregnant before filling out any paperwork.

The clinic was full of sick people, mostly kids whose parents didn't have any money to seek private care. Lana knew she would pick up something from all the sick people in the waiting room. Lana was disgusted seeing babies with rashes on their faces. Watching little kids wiping their noses on their mothers' legs and mothers dressed in clothes without much fashion gave Lana a different perception of motherhood. Admittedly, it was not the perspective she needed at the moment.

The doctor was so busy that Lana never actually got to see the doctor. A nurse came to the door, called out her name, and asked her to pee in a bottle. Lana gave the nurse the urine specimen and was about to leave. When she was almost out the door, the nurse popped her head out the receptionist's window. "I'll have the results tomorrow. I'll call you." Everybody knew what Lana was going through. One lady whispered to Lana as she was leaving. "Good Luck."

Lana couldn't leave that place fast enough. She wondered, what if she ran into Mrs. Davis, Roy's mother. She even peeked outside the window before going out the door. Her better sense came to her, and she thought, what would Mrs. Davis be doing in this part of town?

The telephone rang early. Lana was close by, making sure she answered instead of Alice. "Mrs. Lore?" Lana heard a female voice. Hi, this is Emily from the Wichocoo County Health Clinic. I have your results from yesterday's test. Lana started to sweat, thinking, Just tell me. "The results conclude that you are pregnant, close to three months. Dr. Benhnam Bosamolie suggests you visit your regular doctor and plan your delivery sometime in February. Lana, in shock, set the telephone back into the cradle, forgetting to thank the nurse. Alice walked in just as Lana was starting to sway. She caught her and set her on the couch. "Are you okay? Who was that on the phone?" Alice was scared to ask her sister.

"It was the doctor. Oh shit, I'm pregnant." Lana told Alice.

"Oh shit, pregnant?" Alice had to ask again.

"Roy and I are going to have a baby." A smile came upon Lana's face.

Alice couldn't process the information given. She didn't know whether to start crying or be happy for her sister. "What are you going to do?" Alice asked.

"Well, Roy and I were planning on getting married. Now, we will have to do it right away." Lana smiled at Alice. "Please, can you help me make a big dinner for Roy? I'll tell him tonight."

Alice got off the couch, not knowing what to say to her sister.

Lana broke the silence. "I'll run to the grocery store and buy some steaks." Lana smiled and said it as if everything was all right. "Listen, this is between you and me."

Lana pleaded, "There's no reason we ever have to tell the whole family." Lana was paranoid that this would get back to their father. "Roy and I will get married and tell everybody we got pregnant on the honeymoon. When the baby comes, we'll just say that the baby was premature. Besides, who will care? We'll be married, and Roy and I will raise this baby with lots of love and happiness."

Lana convinced Alice that everything would be okay. She prepared the kitchen for the feast as Lana ran to the grocery store.

Lana prepared the table with the best china they had. She couldn't wait to tell Roy he would be a father. It was seven o'clock in the evening when Roy showed up. The dinner was prepared, and Alice left on a date with Ronnie, which meant they would spend the evening at the family's auto shop with Ronnie's friend Lyle, smoking pot and drinking beer.

Roy was in a good mood and brought Lana a single rose wrapped in green wax paper. The florist left their card between the paper and the flower.

The announcement read: *To my lady forever.*

Lana received the flower, smelled it, and kissed Roy. "Come on in. I have a huge dinner for us."

Roy's eyes got big when he saw how beautiful the table looked. He walked to the table and pulled out a chair for Lana.

She smiled and accepted the invitation, but remembered to serve them both. Lana brought out a bottle of red wine and asked Roy to open it. She returned from the kitchen with a platter of steaks still sizzling in their juices. Roy stood up and helped her set the platter on the table. Lana left and returned with the side dishes, potatoes, vegetables, and bread. Before she took her seat, she served her man, showing her love and appreciation to him. Roy poured Lana a glass of wine, reaching over and placing it on her plate. After she sat down, he lifted his glass into the air. Here's to my beautiful woman and this wonderful dinner she prepared. They both reached over and clanged their glasses. The wine was terrific. The freedom the kids enjoyed allowed Roy to pour himself another glass. Dinner went well. They talked, laughed, and enjoyed each other. After a bowl of ice cream for dessert, Lana picked up the remaining bottle of wine and put it on the living room table. She got two clean glasses and directed Roy to go into the living room while she cleaned up the table. All this treatment was not new to Roy; Lana always treated him special, but tonight was over the line, and Roy could only think that he had forgotten something, an anniversary or a particular date. Lana told Roy she would return and wanted to change her clothes. When Lana returned, she was wearing a black, see-through blouse she had bought for a night like tonight. Roy's mouth dropped open when he saw how beautiful Lana looked. "Wow, I should go home and change, too.

You look way too nice for a homely boy like me."

Lana smiled and sat next to her man. She planted a kiss on him that warmed up his insides. Lana took a deep breath. "Sweetie, I heard from the doctor today. It seems that we're going to have a baby!"

Roy was silent as though somebody had kicked him in the stomach. "You're pregnant?" Roy finally managed the words to escape from his lips.

"Yes, about three months pregnant," Lana answered, letting him absorb the news.

Roy was calculating in his mind if they had been together for three months.

"What are we going to do?" Roy asked.

"Well, we always talk about marriage." Lana squeaked out.

"Yeah, but that was supposed to be after college." Roy pulled away from Lana.

"We can still go to college. We'll just have a little one to care for and love. Alice will help us, and everything will be good." Lana tried to convince Roy and kissed him to ensure everything was okay, but Roy didn't respond and pulled away from her.

Maybe we should talk about adoption.

Give us some time to get our lives together before we have to take on another mouth."

Lana felt the rejection from Roy. She turned away from him, disappointed with what she was hearing. "You do love me, don't you?" Lana had to ask.

"Of course I do." Roy automatically answered.

"And you still want to marry me?" Lana started to cry.

"Yeah, but not today. I mean later when we are older and have direction in our lives."

Now Lana was crying. "We don't have later. We have about two more months before I'll really be showing."

Roy was starting to feel the pressure. "How can we have a proper wedding in two months?"

"Maybe we should just run away and get married, just the two of us." Lana pleaded.

"Elope? I'm the only child. My parents would never forgive us."

Roy stood up, "I need to think about this. I just can't be expected to make the right decision at a moment's notice. Roy started to head for the door. He turned and saw Lana crying, sitting on the sofa. Maybe we should decide to stop this pregnancy right away. I'm sure my parents would have some connection to make it safe.

"You want me to abort our child? First of all, it's illegal, and second of all, the baby is a part of you and me." Lana pleaded with Roy. "Please, let's work this out together. Please don't leave me. I'm scared."

Roy went for the door. "Damn it; I'm scared too. I feel ambushed into marriage. I should go. I'll call you later."

Lana couldn't believe it. Roy ran out on her. All his talks about how much he loved her were lies. Fragments of hot air used to deceive her into believing that he loved her. How could she be so foolish? Seduced by his words, alone to figure out what she was going to do about the baby, Lana cried.

Roy didn't call that night or the next day. Lana got a call from Mrs. Davis, Roy's mother, the following day.

The telephone rang, and Lana answered, hoping it was Roy. "Lana?" A high-pitched voice loudly announced. "This is Mrs. Davis, Roy's mother. Sweetie, we know all about it, and don't you worry, we'll all figure it out. Can you meet me for lunch today around noon? How about at the clubhouse, the President's Palace over by 1st? Street? Just tell them at the guardhouse that you are a guest of mine. They will direct you from there."

Lana feared Roy's mother, but she agreed to be there. "Will Roy be joining us?" Lana asked.

"No, let's make it us girls only." Mrs. Davis strongly suggested.

Lana hung up the telephone and looked at the clock. It was already a quarter to 11, and she needed to prepare herself and figure out where she was going. Lana ran to her room, half scared of what this woman would tell her. Lana kept asking herself, What if she really meant to help us? Maybe with her blessing, Roy will feel better about marrying me. She screamed across the apartment, "Alice, hurry."

Alice jumped out of her room, thinking something was wrong with Lana. "What's wrong?"

"I have forty-five minutes to get ready to meet with Roy's mother." Lana pushed up her hair, trying to figure out how to style it.

Alice had to ask, "Is that good?" Alice was confused, unsure whether Lana was upset because she had to meet with Roy's mother or because there was so little time to get ready. Alice took control of the situation. "Go shower, and I'll lay some clothes for you."

Lana agreed with her, and Alice left, wondering what she would pick out for her.

Alice screamed through the bathroom door. "How about the flower dress you wore to Sally's birthday party?"

Lana yelled from the shower. "No, that's too bright. She said she knows all about the pregnancy, something plain and conservative."

"I have my brown skirt with my tan silk blouse," Alice screamed back to Lana.

"Yeah, that's perfect. Wait! I don't have any brown shoes. Can I wear my black low heels with it?"

Alice thought about it. "No. You'd better wear my off-white sandals."

Lana was frantic. "Oh my God, look in my drawer and see if I have any nylons without runs."

Alice left the bathroom door and opened Lana's dresser. There were three pairs of nylons. One was nude, the other was black, almost a leotard, and the third was sheer white like nurses would wear. "You better wear the nude ones; the others would be inappropriate," Alice called back to her sister. Lana raced out of the bathroom and into her room. Alice had placed the outfit on Lana's bed. "Oh my god, what should I do with my hair?" Lana shrieked.

Alice barged in, grabbed Lana's hair, and twisted it Frenchly. "Here, we'll just pin it up with this." Alice attached a large brooch to Lana's hair. She removed bobby pins from her mouth and stuffed them in Lana's head to hold her hair up.

For a fifteen-minute job, Lana looked great. She got to the club with five minutes to spare. Lana approached the security guard and told him Mrs. Davis requested her presence. The guard had the security arm up before she finished her name.

"Have a great afternoon," he said with a giant smile. Lana parked the car and walked up the stairs to the large white colonial building. She was about to open the door when it was opened from inside by a man in a tuxedo.

"Good afternoon, madam. May I assist you?" The gentleman said.

Lana answered, trying to remember Mrs. Davis's instructions. "I have an appointment with Mrs. Davis." The man understood and requested Lana to follow him. He took her into a dining room full of chandeliers, beautiful table settings, and fine china. The attendant led her to the Davis's table and bowed when he approached Mrs. Davis.

"Excuse me, madam. Your appointment has arrived." The valet performed his duty, leaving Lana alone with Mrs. Davis. Mrs. Davis put on her biggest smile. "Hello, Lana, please sit down. I took the liberty to order you a hamburger, and I hope you like it well done."

The food was delivered just as soon as Lana took a seat. Mrs. Davis ordered a shrimp Louie, which made Lana feel like a child, with her hamburger and fries.

Keeping a smile on her face and picking at her salad, Mrs. Davis began the meeting. "I think it will be best if you just listen, and after I finish what I have to say, you can say what you feel is necessary.

Roy told his father and me about your condition. Frankly, I wasn't surprised. I tried to warn him that dating a girl like you would only end up in hurt feelings for both of you. And now we have a situation. Roy is confused, and I'm sure you are, too. But, sweetheart, you must understand that you and Roy come from two different worlds, and Roy's world is one where situations are fixed." Mrs. Davis continued. "Roy left yesterday for college. We believe it is best not to inform you of our son's location right now, but he is currently at a major University outside of Minnesota. Lana, there will be no wedding. I realize we are talking about a baby, but you are talking about my baby's life and career. As cold as this may seem, I won't let your baby ruin my son's chances in life. Mr. Davis and I believe it would be best for all if you handled the situation as you see fit, but please leave our son out of it. I have a check in my purse for $50,000. You can use the money however you wish. You can do it with the baby at your will. But if you accept this money, we never want to hear your or your baby's name in our home. You will not attempt to contact Roy and release any liability you believe my son may have. If you agree to our terms, I will give you the check today. Our lawyer will draw up the documents and come to your home, and you can sign them."

Lana couldn't take any more. She was already shaking from head to toe. "I love Roy, and Roy loves me. He is the father of my baby, and no matter how much you and Mr. Davis try to buy Roy's doing, he will always be my baby's father."

Mrs. Davis looked around to see who was listening. "Please, keep your voice down. There is no need to embarrass yourself or us. The fact is that Roy doesn't want anything to do with you. He decided to leave and go to college. He also thought I would meet with you and offer you the money. So, I'll give you another chance: take the money for the baby's sake or leave here empty-handed. Either way, there will never be a day when my son will marry you."

Lana started to get up. Mrs. Davis touched her hand. "Lana, don't be a fool. Fifty thousand dollars will buy a lot of good for you and your baby. I don't want to hurt you, but sweetheart, you will not be a part of our family." Mrs. Davis opened her purse and pulled out a check. It was already made out to Lana Lore for $50,000. She offered it to Lana.

Lana stood up and refused the check. "I want your son Roy to tell me, to my face, that he wants nothing to do with his baby. If Roy tells me that, then I will take your offer. Until then, I'll wait until he calls me or comes to see me. It is his baby, your grandchild, that is within me." Lana stood up and walked away from Mrs. Davis. She didn't look back and kept saying to herself, "Don't cry, don't cry."

When she arrived at the gentleman who had walked her into the dining room, she bid him a good afternoon and opened her door. When she arrived at her car, she placed her head on the steering wheel and cried for both herself and her baby. She knew deep in her heart it was over for her and Roy. But she now had to figure out how to raise his child.

Alice was waiting for her sister at the door when she arrived home. Lana entered the apartment and collapsed on the couch, too exhausted to go over it again with her sister. Alice knew right away that it didn't go well. She left her sister alone and went into the kitchen to make a cup of tea. From the dark living room, she could hear moans from Lana. It broke her heart to see her sister in such pain. Alice brought out the tea for Lana. "Sweetie, just sit here and drink this. I want you to rest, and after you get some rest, we'll talk and figure this out. You'll see. It will be okay."

Just as Alice consoled her sister, the front door opened, and John stood in the doorway. "Hey, anybody home?"

Alice sighed, "Hey, John, come in."

John saw Lana on the couch and sat next to her. "What's wrong, beautiful?"

Alice looked at John and asked him to come to the kitchen. John got up and followed Alice.

"Roy and Lana broke up," Alice whispered to John. "It's just a hard time for her right now."

"When did this happen?" John whispered back to Alice.

"A couple of days ago," Alice answered him.

John turned from the kitchen and returned to the living room. "Listen, Lana, it may seem your whole world is falling apart, but he is the loser. You are beautiful and funny; any guy would love to take you out."

Lana turned to John and realized he was only trying to help. "Not if they knew I was pregnant."

John's mouth dropped. "Did you say you're pregnant?"

"He said he loved me and wanted to marry me." Lana cried her heart out.

John sat on the couch and put his arm around her.

"Don't worry.

Everything will be alright. Hey, have I ever let you down yet? My job is to take care of you, girls. I guess I haven't done the best job, but I'm here for you, and we'll get through this." John got up and headed for the door. I'll be back. Alice, you make sure Lana gets some rest. I'll be back in a couple of hours. I'll bring the whiskey for Alice and me. Lana, no alcohol for you," John smiled and left through the front door. Alice and Lana were silent, trying to figure out what had just happened.

"Did he just run away because I was pregnant?"

Lana asked Alice.

Alice laughed. "I don't know what the hell that was." He says he will come back, and you know John, he's good to his word."

Lana tried to figure it out. "Did he leave to get a bottle of whiskey?"

They both had a chuckle. "That is probably the most unusual response from anybody," Alice said.

"That was almost as fast as Roy got out of here once he found out," Lana said his name without bursting into tears.

Alice made dinner for Lana and herself. She made chicken soup from the can and cheese sandwiches. She made a tray from a platter and took it to Lana's bedroom. Lana thanked her sister and set the tray on her night table. From Lana's room, they heard a knock at the door. They both looked at each other, wondering who it could be. Alice made Lana stay in bed, and she went to answer the door.

It was John at the front door, all dressed in a suit and tie, holding a single rose and a bottle of whiskey in one hand. Lana came out of her room, still dressed in Alice's brown skirt and blouse. She looked at John and smiled. "Where are you going?" Lana said, amused.

"Right here," John replied. He walked over to Lana and dropped to one knee. He bowed his head and handed her the rose. "Lana, would you consider me to be your husband and the father of your baby?"

Lana lost her smile and walked over to the couch. "That's not funny, John."

John turned towards her and said. "It wasn't meant to be funny."

"You have a girlfriend." Lana insisted

"Had I broken up with her about an hour ago. I love you as a sister. I don't think falling in love with you as your husband will be too far-fetched.

Lana started to cry. "I can't ruin your life because of a mistake I made."

"Lana, I wouldn't be here right now proposing to you if I weren't serious. I swear I'll love you and the baby for the rest of my life. I'm very serious; please say you'll be my wife."

Alice was in shock, hoping that Lana would say yes, but she stayed silent in the corner of the room. "You're serious, aren't you? You would actually marry me, even though I'm having a baby?"

"Very serious; I'd marry you tomorrow if you'd have me." Lana smiled. "Yeah, I'll marry you."

Alice squealed with joy. "Oh my God, we better open up that whiskey!" She ran into the kitchen and came out with three glasses and one bottle of apple juice. The three of them toasted Lana and John's engagement.

Before John drank his drink, he sat next to Lana and kissed her. First on the cheek, then on the lips. After the kiss, Lana smiled. "I love you, John. You are my hero." They kissed again.

John and Lana decided to have a small wedding. The guests would include John's parents, Alice and Ronnie. Lana wrote to her father to tell him that she and John would be married. She told him that she understood it was all happening so quickly and that she hadn't expected them to attend the wedding due to the distance.

Lana and Alice attended the church on their wedding day. Lana wore a simple, sleeveless wedding dress for the midday ceremony. Alice bought a light green dress with an empire waist that covered her knees. When the service was ready to begin, Lana decided she would walk herself to the front of the church. The music began. Alice started her walk, letting go of her sister's hand. Alice was halfway down the aisle when the big front doors of the church opened, and Michael, their father, wearing his black suit, hurried in. He saw his daughter ready to enter the church. Out of breath, he asked. "Is it okay if I give away my daughter?" Lana cried hard, hugging her father.

"Daddy, you made this day perfect. I wanted you to be here so much, but I was afraid you wouldn't be able to make it. I didn't want you to feel you had to be here, but now you are here." She hugged him again.

"I wouldn't miss my daughter getting married. All my life, I have looked forward to this day. I wouldn't have missed it for nothing." Michael said, trying not to cry.

The rest of the kids came to the front door. Lana's smile grew broader as her sisters and brother entered the church. She asked Steven if he would go up front with John and be one of his groomsmen. Steven nodded and headed to the front of the church. John's family was confused, but after the ceremony, they realized how special it was for Lana that her family had made it to their wedding.

The other sisters grabbed a flower and strolled down the aisle before Lana and her father took a walk. Lana whispered to her father. "Mom didn't come?"

Her father took a deep breath. "It's one of our off times."

Lana grabbed his arm, and they started down the aisle.

He whispered to her. "I love you."

Chapter 22

Checking in with Dorine

2004 Medford, Tennessee General Hospital

Dorine started to wake up. Diane and Kathy were still talking about their childhood pains and gains.

"Alwa! Commo? Commo?" Dorine yelled to the ceiling.

"Mama," Kathy said. "Mama, are you okay? Should I call the nurse?"

"Alwa! Commo? Commo?" Dorine said with tears in her eyes.

"It sounds like the Indian language. You'd better get the girls. I'll call the nurse." Diane ordered Kathy.

"Did you see him?" Dorine said to Diane.

"Who?" Diane asked.

"Chief, Yellow Sparrow, he was right here.

He said I was his daughter." Dorine said, looking frantic as if somebody else was in the room.

A black female nurse came running in and settled Dorine down, laying her flat on her back. "You have to settle down, Miss Dorine. You're going to pull out all your wires. You need to calm down right now."

Dorine lay down and went stiff. Her eyes were so far open that it looked like her eyeballs would pop out. Then a smile came upon her face, and Dorine relaxed, closed her eyes, and fell back to sleep.

The nurse looked at Diane, who was standing in shock. "That sometimes happens when they first wake up. It's the anesthesia they had given her. She'll be fine the next time she wakes up. She'll never remember a thing." The nurse explained.

Diane looked at the nurse. "I sure the hell will," Diane said, still shaken up.

The other girls came running in. But the drama was over, and Dorine was asleep. Diane started to laugh, and then Kathy joined in, not knowing why Diane was laughing uncontrollably. Then Alice joined in, and Susan and Lana looked at each other and shook their heads, allowing a faint smile to sneak onto their face.

The doctor entered and barely said hello when he walked into Dorine's portion of the dorm. All the girls were there, sitting around Dorine. Susan was still embarrassed from the night before when she mistook the doctor for a nurse and called him too young to be good, not because he was black. Alice had to bail her out, explaining to the doctor that this episode with Dorine was too much for Susan. The doctor said he understood that it was a long night for him. As the doctor came to check on Dorine today, Susan was uncomfortable with his presence. Of course, it didn't help matters that her sisters were turning different colors, trying not to laugh at her awkwardness. Let's just say it was hard for them not to make eye contact with the young doctor.

"I don't like the way she is coming down from surgery. He said with a concerned look on his face. She needed to wake up so we could see what kind of condition her heart attack had left her in.

"I think she thought she was the daughter of some Indian Chief." Diane tried to tell the doctor without smiling. "The nurse had a hard time settling her down." Diane pointed out a more serious side of the incident.

"A lot of people have different reactions to the anesthesia. What I don't like is the fact that she is still out of it. Her blood pressure is too low, and her pulse is very faint. I need her to wake up and get her body functioning." The doctor reached over Dorine to buzz the nurse.

He remained silent while writing notes on her chart.

"Is she still going to be okay?" Kathy asked.

The doctor finished his last note. "She is going to live, yes, but I doubt it will be the life she was living before. People her age just don't seem to recover fully. She's going to have to be monitored very closely."

Susan wanted to ask how long she would be in the hospital, but was too embarrassed to say a word.

"Will she be more awake soon?" Lana asked.

The doctor smiled at Lana. "You'll be able to talk to your mother within the hour."

He put the clipboard next to his side. "Now, if there are no more questions, I must finish my rounds."

Susan whispered when it was for sure that the doctor was out of the room. "You all don't think he's too young? And is that the way they wear their hair now?" Susan pulled her hair straight up.

The girls all giggled, shaking their heads at Susan.

Chapter 23

Here's to the Southern Bells

1967, Houston, Texas

Susan, being the fourth youngest in the family, is number three as far as the order of the sisters goes.

It seemed that each of the Lore children had their pet names or duties in the order of the family. Jimmy was the oldest child, a part-time father when Michael was working and Dorine was away. Lana was the oldest sister, put in place as a mother when Dorine was unwilling to be the mother. Alice was known for her kind heart, sharp tongue, and good cooking.

Susan, well, Susan was known for her beauty. She was born with jet-black hair, big dark blue eyes, and skin as white and pure as a snowflake. When Susan was three years old, Dorine entered her into her first beauty contest. Susan won, providing the family with a new sofa and loveseat. Susan took singing, dance, and violin lessons when she was nine. Michael would get up early each day and walk Susan to her prospective lesson.

On Saturdays, he would take all the kids, and they would attend a beauty contest in Minnesota. Susan would stand up proudly, smiling as her mother demanded of her, and be happy to see her father cheering her on as she walked out onto the stage.

For Susan, being beautiful meant extra work, always keeping face, and never complaining about the lack of playtime she desperately wanted. Instead, she practiced the violin in the girl's bedroom, with the door closed at the family's request. She wanted to be an average child. Not set apart for something she had no control over. To Susan, it was creepy that people would stare at her, trying to get close because of her looks. It didn't make sense to Susan, but it made her father proud of her, so she endured their dream.

Susan was fourteen when Michael moved part of the family to Texas. She didn't want to leave Minnesota, but there were no second thoughts concerning Michael. It was hard enough for him to leave Jimmy, Lana, and Alice.

Michael was always close to the older three, confiding in them. He shared his decisions, thoughts, and fears with them, loving the younger ones but not sharing his problems. Now, Susan and Diane had taken the older kids' place. It was a new and positive relationship for them, allowing Susan and Diane to get to know their father.

When they arrived in Texas, they went right to Dorine's house.

She was happy to see them all, especially Kathy and Steven. She held each child, allowing the tears to fall upon them. Acting as though somebody had taken her children away from her, and now they are home. "I can't tell you how much I missed each one of you." Dorine cried, holding her children. She was wearing a red and white polka dot dress. She fixed her hair, pulling it up into a bun and garnishing it with fake white and lavender flowers. Looking worn, way out of style, Dorine's lips were painted a blood-red shade. Her eyes had eyeliner on them, with a cat's tail at the ends. Wisps of blond hair adorned her forehead. She was beautiful, but almost in a trailer-trash kind of way. She was barefoot, feeling like a stranger to her own family.

Michael was in a world of bliss. He stood up strong and handsome, hugging his wife. "I missed you." He told her. He pulled away from Dorine and looked her in the eyes. Michael reached for her hand. "We all missed you."
Dorine learned her cues from the past and cried, begging Michael and the family for forgiveness.

The family, or at least part of the family, was back together. Michael found a job at a local bar, and they all stayed at Dorine's for a while. A few months passed, and things started to turn sour for Michael and Dorine in Texas. Michael, Susan, and Diane moved down the street from Dorine's in a small two-bedroom converted one-car garage apartment behind a house.

Kathy and Steven stayed with Dorine. It bothered Michael to leave Kathy and Steven, but he saw his children daily at some school function, stopping by the bar or watching them around the house, or at Dorine's, where they were watching TV. Now, his relationship with Dorine was more of a friendship. She was over his house, or he was spending time at hers. This type of relationship worked for them, and the kids had the best of both worlds, having a mother and father full-time for the first time in a long time.

At times, it got confusing for the younger ones. They couldn't understand how their parent could be friends but not a married couple. When they saw them drinking, laughing, and having a good time together, they would think that Michael and Dorine were getting back together. But Michael knew his position in Dorine's life, which was number one, but it was Dorine who needed numbers two, three, and four. It was during the night after Kathy and Steven went to bed. Dorine would leave the kids and frequent a local cowboy bar. She would bring home a different guy several nights a week. The kids would wake up in the middle of the night, hearing their mother's drunken laugh, hoping the male voice they heard was their father's.

"Mama," Kathy approached her mother. "I had a bad dream last night. I got up and went to your room, but you weren't there.

I looked all over the house for you. Where were you?"

"Oh, stop this nonsense. I ran to your father's house for just a minute and was back home in no time. Now, you get it through your head right now. I'm no kid, and just because you need to go to bed when the sun sets, that's for kids and not adults." Dorine explained, irritated that her daughter tried to set her in her place. "Besides, Missy, my life can't just be sitting in this house watching you and your brother snoring away. I deserve to have a life, too," explaining to Kathy as if she could understand.

It was Steven, who was now ten years old, who walked into the living room and found his mother in the arms of another man. "Daddy, I had a bad dream! Steven ran to the sofa, thinking his mother's company was his father. When he stumbled to the couch and realized it wasn't his father. He looked at his mother in the eyes, turned around, and went back to his room. Dorine never bothered to explain herself to her kids; it was life, and as far as she was concerned, it was only a lesson about how life was. Several times, Dorine thought she had found a lucky man who seemed to oppose Dorine's whims. She would dress up beautifully and apply her makeup delicately, setting a trap for the new prey. She would cook big dinners, prepping the kids to know what they could or could not say. "You want your mama to be happy, don't you?" Dorine reminded Kathy and Steven. "Now, you excuse yourself after dinner and go right to your Daddy's house.

Now take your school clothes, and I'll see you after school on Monday."

It seemed no man lasted past two Sunday dinners with Dorine. Either they were boring for her, or they were only playing her like a fiddle. What was always the same was how Dorine would run to Michael to regain her bearings and confidence in herself, and how Michael would receive his wife with the hope that this time would be different.

Michael experienced being alone for so many years without his wife. Living with Dorine was better than not being with her at all. He loved her. He loved her unconditionally. Either way, Michael cared for the kids, and Dorine entertained herself, unable to find happiness.

For each of the children, it was a time of survival. There were no older brothers or sisters to help bridge the dysfunction in the family. Susan didn't want the position and clarified that they were on their own. Diane found Charlotte, her best friend, on the first day of being in Texas. I should say that Charlotte found Diane and bulldozed her way into Diane's life.

The family had just arrived. Diane answered a knock at the door. "Hi, I'm Charlotte, and I live across the road down yonder," Charlotte said with a broad smile. "I was hoping that somebody my age would move in here. Mrs. Swinney told me all about your family and that you all would be moving on in."

Mouth wide open, Diane was trying to process what Charlotte was trying to say.

"I mean, nobody is on this street under 30 years old. And now we can be best friends forever." Charlotte reached for Diane's hand, pushing the front door wide enough so that she could wedge herself. "Oh, my lord, your house is so cute. It's just my daddy and me; he has no sense of style. Oh, is that your whole family in the kitchen? I'm sorry; I should let you all settle in. I'll just let myself out. Hey, would you like to come downtown with me tomorrow? I'll show you the wild spots." Charlotte whispered a wild spot. She giggled and left as fast as she arrived.

Steven, who was kind and assertive, made friends and had a special friend who lived across the street from Dorine.

Kathy couldn't seem to make any connections. Her classmates at school were divided into cliques, not wanting to accept any new members. She was on the B squad of life with the girls who still brought dolls to school in the fourth grade. She tried to show the other girls that she was just like them. She would come home and practice jump rope, learning all the cute tunes. "Mable, Mable, set the table. Don't forget the red-hot peppers." When they said "red hot peppers," she would make Steven and his friend turn the rope as fast as possible so she could be ready if asked at school.

Nobody asked her to jump rope. She missed her friends in Minnesota, as well as her brother and sisters. She was ashamed of herself for not coping. Everybody else seemed to find their way, but Kathy wasn't getting any breaks from anybody, not from school or her brother and sisters.

Michael came over to Dorine's house one afternoon before going to work. Kathy was the only person at home. She was sitting alone in the dark, and she wasn't crying because all the tears had long been spent weeks before. Michael had noticed the sadness in his daughter as he entered the room.

Hi, sweetie. Are you okay?"

Kathy didn't answer him, hoping he would just continue, like the rest of them do.

"Why aren't you out there playing ball or whatever you kids do at your age?"

Kathy was silent again. Michael looked at his mail on the dining room table and realized she hadn't answered any of his questions. He put the letter back on the table and sat beside her.

"Sometimes, I have been told that it feels really good when you put your head right here on my shoulder." Michael pointed to his shoulder, "I think Lana used to call it 'The Shoulder of Life and Understanding." Kathy snuggled next to her father. She got on her knees and reached up to set her head on his shoulder, hoping it was true and would make her feel better. "Um!"

Michael sighed. "Do you know how much I love you?" Kathy was shaking her head no, not taking her head off her father's shoulder. "I love you more than dog poop sinks when it gets on your shoes." Kathy gave a smile, not visible to Michael. "God made you special, and then he gave you to me. So, it's time you tell me what seems wrong so we can face the problem together."

"Nobody likes me," Kathy said, wrinkling her face and trying not to cry.

"Oh, sweetie, that's not true. They just don't know you. It's like when your mama makes a new dish. At first, it doesn't look very good. Then you sniff it, and it's okay, but when you finally take a bite, all that silliness about not liking it is all gone." Michael pulled Kathy off his shoulder to make sure she understood.

"You have to give them a chance. When they get around to giving you a chance, you'll see that you'll be the most popular girl in the class. Hey, after all, you're a Lore. Michael wiped the tears from Kathy's eyes.

"Yeah, but look at Diane and Steven; they both found friends right away." Kathy stammered.

"And it will happen for you, too." Michael hugged his daughter. "And if not, you can be my best friend." Michael smiled at his daughter, joking around with her.

Kathy looked at her father. "I may as well get my dolls out of storage and start taking them to school."

"Now, I was just kidding, even though I would make a good best friend." Michael got up from the couch, bent over, kissed his daughter, and headed to the table.

Kathy smiled and appreciated her father's heart. She did feel better. She couldn't help thinking maybe there was something about the 'Shoulder of Understanding.'

***

Susan became popular quickly, mainly due to her stunning appearance. Several boys wanted to date her, but Susan met her sweetheart early in high school. They were known as Barbie and Ken: the perfect couple, the homecoming king and queen, for three years straight.

When Susan was a sophomore in high school, she was offered a modeling job.

"Daddy, Mr. Hunt came to my school today, and they called me to the office." Susan paused, hoping to get her father's attention from the newspaper.

"Who is this, Mr. Hunt?" Michael asked, keeping his eyes on the newspaper.

He's an agent for a modeling agency and wants me to be a model."

"I don't think so."

"Daddy, it's like having a job. I'll get paid for my work." Susan pleaded.

"You have your schooling, and I just don't see the kind of

grades I want from you, and to think that having a job would help this. Well, I don't know."

Dorine walked in from the backroom, overhearing the conversation. "I think a job would be good for her. I remember my first job and the independence of having my own money."

Michael put the newspaper down and turned toward Dorine. "Working at a pharmacy is different from this type of work."

"Daddy, I've been around people like Mr. Hunt since childhood." Susan tried to defend herself.

"You are a child, my child, and I just think you should wait until you are a little older."

Dorine hissed. "My lord Michael, you are so old-fashioned. Let the girl work; she'll be okay."

Michael sighed and stared Dorine in the eyes. "Okay, she can model, but Diane has to go with her."

"Daddy, I can't take my little sister with me." Susan pouted.

"Then, I guess you are going to have to tell Mr. Hunt that you can't do it." Michael gave his final word.

At first, it was exciting for Susan, but the time spent away from her boyfriend, Scott, was a burden more than a pleasure. She resented the fact that Diane had to be there. It was embarrassing to have to drag her little sister.

For Diane, the last place she wanted to be was in a hot studio, watching everybody pay so much attention to Susan.

The pictures from the magazines came out beautifully. The clients loved Susan and requested that Susan move to New York. Michael put his foot down. Susan was not moving to the other side of Houston as far as he was concerned. Susan didn't protest her father's decision, mostly because she didn't want to leave Texas and be away from her boyfriend.

Susan had a lot of potential in an entertainment career. On tour in Houston, she was selected from hundreds of girls at various dance schools to be a background dancer for Ann-Margret. The whole family was excited. Lana and Alice sent Susan a letter of encouragement. Soon after the performance and experience of her life, Susan informed her father and family that she would no longer dance, sing, or play the violin. She was in love, and it took too much time away from Scott.

Chapter 24

Taking One Step, Falling Back Two

After Jimmy passed away, a large piece of Michael's soul was buried with him. He spent most of his time at work. While serving the silence, Michael would drink, drink, and drink. He wasn't physically taking care of himself. Michael allowed himself to become despondent and neglected his responsibilities to his children and himself. His clothes, hair, and general hygiene, were neglected. It was becoming noticeable to those who loved him. He just didn't have the strength to change it. Instead, he would hide, make excuses, and separate himself from his own family.

There wasn't very much supervision for any of the children. Michael was lost in his world, drowning his sorrows in a bottle. Dorine had her own agenda, and that didn't include her kids. The siblings ran their schedules and made their own rules. Rule number one was that there were no rules.

Rule number one was that there were no rules. "You just mind your affairs, and I'll mind mine," Susan said to Diane once when she dared to ask if she was getting serious about Scott. When Kathy tried to get close to Diane, she would reject her sister, placing all her energies on her best friend, Charlotte. The only bond the sisters shared was their last name, Lore. Without parents setting guidelines and rules, the children ran free, seeking stability in their friends and families.

When you have dysfunctional parents, it makes it hard to know what the norm is. Maybe the freedom that Michael gave Dorine was a good thing. After all, if you talk to Dorine, she believes in no barriers or restrictions in one's life, especially hers.

It just wasn't the Lore family. It was a political fever that was blazing through the country. We have just emerged from the era of peace and love. Daming the hippies and now let all express love and peace. All to hide the fact that we are in a war that is probably going to take our lives before we can legally buy a beer. Kids manipulate parents from their ability to control the behavior of the young's choices by demonstrating their rights to say no to war and yes to drugs and rock and roll.

After losing their child and brother, the Lore family was no different and followed suit in demonstrating rebellion against their parents and God himself. The only difference with the Lore family was that the parents didn't care. The pain from Michael's personal loss paralyzed him from any thought of what was right or wrong. Dorine only thought of her own morality, believing that, finally, the world would see what is truly important in living life to the fullest every day. Love the one you are with. Peace and love.

Chapter 25

Raising Kids is Hard To Do

1972, Houston, Texas

By the time Diane was 16 and Susan was 18 years old, they knew that it. All was bullshit. They knew their mother was a sex-crazed lunatic who only thought of herself when making decisions in life that affected each of them.

Then you have people sharing the Bible with you from their hearts. Sweetly telling you that you have parents from hell.

"Diane asked one lady who came to their door. "Didn't Jesus drink wine?"

"Oh, sweetheart, in those days, it was grape juice. It's not the same as what we call wine today."

To the kids, it was confusing what was right or wrong. So, most of the time, they were wrong. It wasn't as though they didn't discuss things with their father. He was a man who unconditionally loved them, and nothing they did would ever come between his relationship with each of them.

He was very supportive of anything they tried. And if they failed, he was right there picking up their tears, and shoveling the shit under the rug, especially his own.

Maybe it was too much, at least for Susan, not having boundaries. She was always venturing into areas with no idea of the consequences. In her young mind, there were only a few solutions to her problems. Failing to recognize that experience and confidence are essential for making informed moral decisions. In Susan's mind, she lacked confidence; she only wanted to be Scott's wife and was willing to sacrifice who she was to achieve that goal.

Susan, trying to please her boyfriend, became submissive too, whatever pleased him, always thinking that she was going to lose him. It seemed she would find herself in positions that she knew were wrong, like drinking, smoking, and having sex. In her senior year, Susan became pregnant and planned to get married in early June, right after graduation.

Even this situation didn't seem to slow her down. It was like, "Oh well, we were going to get married anyway." Life had been taken for granted, and Susan was only a pawn on a big chessboard. She didn't know how to take control of her life. She allowed Scott, who had a controlling personality, to make all the decisions concerning Susan and him.

At her father's house, Michael woke up late in the morning, nursing a hangover. Diane had already left for school, and Susan needed to tell her father she was pregnant.

"Daddy, I need one of your hugs that Lana always talks about," Susan said.

Michael looked up slowly, seeing if this would be a mind exploder or just

It's simple: let me kiss it and go and play.

"I think I'm pregnant." Susan softly said.

Michael grabbed his head before it flew off into the universe. "You think, or do you know?" Michael asked her.

I'm pregnant." Susan tearfully admitted to her father.

"Um. Do you have a plan?" Michael inquired.

"Scott and I want to get married after graduation."

Michael was silent. "You know what bothers me the most?"

Susan shook her head no.

"How come to the boy who got my daughter pregnant is not the one here telling me that he is going to marry you? Are you marrying him because you're pregnant?"

"We've been boyfriend and girlfriend for three years now." Susan boasted to her father.

"Do you love him?" Michael asked.

"I think so. Everybody says we should marry because we are both alike." Susan tried to explain.

"Because you are beautiful, and he is handsome, doesn't mean you are suited to get married. Marriage, as you know, is hard, and without love, it is impossible."

"That's why I'm scared. Look at you and Mama. What happens if my marriage turns out like yours? I don't think I could be so forgiving as you are."

"Believe it or not, your Mama and I love each other. All I want for her is to find happiness, even if that means her not being with me."

"When Mama would tell you that she was pregnant with each of us kids, did you get a big lump in your throat?" Susan smiled, asking her father his reaction to being a father.

"Weak at the knees, happy, but weak at the knees."

"How did Scott take the news?" Michael needed to know.

"Very loving, he decided we must marry as soon as possible. You know, not even considering running like Roy did to Lana. Can I marry him, Daddy?" Susan, very seriously, asked her father.

"I love you so much. I want you to be happy. If you want to marry Scott, I'm right behind you. If you have one doubt, wait, have the baby, and if you and Scott still feel the same way about each other, marry him." Michael smiled at his daughter, "Does he treat you right?" Does he give my baby the love she needs?"

"It's me. I'm so afraid of losing Scott. I'm afraid I'm going to drive him away." Susan tried to explain.

"All your beauty, and yet you act as though you are the most worthless person on earth. Don't you know how special you are? That this little snot-nose kid that got my daughter pregnant doesn't realize what a wonderful young woman he is about to marry." Michael was upset with Susan because of her lack of self-esteem. "I didn't stay with you kids all those years so that you would be afraid of being abandoned. You and your brothers and sisters gave me special love that your mother has missed. You were my life, the daily water that I needed to survive. Have confidence in yourself, Susan. Look at your inner self. It's even more beautiful than your outward self. You are the prize, not him. He better hope that he can keep you. You'll see it will all change around. And I just hope he really does love you because if not, you'll do the right thing for Susan, and he'll be gone."

"I know, but I get so jealous; half the time, it's not even his fault. Girls just find him attractive, and I feel like I'm running a race trying to stay ahead. And if I trip or fall, the girls will win."

"If you trip or fall, who says that he won't stop and pick you up? The girls will always be there. They are the chocolate of life. For the rest of his life, you are his diamond, something special to him."

Susan got up and hugged her father. "How come you always have the right words to say? I love you, Daddy."

"I love you, too. Don't worry; we'll get through this one."

"Daddy, can I say one more thing?" Susan whispered in Michael's ear. "Please slow down on the drinking. We need you, Daddy; we are lost without you. Steven is starting high school next year, and he only has us, girly sisters, to annoy him. He needs his father to help him to transcend from a boy to a man."

Michael stayed in the chair and grabbed Susan's arm. "I know that I have to pull it together. Sweetie, I wish I were as strong as you are, but I'm weak. You're right. I have to make sure that I'm here for all of you kids."

Susan kissed her dad's cheek. "I love you, Daddy, but I have to run."

Hey, no more running; you'd better learn how to walk." Michael smiled.

"I know, it's not wise to run when one should learn how to walk first," Susan said, imitating the popular Kung Fu man on television.

Chapter 26

Diane Lore

2000: Medford, Tennessee

Diane was two years younger than Susan. When it was time for her parents to give her individual time, Michael and Dorine were worn out. But somehow, Diane turned out to be the sweetest, down-to-earth, and caring person among all the sisters, even though she was too insecure to recognize these attributes within herself.

She was an excellent businessperson. She taught herself how to manage her husband's business, keeping him organized and free to succeed. Diane could turn a bad situation around and make it smell like roses. Being a good mother was at the top of her list. It didn't matter how successful she could have been as an individual or woman. It was far more critical to her that her children were appropriately raised by a loving mother and a hard-working father, even though he was on the road most of the time. Her family was much more important to her than having the material possessions they could have obtained with a two-income family.

It wasn't until Tom, her husband, had his first heart attack that Diane had to look at life from a different perspective. Her two boys were already in college, and she needed to take over the role of financial caretaker. Diane was in her mid-forties. She possessed all the necessary skills required to become an executive, but on paper, she had no experience over the past twenty years to qualify for such a position. She was lost and oblivious to how to get a job. When it came down to a simple job application, she had no more experience than a fifteen-year-old looking for their first job, making minimum wage.

Diane wouldn't let other people's perceptions stop her from making a living. She was a Lore, and power and determination were innate in each of her sisters. If nobody wanted to give Diane a job, she would create her own source of income. Diane registered for a quick course in real estate; before she passed the test, she had already secured a position with one of Tennessee's largest real estate houses. She passed the test on the first try and became one of the leading salespeople in her office. She allowed her mother's ambitious spirit to enter her mind, pushing her to a higher degree.

Chapter 27

Diane Subject To the Boundaries of Dorine

1969, Houston, Texas

When Diane was a child, Dorine was not emotionally close to her. Even when they lived together in Houston, there was a sense of boundaries regarding how close Diane could get to her mother. Dorine's rejection of Diane hurt her, but that was okay because she had her father and her friend, Charlotte. Dorine chose her children, at least which ones she would keep, and Diane wasn't one of them.

"Sugar, your father and I just can't seem to live together and be happy. He will move and wants you and Susan to move with him." Dorine tilted her head so Diane could understand that she was being relocated.

"What about Kathy and Steven?" Diane felt angry that she was separating. The family was reduced to a smaller size, all because she wasn't happy.

"Kathy and Steven need their mama; besides, you'll be just a yonder, maybe a block or two away," Dorine said, annoyed with all this questioning. It really didn't matter; the family, or the sense of family, was gone. Nobody cared enough to bring it back together. Everybody was trying to find their way.

The house that Michael rented for Susan, Diane, and himself was a dirty, small two-bedroom house. It was a house built behind a home. At one time, it was a garage with the ability to hold one car and storage on the side. But to Michael and the girls, it was their new home.

Susan, Kathy, Steven, and Diane began cleaning the house. Susan got on her hands and knees and washed the grime from the floor so that Michael could bring over the extra furniture from Dorine's garage. Diane and Steven helped Michael carry in the mattresses and the kitchen table. The top of the table was all scraped up, but Kathy created a beautiful tablecloth out of string. Diane and Susan were furious with their mother. She knew what kind of place Michael could afford, and still, she allowed them to move to such a place.

"This could be nice," Dorine said when she came over for coffee. Diane had no patience for her mother, blaming her for putting them in such a hellhole.

"Diane, come over here and tell me what you and this, um, what's her name, have been up to," Dorine said with a large bite of toast in her mouth.

"Her name is Charlotte, and we just go to school and stay out of trouble."

"That's the trouble with you kids nowadays. You get a good education and don't appreciate all it takes to get you to those schools. Look at your sister, Susan. All those damn years, we paid for her lessons, and now she doesn't want to invest the time and hard work it takes to become successful. You gotta be able to face "no" in the eye and spit right back into it. My children are go-getters, and for Susan to quit because she doesn't have enough time to spend with her boyfriend is unacceptable. Well, that gets my goat." Dorine lectured Diane.

Diane wanted to tell her many things. Like, since when did you start caring about your children? Or that maybe Susan has learned by example from her mother how to become a loser in life. But instead, Diane agreed with her mother. "Susan will find her way; when she does, she'll be able to use all those lessons inside her."

Dorine looked at Diane to see if that was a smart-mouth comment or if she agreed with her. "Either way, I only wish I had half the opportunities that you kids had while I was growing up," Dorine said, sipping her coffee.

Diane couldn't hold back her tongue and decided to leave the table. Dorine was known to take a slap at her children for just looking like they were disrespectful.

"I've taken too many beatings from my daddy to allow my children to be disrespectful." That was Dorine's most significant issue. She wasn't going to raise children who didn't know their place.

Diane hated her mother. She wasn't a person you could respect. She was a self-centered, manipulative woman, using her body for self-gain. Diane had to keep herself intact and make each day a positive day that meant something to her. Not allowing this woman to destroy her life, like she did to her father's.

Chapter 28

When You Stop Believing In Yourself, The Devil Will Come In

1972 St Paul, Minnesota

Winter brought on a depression that kept Alice locked in her room. Her relationship with Ronnie came to an end. In her heart, she just didn't feel that Ronnie was totally in love with her. Too many lies and too many secrets crept into their relationship. Alice was still in love with the boy, who did not accept other people's outlook on his potential in life. He was passionate about overcoming discouragement, poverty, and societal predictions of failure. He had the attitude that he would show the world he was different from others, unlike his parents, who had settled into a state of disbelief. However, as kids, Alice celebrates Ronnie's passion and encourages Ronnie to stand up to those who believe differently. However, over the past few years, Ronnie had allowed discontent, struggle, and a loss of faith to creep into his life.

Maybe when they were seniors in high school, Ronnie's love for Alice was always there, but Ronnie gradually gave up the dream. If Alice offered any encouraging words for Ronnie to hold on to, he would explode in anger, claiming she had no idea how life could smash one like himself. When reality happened, Ronnie would not have gone to college. It wasn't just the money; although he had none and nobody was willing to sponsor him, Ronnie tried hard but didn't have the grades that would impress anybody. That was the final call; Ronnie gave up. He accepted himself as a loser, brought on loser friends, and got himself medicated with drugs to keep himself surviving from day to day.

Alice thought it was just all the disappointment he was facing, and she stayed by his side, though he was smoking marijuana and drinking. He was still holding on to his lifeline, Alice.

Time passed, and Ronnie's behavior and attitude changed rapidly, treating Alice with no appreciation or love. Alice came home crying one night, and Lana was up with a crying baby. When she saw the need, she put Junior in bed and came out to love her sister, who was in need. Alice broke down and told Lana, "He treats me as if I'm his biker mama. Instead of love, I see hate in his eyes."

Lana faced her sister. "Listen, do you want me to have John go over there and kick his ass. Nobody is going to treat my sister like this."

Alice thought about it and laughed. "Do you think that is what Jimmy would have done?" They both laughed and hugged each other. Alice softly said, "I miss my big brother."

Ronnie had called Alice on the telephone. His intention for the call was to tell Alice that he was going to a party with Lyle. When Alice didn't protest, Ronnie knew something was wrong. "Okay, what's the problem?" Ronnie hissed at Alice.

"I think we need to go our own way," Alice whispered over the telephone.

"What the hell do you mean?" Ronnie started to get upset. "Just because I want to spend one night with my buddy; you get all pissed off." Ronnie continued.

"It has nothing to do with you and Lyle. I thought you loved me, and now I can't see that love." Alice cried.

"Oh brother, I'm so tired of all this bullshit. Maybe we should go our own ways."

Alice was crying hard, not knowing what she wanted. "That's just the point. You don't know how to fight for us. Instead, you would rather leave me behind."

"You're psycho. I can't keep up with what you want." Ronnie ready to end the conversation.

"I would never leave you, or hurt you, or disrespect you, and Ronnie, you have done all these things to me. And don't you think I know about all the drugs you are putting into your body?

Where is my man who fought for life, fought for me?" Alice was giving him her final words.

"Right, I don't need this; it's over," Ronnie screamed and slammed the telephone.

Alice hung up her phone, quietly walked to her room, and closed the door.

Lana felt responsible for breaking up Alice and Ronnie. She thought that all the grief she gave her about Ronnie was the reason Alice broke off their relationship. Lana felt such a need to fix Alice that she thought she needed to call her father. "Daddy, she hardly comes out of the bedroom," Lana explained over the telephone, knowing that if anybody could help her, their father always seems to have all the right words to say. "I'm starting to get worried. She looks horrible, like she has given up on life. She won't tell me when I try to ask her what's wrong."

"Maybe she needs to come down here," Michael said.

"She is only working with one old lady, and I can take that over until she returns. "How are things down there?"

"Not too good, ever since Jimmy died, it's been hard for all of us.

Your mother and I have split up, and the kids all seem on their own."

"Daddy, that sounds horrible. I don't know if that would be a better situation for Alice. She needs something."

Lana pleaded with her father. "She needs you."

Michael was silent for a moment. "I'm coming up."

It was a Tuesday, a week before Christmas, and Michael showed up at Lana's, John's, and Alice's apartment. He was by himself, half-frozen from the cold. Alice answered the door, and when she saw her father standing there, something inside fell apart, and she just leaped into his arms.

"Daddy!" She cried.

Michael held his daughter and led her to the couch. Lana and John were taking Junior out to an indoor mall. Leaving Alice and Michael alone.

"Where is my strong little girl?" Michael said, not knowing where to start. Alice buried herself in his arms. "I don't know what happened to that girl. Somewhere, she got lost."

"Tell me, sweetie, tell me what happened."

After a good cry, Alice told Michael about the break-up and the depression she had been going through. They both ended up in the kitchen, sharing a bottle of whiskey. Michael listened to his daughter and assured her of his love. He tried to help her, but the best medicine was him being there for her in times of need.

After several shots and a lot of tears, Alice managed to smile. "Everything seemed so wrong, Jimmy's death, Ronnie's insensitivity to my sadness, and treating me as if I were worthless." Alice started to cry.

Michael got out of his chair and put his arms around Alice. "I know how hard it's been. And I can't say I have dealt with it any better than you. We both need to bite our lower lip and move forward. You have a life you need to get on with, and I have my kids, all of you who need me. So, sweetie, let's both start right now and get ourselves together."

Alice wiped away the tears. "Right now, both of us?" She smiled. Michael grabbed his shot glass and raised it to the sky. "Here's to today. And tomorrow will take care of tomorrow." Michael slugged down the drink.

Michael stayed with Alice, Lana, John, and the baby for three days.

When it was time to say goodbye, he wouldn't allow them to be sad. "I'll never leave my girls alone. I'm always here with you both." He whispered to each of them, giving them a final hug.

Lana, bundled up in a winter coat, gave one last yell to Michael in the car.

"We love you, Daddy."

Michael waved as his car disappeared around the corner.

After Michael's visit, Alice came out of her depression and decided she needed to get back to taking care of her patient. It had been several months since the separation of Alice and Ronnie. The winter still lingered, but the hope of spring was always around the corner. Alice had several bouts of thinking about Ronnie, but she felt it was good to understand her love for him. Was she ready to move forward? The pain of the breakup and her weakness in handling it made her think she would be better off giving herself more time to recover. Of course, Lana and John tried hard to persuade her to let them find the perfect guy for her. But it was a little scary to think they knew the perfect guy, and she still couldn't answer that question for herself.

It seemed that no matter how warmly Alice dressed, she was always cold. With the holidays coming and going, Alice still had much to deal with, especially since Ronnie did not attempt to contact her.

She still loved Ronnie. However, wasn't sure if he always loved her. It had been over four months since they broke up, and she hadn't received one telephone call. He gave her no indication that he wanted to get back together. Lana was right. He didn't treat Alice special; he was verbally abusive to her, especially around friends and his family.

"Hey, why don't you get off your lazy ass and get me a beer?" He would Command Alice.

Alice would look around, thinking that he wasn't talking to her. Everybody in the room would hear and look at her, silently telling her to say hell no. But Alice would get up and retrieve his drink.

"You're a good bitch." Ronnie would say, laughing and kissing her as if she was a biker mama.

And then there were times when they were alone, and Ronnie would hold her and tell her how much he loved her. That life, without her, would be empty for him.

Alice was too confused to know what she wanted, but being alone didn't help matters. Her mind warped around who Ronnie was and wasn't, the sin of not loving oneself.

One day after work, Alice was halfway home. Ronnie was waiting behind a parked car, hoping to catch her alone. Alice, with her head down, endured the cold, not seeing him, and was startled when he appeared beside her.

"I saw you were coming. Do you mind if I walk with you?"

Alice wasn't sure if it was okay. She didn't say a word.

"How are you doing? I missed you the last few months." Ronnie muttered.

Alice stopped and looked at Ronnie. "Why do you say things like that? You haven't even tried to talk to me."

"I'm here now."

"Well, maybe now, it is too late," Alice said.

Ronnie placed his hands deep into his pockets. "I still love you."

Alice stopped, looked at Ronnie, and knew she still loved him. "I love you, too, but sometimes that's not enough. I don't know if I ever can be enough for you." Alice started to cry.

"I want to be with you. I want to be the one to make you

happy." Ronnie pleaded with her. "I'm lost without you." Ronnie continued to face Alice, touching her hand, which was covered by her mittens. "I don't want anybody else. I'm sorry that I hurt you. Please take me back." Ronnie begged Alice, hoping she would forgive him.

Alice looked at Ronnie in the eyes, "I need somebody who will stay with me, no matter what, who will protect and respect me. I need somebody who will love me more than himself. Do you know what I mean? I loved you, Ronnie, but you allowed us to be apart. And now you want me just to forget about the last few months that have passed? That's not right for you or me." Alice said.

"I'm a kid, and I'm stupid; there's no excuse except that, as much as I tried to move on, I realized I still loved you. And nobody can ever fill that space you have in my life."

Alice sighed. "Don't ever leave me to fend for myself. I'm not your mother, and don't treat me like I'm your servant. You gotta show me this love. Without action, you're only blowing bad air into the sky."

Ronnie nodded, accepting her demands. He leaned forward and brushed his lips against hers, reminding himself of the sweetness of her lips.

Alice received Ronnie's tenderness, remembering how much she loved him. They held hands while walking to Alice's apartment, catching up with all they had missed.

Alice put her head on his shoulder. "I missed you."

Ronnie squeezed her hand. "I missed you a lot." Ronnie stopped at the corner and asked Alice if they could stop before reaching the apartment.

"Listen, I got myself in trouble."

Alice with a frightened face. Replied, "With the law?"

No, with my life." It had been going on before we split, but I was trying to get past who I am by feeding my veins with poison. I was mean to you and everybody, and it got to a point where I needed the high to make it through the day. I loved it, I hated it. The more I used it, the more I hated myself. I blamed everybody, including you, for causing me to get hooked. I cared about nothing other than getting inside of me. But when I was down off, all I could think about was getting back on the horse. Alice, I need you. I love you; only you mean more to me than the high. Please stay with me. Help me to find my way home again.

Alice, in shock, shed tears of fear for herself and Ronnie. "Are you still on it? Are you on it right now? Is this why you are telling me all this?"

No, I am going crazy, but I haven't had a needle for 4 days now. Alice, my only hope that makes it worth living is you." "What happens if I'm not enough? How am I supposed to survive losing you again?'

I'm afraid, Alice, without you, it's going to kill me."

Looking slowly, Alice got off the bench and stretched her

hand to Ronnie. He looked at her and cried as he took her hand.

When they arrived at the apartment, nobody was home. Alice kissed Ronnie hard, leading him to her bedroom. Recognizing what was familiar, they made love, holding each other throughout the night.

When Lana left her bedroom in the morning, Ronnie was leaving Alice's Bedroom. She looked at Ronnie, surprised to see him coming out of Alice's bedroom. "You don't even realize how much you hurt her." Lana quietly said to Ronnie.

Ronnie was silent. He stood there, letting Lana know he wasn't going anywhere.

"How much more do you have to take from her? Let her go, find somebody else to abuse."

Ronnie turned to leave. "Get used to it, Lana; I'm here to stay." Ronnie opened the door and left.

Lana went to Alice's room. "Alice, can I come in?"

Alice, still half asleep, answered Lana. "What?"

Lana opened the door and entered the room, sitting on her bed. "Are you Okay?" Alice nodded yes. "There's no telling you, is there?" Lana asked. Alice rolled her eyes, ready to strike. Lana caught herself thinking she caused all the trouble in the first place. "Sweetie, I won't tell you who to be with. If you love him, then I'll love him. I still think you deserve better. But if Ronnie is your choice, I'll try to accept him because I love you."

Alice smiled and reached out to her sister for a hug. "He needs me, and I need him," Alice whispered to Lana.

"Why do we, Lore's, have to be caretakers? I hope he's brave enough to take care of you." Lana said, getting up from the bed.

"All I know is right now we need each other," Alice assured Lana that she had it under control. "He makes me happy. And I haven't been happy in a long time."

Lana stopped at the door. "Okay, sweetie, then I'm happy too." Both the girls smiled, feeling their bond of sisterhood.

***

Summer was almost over. Ronnie and Alice survived their first six Months back together. Oh, understand there were battles to be told, but no drugs, no heartache, just gratitude as they reached out for the next 6 months.

Alice didn't see herself continuing to college, even though John encouraged her to get more education. Ronnie and Alice are always together, and Ronnie asks Alice to marry him. Alice accepted, only to find out she was pregnant.

Alice was up early, cooking herself some breakfast. John rushed in, grabbed some coffee, and went off to school. Alice set a plate of food at the table, not feeling the urge to fill her tummy, but ate because the food was there. Lana entered the kitchen, went to the cupboard, and got a cup. She poured herself a half cup of coffee and filled the rest with milk.

"Ronnie asked me to marry him."

"What did you tell him?"

"Yes," Alice answered her.

Lana went to the table, pulled a chair, and sat across from Alice. "When is this going to happen?" Lana asked.

"I think soon. We're just going to the courthouse."

"What! Why? Can't you guys wait and have a wedding?" Lana started to get upset.

"We can't afford a wedding," Alice told Lana.

"Did you tell Daddy?" Lana asked.

I'm going to call him today. I think it would be best for all of us if we just got married and moved on with our lives."

"It's a celebration of love. It's your chance to tell the world you are getting married. To the man you love." Lana started to get excited.

"Both of us feel that being together and getting married is more important than inviting many people to see us say I do."

"Are you going to live hereafter?" Lana asked.

"No. There's an apartment next to the shop. Ronnie is going to fix it up for us."

Alice smiled. "I figured John is graduating. Besides, you guys need the room, and it's about time the two of you got a real start without your sister hanging around."

Lana shook her head no. "It's far more important that you take your time to make such a big decision."

"Ronnie and I have been together since I was a freshman. We know that the time is here, and both of us want it." Alice started to get a little defensive.

"Can I at least make you dinner? We can have his family over with me and John. Maybe daddy can come with the kids." Alice nodded and approved the plan. "Oh, between you and me, I'm pregnant."

Lana's jaw fell to the ground. "Does Ronnie know?"

"Yes, but he asked me before he even knew that I was pregnant, so we'll continue with the plans we had and make it official."

"Where's the joy? I know it's early, but we have a million things to do before the wedding." Lana was already two stages ahead.

Alice smiled, happy that her sister was standing beside her.

Chapter 29

Mama Dearest Comes to Visit

1973 St Paul, Minnesota

Lana and John were married for a couple of years and had a baby boy. They decided they would call him Junior, and now she was pregnant with her second child.

It was a hot summer night, and the sun was still trying to shine even though it was close to 9:00 p.m. The telephone rang when John was with Junior, trying to put Jr. to sleep.

"Hello," Lana answered the telephone.

"Lana, it's Mama!" Dorine squealed over the phone

"Mom?" Lana asked, surprised to hear her voice.

"Listen, honey, I'm in Minnesota, just taking a vacation, and, well, I was wondering if I could stay a couple of days with you and John and visit with my grandchild."

Lana was shocked and touched that her mother tried to do something nice.

"Um, yes, of course, I mean, sure. Where are you at?"

"Here in St Paul." Dorine slurred.

John entered the room and saw that something was amiss with Lana. He quietly asked if she was okay.

"It's my mother. She wants to come over and spend some time with us."

"Tonight?" John asked

Lana nodded her head yes.

"Yeah, Mom, it will be good to see you." Lana lied.

"Great, then I'll be there soon."

Lana ran around the house, making it perfect. "It's so typical of her just to show up. She must have known she was coming to St. Paul before she left on her vacation. She could have called me before she left."

"And tell me, you would have been home." John smiled at his wife. "It's a good thing that she is trying to make amends." John reached and touched Lana's hand.

"I wonder if Daddy is with her?" Lana thought out loud.

The doorbell rang, and Lana took a deep breath. "She's here." Lana opened the door and saw a drunken Dorine in the arms of some stranger.

"Sweetie!" Dorine overstated. "Don't just keep us out here in the cold," Dorine giggled as she pushed past Lana and made her way into the home. "Oh, this is beautiful. John must be doing pretty good for himself."

John came to the door and immediately saw the problem. "Hi Dorine," John said, not knowing what to call her.

"Now, you just call me Mama, like the rest of the kids." Dorine slurred. John just smiled and moved closer to his wife.

"Oh my God, where's my manners? Everybody, this is Chuck. Chuck and I are on vacation. We left over a month ago, and I'll tell you, this country is bigger than I ever imagined. Can you believe, child, I made it to California?" Dorine went into the living room and took a seat on the couch.

"Mama, what about daddy?" Lana managed to get the words out.

"Oh, sugar, you know how your father and I have our ins and outs. And Chuck, well, we met dancing at a country-western club. Well, from the first night, we have hit it off."

"Sugar, can you show us to our room?" We are bushed from all the sightseeing we did today." Lana was at her limit. To think she would allow her mother into her home with some man she is entertaining. Well, it just wasn't going to happen.

"Mom, either you come with me to the kitchen, or I'll tell you right in front of your friend. But there's no way in hell you're staying in this house. I can't believe you would think it was okay to come to my house with a man who's not my father." Lana said, shaking from head to toe.

Dorine looked at Lana and started to take a slap at her, but Lana caught her arm early. "Don't you dare think you are going to lay a hand on me.

I won't say it any other way, but get the hell out of my house."

"Now, that's no way to be a talking to your mother," Chuck said, trying to Defend Dorine.

"John rose to the occasion and said, "Sir, I think it would be best to listen to my wife. You are not welcome in our home. Lana has a father, and you are not him."

Dorine huffed. "I have never been so insulted in my life. And to think that my own daughter is throwing me out into the streets. Well, it breaks my heart."

"That's right, mother, and don't let the door hit you in the rear," Lana said as she walked to the door to throw them out.

"I haven't even had a chance to see my grandchild." Dorine pleaded on her way out.

"Thank God, my child doesn't know his grandmother," Lana said, slamming the door behind them.

John walked over and held his wife. "I'm sorry, sweetheart," John said.

"It never changes. When I think my mom is going to start being a human being, she pulls some kind of bullshit. But this one is over the top." Lana shook her head and started to laugh. "I can't believe I just threw out my mother. She deserved it." Lana said with a smirk.

Chapter 30

Making Money, and Having Fun

1974, Houston, Texas

It was 1974, and Diane was 20 years old. Lana, Alice, and Susan were already married. Kathy and Steven lived with Dorine, and Diane lived with her father. Still in the little house behind the landlady's house. When Diane graduated from high school, she decided she would be the first Lore to attend college. Diane carpooled with Charlotte, even though she seemed to drive every day, because something was always wrong with Charlotte's car.

Michael still worked at the neighborhood bar, and Diane and Charlotte clean the place a few days a week, mainly because it helps Michael and gives them some pocket money.

When Charlotte first asked her father for permission to work at the bar, he adamantly said that no daughter of his was going to be a barmaid. Charlotte started to pout and shouted on the way to her room. "But Mr. Lore is the manager, and we'll only work when he is around."

Charlotte stopped and was surprised by the silence. "Michael Lore is the manager? Why didn't you say so in the first place? When do you start?"

Charlotte ran back to the front room. "You mean I can work?"

"Only if Mr. Lore is there while you're working. He's a good man, and he'll take care of you."

Surely it wasn't Michael's idea, or fault, that Diane and Charlotte would pour a couple of beers or wink a few tips when Michael was in the office, trying to finish his ordering sheets. The locals loved the girls and kept a watchful eye over both. When a stranger entered the place, they began getting a little too close to the girls. A few regulars would also give the boys a nice talk. They would buy them a drink and set the rules straight; Charlotte and Diane were off-limits. The girls took care of the regular customers. If one happened to overindulge, the girls would help them into the back seats of their car and take them home.

"I don't know what I would do without you girls. You know my Emily, she told me, don't even wake me up in the middle of the night to 'come' a picking you up." Gary Swanson, a regular at the bar, explained.

"Oh, don't you worry, Mr. Swanson. We'll get you home safely, and you can sneak into your bed without Emily ever knowing." Diane and Charlotte helped Gary out of the car and to his front door. Gary pulled out the standard $5.00 tip, and the girls refused. Gary became insistent, and the girls accepted the money, running to the car laughing, loving their new job.

Michael and Diane save every Tuesday night just so that Father and daughter could catch up on what was happening outside of the bar. There was a neighborhood Jack in the Box a block away from their home. On Michael's day off, they would sit in the restaurant for hours, eating tacos and talking about the previous week. It turned into their time, which Diane looked forward to each week.

"I met a guy the other day." Diane started the conversation of the night.

"Oh yeah? You mean, you're considering giving some guy a chance? Oh, boy, he must be special." Michael said, half jesting.

"It's kind of funny when he walked into Shooters the other night; I noticed him and told Charlotte that I was going to marry that man. We both laughed, and the next thing I knew, he was right behind me. He asked me to dance, and I spun off my chair, and we flirted with each other while dancing to a song. He walked me back to my seat and took Charlotte's chair, who conveniently went to the bathroom," Diane explained, still dazed by the young man.

"He bought me a drink and talked to me as if he knew me for years. I don't know Daddy; he was just different."

"Are you going to see him again?" Michael inquired.

"Oh, you know how those boys are; a peck on the cheek, and they're off to the next girl."

"Oh! So, he got a kiss?"

"Oh, Daddy, he could have gotten a lot more than that if he had played his cards right. Just kidding." Diane teased her father.

His name was Tom, and he was a special person. He was tall, almost 6'6", and so handsome that he could turn every head in a room. He had a great personality, and by the night's end, everybody wanted to be Tom's friend. He was a real leader, a man with a big heart.

Tom took the town by surprise. Outside of the club, everybody was asking, "Hey, have you met the new guy, Tom?" Diane didn't realize they were talking about the same guy she met at Shooters.

One evening, her friend Fern called her and said, "You all have to get down to Shooters right away." Fern wanted to introduce Diane to this special guy.

Diane and Charlotte were working at Michael's bar. "We're working right now; I can ask my Daddy if we can get out of here early."

"You have to, Diane; this guy is perfect for you."

"Okay, just as soon as we can break away, we'll be on our

way," Diane told her.

"Great, don't worry; no matter what, I'll keep him fresh and alive for you."

If necessary, Fern promised to block the door to hold this one hostage. Diane laughed and assured her that they would be there just as soon as they could.

When Diane and Charlotte made it to Shooters, they saw Fern almost falling out of her chair, drunk as can be, waking up every few moments, willing herself to be conscious. "Now you just wait here, my friend Diane; I mean, she's perfect for you. She's pretty and funny." And then she would pass out again for a few more minutes. Tom was talking to Fern's boyfriend, Bill, while Fern was trying to be a faithful friend, challenging Tom to a drinking contest. She was willing to do just about anything to keep him there. That was why Fern was so drunk. She lost the battle; however, she managed to stall for time. At one point in time, she figured Bill wouldn't be able to keep him there, so she passed out right on top of him. Of course, Bill was embarrassed and peeled his girlfriend from Tom.

Diane and Charlotte walked up to the table; Bill stood up to greet the girls. Diane saw what condition Fern was in, and as she was just about to ask what had happened, Tom stood up. And Diane met his eyes, and they both smiled.

"You're the girl Fern has been talking about?" Tom said, extending He gave Diane a warm welcome hug.

"Fern's been talking about you all week. I had no idea it was you." Diane blushed with embarrassment. "I've been coming every night, hoping you would be here. When Fern told me about a girl I had to meet, I was trying to be nice. Well, I guess we are here now." Tom smiled and continued. "Besides, I don't know what she would have done next to keep me here for you. I think she went to her car to try to find some rope." Tom said with a chuckle.

Diane started to laugh. "Yep, Fern is a good friend. Diane said as she turned to Bill and leaned over and hugged him. Diane whispered into Bill's ear. "Good job, Fern!"

Tom and Diane talked in Tom's car, in the parking lot of Shooters, until the sun gave a morning smile.

Diane had several boyfriends in the past, but Tom was the first man she ever dated. Tom was new to Houston, coming from California. He was sent by God to meet Diane.

The new couple united with a fresh sense of fun understanding, and a new love bond blossomed between them. They didn't demand but craved the time together. Tom spent a lot of time with Diane at Michael's bar, just being present with her. After a short while, Tom helped them with much of the physical work the bar needed. His payment was just being allowed to be with his girlfriend.

Tom came with a lot of baggage from California. He previously married his high school sweetheart and had three boys from this marriage. The break-up of the union was hard to accept, and to leave his boys behind was almost impossible. However, his ex-wife was terrific with the boys, and he knew they were in good hands with her.

Tom needed Diane to know and understand his past. He explained his love for his children, and his hope for a future is a significant part of his boy's life. Diane listened and thought about what this meant for her. She appreciated Tom sharing his past with her before either of them made a commitment of love. Tom's honesty and sincere appreciation for his children made it difficult for Diane to use this information against her decision to fall in love with him.

***

Tom was the healer of all bad situations, and when it came to Diane'sfamily, he couldn't accept the fact that they were a fractured family. Spending so much time with Diane meant spending a lot of time with Michael. In doing so, they became friends. Many nights, Tom and Michael sat at the bar, sharing each of their past. Michael shared with him the damage done to his family and, for many reasons, how he felt unable to fix all the problems. Tom reached out and wanted to help Michael and his family. Michael was eager to let Tom try to reconnect with them all.

"Sir, I'll never try to undermine who you are and your relationship* with Your kids, but they need to see how they are special," Tom said, drinking at the bar with Michael while Diane worked in the back with Charlotte.

When Tom met Dorine, he knew her past and truly loved her for who she was. He shared his history with her, and the two of them had a special bond. "You are who you are, and there is no changing that, but now you have a chance to be a good mother, especially to Kathy and Steven," Tom told Dorine, sitting at her kitchen table, both enjoying a good cup of coffee, with a dab of whiskey to square the corner off.

Dorine accepted what Tom had to say to her. Their relationship was not about how bad Dorine was. It was an enlightening time sharing the good and bad events of life. Most of the time, they would crack up over the silliest things. Laughing until tears appeared in both of their eyes. Dorine saw happiness through Tom's eyes. She realized that there was hope for a real relationship between herself and her children in the future. Listening to Tom's hope and love for his boys, he showed Dorine that it was never too late. As Dorine often said, "Time to take the bull by the horns."

There were many late nights when Tom, Diane, and Michael would end up at Dorine's after the bar was closed. She would get up and make a giant breakfast for them all. When many laughs and a good meal were over, Tom and Diane would leave, giving Michael a lift to his house down the street. Tom, Michael, and Dorine were becoming good friends. Michael appreciated Dorine's time with him, and even though he respected her space, he loved the closeness they experienced again.

Each of Diane's sisters met Tom, and before the end of their first visit, they loved Tom. Tom recognized all the good in each of them and brought peace to their broken hearts. He mended years of rejection and showed them how each sibling was unique from the other. "Of course, you're special, each of you guys is Lore's." Tom would remind them.

Tom's heart went out to Kathy and Steven. Kathy was always crying, whether it was because of her family or her place within herself. Tom would spend time with her, encouraging her to be the best she could be. Diane never realized how much she hurt Kathy as a child; she reached out and learned to love her sister. In a short period, both Diane and Kathy found a new love between the two of them.

Through love and wisdom, Tom was able to reunite the Lore family. The Lore's realized their love for each other was always there. It just took some work to put it all together.

Chapter 31

Steven's Love For His Family

1973, Houston, Texas

Steven was in high school and turned sixteen. Tom bought him his first car, a 1963 Nova. His new ride was a dark blue-green on the outside, with a green vinyl interior. Steven loved the car and loved Tom for being there for him. Tom had a way of showing his love without overpowering or making Michael feel threatened. Tom empowered Michael through encouragement. He truly respected him for all the love he gave to his children. Unfortunately, Michael had a drinking problem and found it hard to be a father to Kathy and Steven. He loved his children; they were always his life, but for his two youngest children, he had a hard time connecting with them, mainly because his self-esteem was so off-balance. Michael felt they were embarrassed by him; after all, he was ashamed of himself. Michael stepped aside and became a passive parent. Most of the time, Kathy and Steven didn't realize their father was present.

They often mistook his lack of participation as a lack of love, but for Michael, it was a result of a lack of confidence and feelings of worthlessness.

Many afternoons, Michael would go to Steven's football practice, watching a workout at the far edge of the field behind the chain link fence. He was proud of his son and would do anything to avoid embarrassing Steven.

Steven was popular, a quarterback, and loved by all for his humble spirit. Everybody knew he was raised in a dysfunctional home and grew into a positive person. He carried no bitterness toward his parents and loved them both.

Kathy, Susan, Tom, and Diane became Steven's fans. They would line themselves up with the cheerleaders and scream throughout the game. Michael would attend every game and silently cheer his son on from a distance. When it was time for a father-son moment, Tom was there to cover for Michael, giving Steven the strength to be all he could be. Steven was a real achiever in both sports and academics, and he made his parents proud.

In one game, Steven tried to concentrate on the moment of action. He looked past the goalpost and saw his father standing beyond the end zone, watching the game himself. Steven turned to see his father gone after the team gathered and gave a final cheer. The next game, when he saw his father alone, hiding from the crowds, he ran to his father instead of joining his team for the last-minute instructions in the 2nd quarter. Michael was upset that Steven didn't go with his team, holding on tightly to the chain-link fence. Steven approached the barrier, greeted his father, and touched his hands through the links. "Hey, thank you for coming to my game," Steven said, not knowing what to say.

"You're doing great, son," Michael told him. "But you need to be with the team."

Steven smiled at his father. "You're more important than anybody on this team."

Michael smiled. "You're like your brother, so talented." He caught himself because he was starting to get choked up. "Now get out of here. They need you over there with the team." Michael squeezed his fingers against Steven's.

Steven nodded, "Thanks for coming, Dad." He turned and ran back to the sidelines with the rest of the team. A few of the guys were wondering who the man was. Steven proudly said, "Oh, it's my Dad."

After several years of heartache, the Lore family experienced peace. Each of the children understood that nobody was there for them more than their siblings. They loved each other, became deeply involved in each other's lives, and helped and encouraged one another to be the best that God had made them to be.

Diane and Tom became more serious; they both fell in love. Never being in love, Diane struggled to accept this sensation as reality. Love for Diane was an emotion only pure in fairy tales. Tom was like her Prince Charming, allowing her to rest within his soul. The whole situation was scary for Diane. She had exposed herself to happiness and pain, never regretting her love for Tom. The healing power she demonstrated was a pure motivation for him to fall in love with her. Diane trusted Tom with her love, his past, and her family. Tom respected this trust and gave his heart to Diane in return. A perfect couple, everybody would tell them. In Diane's heart, she knew that Tom was her man forever.

The two spent most of their time at Michael's bar, helping him by keeping him company and taking a lot of the workload away. Steven and Kathy would often hang out after school and stop by most nights to bid their father goodnight. Michael had started to slow down on his drinking, as he had promised Susan, and was happy to see his family coming together. He wanted to be a part of this new family relationship. With everybody talking and loving, Dorine found a new respect and love for Michael, and several nights a week, she would be at the bar with her family, enjoying the new life she had found herself in.

Steven was the youngest of the Lores. He was the family's pride. He was always smart and knew they had it tough, but somehow, as a child, he could see the good in his family and continue to be himself, as Steven. When Tom came around, it was Steven who felt complete, having once again a family to lean on and to love. Steven always showed his love to his mother. He knew what kind of woman she was, but that didn't stop him from loving her.

All the kids think Steven was too generous with his love for their mother. And that Dorine would someday take advantage of this unconditional love and hurt Steven. However, Steven never considered the consequences and gave himself as a gift to his mother. Maybe it was because everybody else was against Dorine that Steven felt she needed somebody on her side. Perhaps it was because Dorine reached out to Steven and Kathy that he felt a bond between them. He just loved his mother more than anyone else could.

Kathy would often tell her sisters that they didn't know their mother. Lana would slam that idea out immediately, saying she was never around long enough to get to know her. In their own way, Kathy, Steven, and Dorine are a little family of their own, and Dorine treats them as if they were her only children. I'm not saying she changed her ways, but she would play mother to them when she was home

When Steven was sixteen, he had a girlfriend. Her name was Shelly, and she was a sweet girl who was always by Steven's side. When they were together, they never let go of each other's hands.

Steven was very popular in school and was approached by several girls, but he gave his heart to his girlfriend and was sincere in being faithful to her.

Diane was having breakfast with Steven and Kathy before they all had to go to school.

"You know you are too young to spend so much time with Shelly. You need to experience a lot of girls to see what is special and find the right girl who has it all." Diane tried to explain to Steven.

"Steven just laughed and said. "Shelly is the one. She makes me laugh and feel special. I don't want to date anybody else."

Kathy was eating her Cheerios, "I wish I could find somebody special. You're lucky, Steven, to have Shelly, and Diane, you're lucky to have Tom. I know someday, even if I'm hiding under the bed, the right guy will find me, and he'll be my special guy." Rolling her eyes up, she lost her smile. "It seems I can only find the jerks. And when I think he's the one, he only wants me in bed. Guys are jerks." Kathy said, pushing her bowl of cereal away from her.

Steven reached out to his sister. "Why has life always been so hard for you?" Steven said, chuckling.

Diane stepped right in. "Stop looking so hard. How do you expect somebody to love you if you don't love yourself?" Diane was sincerely trying to help, not being overly critical of

Kathy.

"Sometimes, I think there isn't much to love. I mean, look at Susan; she is so beautiful. Diane, you are so smart and full of confidence, and you, Steven, have the world by the tail. What happened to me?" Kathy smiled, knowing she was making more of this than it was.

I love you," Steven said very seriously. "You are pretty, smart, and fun to be around."

"Of course. You do, you have to, you're my brother." Kathy, feeling awkward, pulled away from the table.

Diane wasn't going to let Kathy get away. "I think the same way as Steven.

It's only you who sees yourself differently. You're not that whiney little girl anymore. You'd better stop and listen to us. Stop being so destructive to yourself."

Kathy pushed some hair from her face, picked up her dish, and took it to the sink behind them. She was facing the window, looking at the backyard. "Thank you both; I'll try to have a better outlook."

"At yourself, not others." Diane had to add.

Kathy nodded her head and turned, smiling at both. "Hey, I thought we were talking about Steven and Shelly." Kathy smiled.

"Steven is happy right now, at least until our next conversation." Diane took her brother's hand and smiled.

Steven looked at his watch. "Hey, we all better go, or we'll be late." Steven got up and hugged Diane, then went over and spanked Kathy. "If you want a ride, you better hurry up."

***

Kathy was in her senior year and found a special guy. He was on Steven's football team. Kathy, her new boyfriend Alan, Steven, and Shelly were always together. The boys were always talking about football, and the girls complained about the boys always talking about football, but the four of them were happy. Whether they were at Dorine's house doing homework or cruising the streets at night, life for all of them was exceptional.

Before the first football game of the season, Steven came to the bar to ask his father to attend the game the following day. Michael smiled and told his son he wouldn't miss it. Michael purchased a ticket, entered the gate, and joined the rest of the family on the bleachers. Steven turned from the team when they settled and started waving to his family. He pulled a couple of guys to the side and pointed up to the stands. Steven was proud of his family and wanted them, as well as others, to know that he appreciated them for being there and rooting for him.

Steven was not the quarterback because of his popularity. He was talented and had an arm that could accurately throw the entire football field. Even though he was only a junior, college scouts were already approaching him to discuss the possibility of

268

him attending their school. Steven understood the offers made to him but didn't allow himself to be distracted by the attention. He was very level-headed and knew he was a part of a team. He realized that he had to concentrate on the moment and be a team player so that everyone could be successful. Steven was very humble with his talent and saw it as a gift not to be abused.

The newspapers loved Steven. They would write articles explaining who this boy was. They would use such expressions as 'Wonder Boy here in Houston.' 'Hometown boy brings hope to the community.' Somebody wrote a story about Steven, his talent, and his humble spirit in the editorial section. The community fell in love with him. Steven was embarrassed by all the attention, and everywhere he went, people recognized him. They would wave at him and approach him as if he knew them. Though Steven felt uncomfortable, he always smiled, shook their hands, and thanked them for saying hi.

Chapter 32

Checking in with Dorine

2004: Medford, Tennessee

The afternoon was almost over by the time Dorine finally woke up. The young doctor ordered Dorine to stay in the hospital for several more days. Dorine was weak and sore and didn't want to do much talking.

"Mama, are you feeling okay? Kathy asked

Dorine blinked her eyes twice as if she was preparing to lose her speech.

"You sure did scare us," Diane told her mom.

Lana was trying to find the right words to say to her mother. "I'm glad you're okay."

Dorine didn't say anything and reached out for Lana's hand. Lana accepted her mother's gesture and smiled.

Dorine opened her mouth to speak. "I knew someday you would forgive me."

Lana stopped the tears from falling from her eyes. She let Dorine's hand go and walked out of the room.

Alice went after Lana as the rest of her sisters watched with open mouths.

"She'll be back, Mama, just rest." Kathy took her empty hand. Dorine just shook her head and didn't try to say a word.

Susan approached the bed and said. "Mama, you just worry about getting better. When you get well, there will be plenty of time to deal with Lana."

Dorine closed her eyes, telling the girls that she was tired.

Chapter 33

The Sweetness of My Child

It was October 17th. Around 11:00 p.m., Steven had just taken Shelly home from the football game. He was going home, feeling elated and full of energy, when he decided to stop at his Father's bar to thank him for coming to the game and to bid him a good night. The bar was full, and everybody knew of Steven's success. Steven shook hands, received back pats, and made it to his Father. Michael smiled at his son, took a moment, and hugged and kissed his son on top of his head. Steven loudly told Michael that he loved him, but he did not know if Michael heard him over the bar noise. Steven smiled and kissed his Father on the cheek, explaining that he was drained and was going home. Michael smiled and nodded, slinging drinks down the bar to his friends. Steven left the bar from the front door, once again receiving accolades from the customers who knew they were in the midst of greatness. Steven smiled, knowing this was a testament to his father's greatness His friends, his peers, who truly loved Michael. Steven left the bar.

The night was pretty clear, with a touch of crispness coming upon them, considering winter was approaching them strongly. Steven was traveling North on Rose. He was stopped at a stoplight. All he would think about was how special this night was and how blessed he was to be held close to God. His signal light turned green, and Steven proceeded to cross the intersection of Highway 7. He didn't expect a car to ride through the red light, crashing into his side door. The sound of metal bending and glass exploding was the last sound that Steven heard. The opposing vehicle rolled over Steven's car, squashing Steven in his seat. Steven was instantly killed as the drunk driver was carried away to a local hospital.

The police officers were reported crying as they tried to get Steven out of the vehicle. By the time they got to him, Steven was already dead.

It was a passerby trying to be helpful who recognized who Steven was. He ran to the corner right away and called Michael at the bar. He told him he had better come to the intersection because Steven had been in an accident.

Michael removed his apron and opened the hatch that let him out of the bar area. He ran outside the bar's door. His car was parked in the back lot, and he ran his heart out, praying directly to God to be with Steven. Michael ran a couple of blocks to the intersection of Rose St. and Taylor. When he got near, he saw Steven's car and a body on the ground covered in front of

Steven's bumper. Michael first went to the car's passenger side and searched through the window, hoping to see his boy, but an officer approached him. He was angry that Michael was there.

"Hey, get the hell out of here." The officer screamed at Michael.

"This is my boy's car. Where is he?" Michael cried. The policeman grabbed hold of Michael and yelled on his walkie-talkie. "Hey, somebody come over here; it's his father." The officer called for assistance.

Michael was frantic and wasn't going to be restrained by anybody. He slid on his knees to the body on the ground. "Please, this can't be my son!" Michael uncovered the body and saw Steven's beautiful face under the blanket. He fell backward as if somebody had shot a bullet through him. Michael lost his breath and blacked out for a moment. When he regained his conscience, a policeman dragged him away from Steven.

Michael felt such an enormous pain that he was unable to fight. He was inshock and stood by the car, not believing his son was dead.

Diane and Tom were in the bar's storeroom, taking an inventory for Michael. They questioned several guys when they came out and saw the bar unattended. "Where's my Daddy?" Diane asked.

"He ran out of here like smoke coming from a fire."

Diane looked at Tom. Tom ran outside to look for Michael. "Was he sick or something?" Diane asked.

Another guy at the bar said, "Somebody called, and when Michael hung up he left."

Diane went out looking for Tom. He was outside the door, trying to figureout where Michael was. "They said he got a phone call and ran out of here." Diane started to get upset.

A man in a car pulled up to the curb. He rolled down his window and screamed at Diane that there was a car wreck. "Your Daddy is on Rose St. and Taylor, and he's all shaken up. I thought I'd better find you all so that you can help him."

Tom took off running, and Diane thanked the man, took a deep breath, and ran after Tom.

When they got to the accident scene, Tom and Diane saw Michael against the car.

At first, Tom and Diane don't recognize the car until they get up close and realize it is Steven's car. Tom ran up to Michael, not believing what he saw.

"Michael, is it Steven?" Tom yelled at Michael above the din of the street noise.

Michael didn't answer. He couldn't make the mind process that he had lost his son.

Diane came up behind them, jumping and screaming for Steven. Tom Diane was grabbed as a policeman approached.

"I'm sorry you can't stand in the middle of traffic." The officer Instructed.

"Is Steven okay?" Tom asked the officer.

The officer was silent and pointed to the covered body. Tom got up and leaned down over the body. Diane, horrified, put her hand over her mouth. Tom pulled open the bloody cover. When he saw it was Steven, he put the sheet back over him and loudly yelled. His eyes bulged as his mind exploded, wanting an explanation. "Where's the person who did this to Steven?" Tom managed to get out of his mouth.

The policeman turned back to them. "He's on his way to the hospital. He appeared intoxicated, and a witness said he ran the red light." The policeman wanted to tell the whole story.

Tom looked once again at Steven and turned back to Michael. He grabbed Diane's hand and pulled her into his arms. Michael was softly crying, killing himself from within.
"Michael, I'm sorry," Tom cried to Diane's father. "I swear I'll kill the bastard who did this to Steven."

Diane fell to her knees, holding onto Tom's legs. Tom stooped down and held his girlfriend.

Diane asked Tom, not allowing herself to comprehend or want to understand. "Is Steven dead?"

Tom held her tight and cried in her ear. "Yes, your brother is dead."

Diane was so upset that she fought her way free from Tom's arms and ran to her father. "Daddy, make it stop. Make this nightmare stop now!" Diane cried to her father.

Michael just looked past Diane, knowing it was too much for him to handle.

A police car pulled up in the middle of the accident scene. Several officers jumped out of the car and came over to assist Michael. They guided the family to their police car and sat them in the back seat.

"Now you just wait here until we figure out what happened." The family was silent, unsure of what to say to each other.

"I feel like we are the ones who did something wrong," Tom told Diane.

Tom went to open the door, but the criminal-proof locks were working inthe back seat.

An officer came up to Tom's side of the car. I'm sorry, Mr. Lore, talking to Michael, why don't you let me take you all somewhere other than here? It's too late for any of us to help your son." The policeman said, feeling responsible for getting the family to a safe place. "Is there any place that I can take you all?"

Michael was silent, and Tom instructed the officer to go to Dorine's house.

When they arrived at Dorine's, Michael started walking

278

down the street from the house.

Diane began to go after her father. "Daddy, where are you going?" Michael stopped, and in a very composed voice, he said. "I need to do some walking. Go in and tell the rest what has happened. I just don't think I can do that right now."

Diane made her father hug her as she let him continue down the street. She returned to Tom, and the two entered Dorine's house, waking her up.

Chapter 34

Saying Goodbye to My Son

It was Kathy who called Lana early the next morning. It just didn't make sense to any of them to wake up Lana or Alice since Steven was already dead.

"Hello," Lana answered the telephone.

There was a moment of silence as Kathy tried to regain her strength. "Lana, it's me, Kathy."

"Oh, hi, sweetie." Lana didn't detect anything wrong.

"There's been a horrible accident, and Steven was killed." Kathy couldn't stand her words and cried over the telephone. She almost hung up the phone, but Lana pleaded for her to hang on.

"Kathy, please catch your breath and tell me what is happening," Lana commanded.

"Steven was in a car accident last night. A drunk went through a red light and ran into him. The crash killed him."

"Where's daddy?" Lana asked right away.

"He's at his house, but somebody needs to make the arrangements. He's a mess, and Mama, well, she just doesn't believe it happened, and she hasn't come out of her room this morning." Kathy said, trying not to cry, but she was scared.

"Listen, sweetie, and I'll be right there. Tell one of the other girls to stay with Daddy. I don't know how he is going to handle this." Lana said, concerned for her Father. "I'll catch a plane and be there this afternoon."

Lana hung up the telephone with Kathy and immediately called Alice. "There's been an accident, and Steven is dead. Alice, is there any way you can come with me to Houston?" Lana said pretty much in one sentence.

Alice was still not fully awake, considering she was on the late shift at the Downtown Café. "I have the next couple of days off. I'll try to get a replacement for me. Are we going to drive?"

"No, we better fly. The family all sounds like a mess down there." Lana explained.

"I don't have the money to fly. And I need to talk to Ronnie. Are you going to take Junior and Steven with you?"

"I haven't gotten that far. I'll loan you the money. Maybe I can get John's sister to watch all the kids for a few days over here." Lana tried to make arrangements so she wouldn't have to think about the tragedy they were about to experience.

The night Steven died, Diane and Tom told Dorine

and Kathy. Of course, everybody was in shock. Diane called Susan, and she rushed over by herself, leaving her baby with her husband at home.

Tom left the family and went in search of Michael. He stopped at Michael's house, but he wasn't there. He continued his search and ended up at the bar. Tom looked through the window. Most of the lights were out, but Tom could see the shadow of a man sitting on a stool leaning against the bar. Tom walked in and called out to Michael. "May I join you?" Tom asked.

Michael didn't say a word. He got off the barstool, went behind the bar, and got Tom an empty glass. Tom went up to the bar and sat next to Michael's seat. Michael came around the bar, picked up a bottle of whiskey, and placed it in front of his charge. He poured Tom a drink.

"When I got here, the lights were all out, somebody put all the money in a bag, and they locked the front door. Michael took a swig of his drink. "Look, they left their drink money here on the bar." Michael appreciated his friends and his customers in this time of need.

Tom, not knowing what to say, belted down his first shot. "I didn't eventhink of the bar when we ran out of here. The guys must have closed us down."

"He was really a good boy," Michael whispered, not crying but giving honor to his son.

"Yes, he was a good boy." Tom had to catch himself from crying.

"He's with his brother now. Jimmy was a good boy, too. He'll take care of him." Michael said into his glass.

"I know it's hard to accept, and believe me, I don't understand, but they say he's in a better place. I mean, with God and all." Tom tried to understand for himself.

"It's me. God knows that I'm not the best father, and he took my boys from me." Michael started to break up.

"No, Michael, you're a great father, and your kids love you." Tom looked Michael in the eyes.

"Yea, Yea, Yea." Michael pushed the air away from him. He pulled out a cigarette from his shirt pocket and offered Tom one. "In the bible, there is this character named Job. He was a good person. He worked hard and loved his family. And for some reason, the devil had to get onto him. And God listened to the devil and took away everything that meant anything to Job. Michael said, taking a big puff from his cigarette. "I don't understand a God who would listen to the devil like that and destroy a man's life. Why?"

Tom didn't know how to answer Michael; all he could do was listen.

So, all I can figure is that God is mad at me, and He's punishing me for being a drunk." Michael grabbed the bottle, poured himself another, and lifted the bottle, saluting God. "At least that's how I see it."

Tom took the bottle and poured himself another drink. "I don't think God took Steven to punish you," Tom said. "I think each of us has our time here on earth, and as sad as it is, it was Steven's time."

"You don't see that as being cruel?" Michael asked. "God gives you a boy and makes him joy in everybody's life. Then He takes him away." Michael took another drink. "God forgive me, but I don't find any humor in that."

Michael got off the barstool and almost fell to the ground. Tom jumped off the stool to help Michael. Michael, with his cigarette hanging from his mouth, muttered. "I have to use the head."

Tom backed off and got back on his stool. The bar's emptiness and the night's spooks haunted Tom as he tried to understand the only God he knew. He understood what Michael was saying. It hurts to be allowed to love and then have it taken away. Tom looked around and started to pray to God for help. "God, I don't understand, but who am I to question you? Please help us here. All loved Steven, as I'm sure you love him."

Tom heard a roar as Michael was throwing up in the bathroom. "Please give us the strength to endure this." Tom prayed to God.

Susan arrived at Dorine's house, running in, still in her bathrobe, with a pair of jeans underneath. She cried out to her sisters as they met her in the living room. The three cried together, not even trying to make sense of what had happened.

Dorine was still in her room. The pain she felt came in waves as she muffled her screams into her pillow. Her heart was broken; her baby boy was dead.

Morning hit Diane hard. It was 9:30 a.m., and she realized that it wasn't a dream and that Steven was dead. She got up to check on her father, whose bed was empty, looking as though it had not been slept in. Diane walked to her mother's house and found Susan asleep on the couch. She peeked into her mother's room and found her sleeping alone. Diane left Dorine's home and decided to try the bar. When she arrived, she found her father and Tom slumped over the bar, with an empty bottle of whiskey between them. She reached into Tom's pocket, got his keys, entered the alley behind the bar, and got his car. Diane pulled up to the front door. She left the engine running and woke up Tom out of his stupor.

Tom's head was pounding. He could barely focus, but saw an angel before him as he hugged Diane.

"Let's get my dad home," Diane whispered to Tom.

Tom nodded and put Michael on his shoulder. Michael woke up miffed, but when he realized it was Tom and Diane, he

286

allowed Tom to pull him to the car.

When they got Michael settled at home, Diane took a cigarette from Tom and sat at the kitchen table. "I think we have to make the arrangements. Mama never came out of her room last night, and Susan and Kathy are a wreck." Tom pressed his hands against the sides of his head, trying to keep it together.

"We have to do it for Steven." Diane continued. "We must be strong and make this farewell honorable to him."

Tom reached over and took Diane's hand. "I love you." Tom took a deep breath, lifted his head, and stood up from the table. "I'm going to go home and take a shower. I'll be back in an hour, and then we'll figure out exactly what we can do."

Lana and Alice's plane arrived mid-afternoon. They took a taxi from the airport to Dorine's house. When they arrived at the front steps, Lana stopped, unsure whether to knock or walk right in. Alice gave a hiss, stepped before Lana, and opened the door. Dorine was the only one in sight, sitting on the living room couch dressed in blue slacks and a white blouse. Her feet were sockless, tucked under her on top of the sofa. She looked up and saw her daughters entering the living room.

"Mom." Alice started to cry, looking for comfort from her mother. She hurried up to Dorine and hugged her. Lana stood there, not expecting to be confronted with her mother as soon as they arrived. Dorine looked up at Lana, not being the first one to say hello.

"Hello, Mom," Lana said. "Where are the rest of the girls?"

Dorine perked up, releasing Alice to sit next to her. "They all went to the mortuary to make the arrangements."

A knock at the door broke the awkward silence. Lana turned and opened the front door.

A young girl was shivering on the porch, as if it were midwinter. "Hello, my name is Gabby. I'm sorry to impose, but I represent the Herald Times here in Houston, and we loved Steven and would like to know if there is anything we can do to help in this time of need."

Lana was touched by this young girl and asked her to come in.

"I spoke with the high school, and since we all loved Steven, we were wondering if we could have a type of memorial at the school for him. You wouldn't believe all the people who have called and just want to say how much Steven had touched them."

Lana led Gabby to her mother. Dorine tried to hold herself together. "I think a memorial for my Steven at the high school would be nice."

"Mrs. Lore, I know this is a lot for you, and believe me, we'll make all the arrangements, and the Herald has already agreed to pay for all the costs."

Dorine was overwhelmed and slowly nodded her head

yes. She smiled in gratitude, not able to express her feelings in words.

As Gabby left, Kathy, Susan, Diane, and Tom came up the walkway. Lana and Alice met them at the front door, and the girls hugged each other. The kids entered the living room and found a place to sit wherever they could. They shared their hearts, and all agreed it was time to think of Steven and make the right decisions.

Dorine was silent, watching her children love each other. She knew each was her own but felt like a stranger, not a mother. Lana was taking charge, as she had been when they were growing up. She provided the final answers to what was right and what was not. But together, they decided that Steven would be buried in Rutterfield with Jimmy.

It was a Monday evening in mid-November. The school allowed the newspaper will provide a memorial in the school gym. The bleachers were set up, and a table was decorated with a large picture of Steven in the middle. The crowd was sullen as they entered to pay their last respects. The family, minus Michael, was led to the center court and asked to sit beside the table. Michael could not bring himself to attend a public memorial. He was too grieved to accept that anybody could feel the loss as much as he thought, and he wasn't going to display his grief to the public. The service commenced without Michael.

Several clergypersons gave insight into God's purpose in taking such a young man. The words were hollow, lacking any real meaning to anyone The principal came forward, shook hands with the family, and spoke about Steven as if he had a personal relationship with him. What was impressive to each of the family members was the outpouring of love from Steven's students and friends, who stood up in tears to share their stories of their relationship with him and how he had affected them forever. At the end of the memorial, the school choir emerged and sang a deeply spiritual song, bidding farewell to their friend and classmate as he was laid to rest. It wasn't until the end of the ceremony that Alan, Steven's best friend, got up from the bleachers, walked onto the court to the table, and placed Steven's football jersey next to his picture.

Alan fought back his tears as a puncture dam held back tons of water. "Steven was my best friend and the greatest football player ever." Alan couldn't say anymore and was overwhelmed with grief. When he finished, he bowed his head. The room went silent, then one person clapped, and the whole gym exploded, raising their voices to bid their friend goodbye.

The family left the memorial feeling so proud of Steven. There was peace in their hearts that, despite Steven's short life, he touched many lives and made a difference in the community.

When they got home, Diane and Susan went to Michael's

house to ensure he was okay. He was sitting at his table. Still visibly upset from the past few days, Diane and Susan tried to tell him all the good things they said about Steven at the memorial, but Michael didn't want to hear about it.

"You know I love you both, but I need this time alone." Michael tried to explain.

Diane stood up from the table. "Some of the neighbors have brought over food to Mama's house. I'll go over there and get you a plate." "No, that's okay."

"No, I insist." Diane started to cry. "Can't you see, we all are sickened by this, Daddy, don't make it your pain. We need you."

Michael set his head between his hands, leaning on the table. "I need time."

Susan stood up and hugged her father's back. The two girls left.

People were dropping in and out of Dorine's house. Everybody paid their condolences, but the family just wanted to be left alone.

Lana was tired of avoiding Dorine and snuck out of the house. She found her way to her father's house.

She softly knocked, but nobody answered. She poked her head in and saw her father sitting at the table, crying in his hands. Lana walked over to him, hugged him, and told him she loved him.

She saw the bottle of whiskey on the table and poured herself a glass. She scooted a chair beside his, sat down, and placed her arms around her father.

"I know how much this hurts. When we lost Jimmy, I thought I lost my own life. I loved my brother so much. And it hurt, and I was mad and angry with God. It seemed so unfair. So many scum balls in this world, and God picked on my brother. Maybe Jimmy was the lucky one. Maybe it was a blessing that God took him out of this world. Maybe Jimmy is in peace, the kind we find only in dreams. Daddy, you know what makes me feel more horrible about Steven? Our Steven, I didn't know him. He was my brother, almost like a baby of my own, when Mom decided to be on her own. All these years have passed, and I have allowed my brother to grow up without me. And Dad, that is horrible. Lana started to cry. I feel like a worthless piece of shit, not taking the time to know my little brother. Daddy, you are blessed to have known both of your boys; they loved you and took pride in being your children. And instead of condemning God, you should thank Him for giving you all the time you had with each of them."

Michael looked up from the table with a tear in his eyes. "I know how much Jimmy loved you very much. He wanted to be your big brother because he was proud of you. Steven also knew who you were. No, you hadn't seen each other for years, but he understood who you were in his life. And there was love in his heart for you. It's a shame that you didn't get the time to know your brother, but Steven understood, and it never stopped him from loving you."

"Do you know the first year you all came down here, Steven painted me and Alice a picture of poodles? To this day, I still have that picture framed and hanging in my bedroom. Daddy, I wish I had known him; he sounds like a wonderful boy." "He was a good boy who wasn't afraid to show his love." Michael pushed His lips were pressed together to try to subdue the emotional anger.

He was speechless as he reached out for his daughter. "I can't tell you how much I missed you. You'll always be my little princess."

Chapter 35

Back to Rutterfield

Tom rented a van for the whole family. They all traveled together to Rutterfield to leave their Steven in peace with Jimmy. Lana remembered the last time they were together in a car. It had to be their old station wagon before Dorine ran off to Houston.

The family grieved for Steven. However, in Steven's honor, as a family member, they shared their lives with each other, including those living in Minnesota and Houston.

Susan told them about her baby girl and how she was a fighter. She smiled. "The baby is just like her grandmother, independent and stubborn." They all laughed. Dorine found a sense of pride in Susan's comparison. Even Michael joined in. "Thank God she got her grandmother's looks and not mine."

Lana shook her head, thinking that man was always faithful to that woman.

"Junior is going to be starting school this year. Can you believe it? I hate the thought of them growing up so fast. John thought that we should put him in a private school.

Can you imagine a private kindergarten school?" Lana laughed, thinking that was typical of John.

Alice was not as talkative as usual. She was preoccupied with thoughts of home. Her son, Alex, who was about to turn four, and her daughter, Christy, who was two, needed their mother. Even though she had to work two jobs, Alice was the primary caretaker. Ronnie loved his children but wasn't one to care for their needs, at least not to Alice's standards.

The burial was long and loathsome. The same priest who presided over Jimmy's funeral gave a graveside service for Steven. Steven was buried next to his brother Jimmy, whose grave still hadn't been marked with a gravestone. Lana made a mental note to purchase them for both Jimmy and Steven.

Michael stayed up all night with Steven, just as he had for his son Jimmy. At the funeral, Michael offered his baby to his oldest son to watch over him. The whole family felt the loss, realizing that Lore would not carry on further past this generation.

After the funeral services, Lana and Alice decided to take a taxi to Nashville and fly home. The hugs and kisses were endless. Michael walked both girls to the cab.

"Daddy, promise me that you're going to be okay." Lana reached out for her father's hand.

Alice put her suitcase in the back seat while Lana said

goodbye first.

Lana kissed her father and slid into the back seat.

Alice stepped forward and gave her father a big hug.

"I love you, daddy." Alice couldn't say any more without breaking down. She hugged her father tightly, released him, and jumped into the taxi. Both girls waved as the cab drove away. A sense of sadness overcame both as they wondered if their father's broken heart would ever mend.

Chapter 36

The Joy of Christmas is Gone

1975, Houston, Texas

The winter of 1975 was harsh. The Lores survived Christmas, even though they each mourned their son and brother with all their heart. Michael caught the flu, which kept him from working. The only medicine he swallowed was a bottle of whiskey. Hoping the alcohol would kill the bug. But more severe than the flu was Michael's mental state. He didn't care if he recovered or not. It was mid-January when Michael lost his job at the bar. The owner didn't want to let Michael go, but he had no choice. Michael just wasn't showing up. By February, Michael's savings account had run out, and he couldn't pay rent. The landlady, who lived in the front house, asked Michael to move out because she needed somebody to pay the rent.

Michael was trapped in a pit of depression and simply walked away from his life. Diane, Tom, Kathy, and Susan searched everywhere but couldn't find him.

Susan called the police, but they told her that unless he was forced or disabled, he had the right to be wherever he wanted to be.

Diane called Lana and Alice and told them, thinking that he might head their way. Both girls were sick about the news and felt helpless, knowing that nobody knew where their father was.

Officer Brady, the same policeman who had supported the family during Steven's accident, got in touch with Diane and told her he thought he knew where Michael was. Diane called Tom, and they rushed to the police station to talk to Officer Brady. "I was on patrol over by the condo district. You know, Paper Jack Canyon, where all the homeless people live? I was checking up on the ships when I could have sworn that I saw your father. I circled the corner, thinking I was seeing things, and returned down the street, but he wasn't there. I stopped the car and asked one of the residents if they had a new neighbor. The guy started scratching himself and finally said, Yeah."

"I told him this is my place, but he pushed me, and he's been sitting there against the wall for at least forever." The deranged man said.

The officer gave a half-smile. "I saw the report that he was missing, so I thought I'd better call you."

Diane tearfully thanked the officer. "We have looked

all over for him. He just disappeared. Thank you for the information. If you see him again, please call me. We're going to start searching again."

"Check the shelters. Sometimes, they get tired of sleeping on the streets and move inside, especially this time of the year." The officer told them.

Tom grabbed Diane's hand, and they walked out of the station. "Let's go downtown and see if we can find your father," Tom said.

"Why would he do this? He knows that we all love him." Diane said, trying to understand her father's actions.

"He could be just out of it. A lot has happened to him. Let's just find him and bring him home." Tom said, opening the car door for Diane.

The sun barely peeped through the thunderous clouds. Tom had never been to Paper Jack Canyon, even though it was only a few blocks east of Michael's bar.

The streets, littered with discarded clothes, newspapers, and empty boxes, lined along the front of several buildings. The residence sprawled along the curb, and sidewalks allowed the days to become nights. They only tried to gather enough money for the next fix, drink, or bottle of wine. Tom and Diane searched the streets, looking for Michael. They were going so slow that a couple of men approached the car asking for money. Diane rolled up her window tightly and locked her door.

She was scared these characters might try to open the door and pull her out. When they rolled mid-block, Tom spotted Michael sitting against the wall, bundled tightly, reserving his space from all the unfortunate ones.

Diane wanted to go to her father, but she was afraid to step outside, as if someone would grab her before she could reach Michael.

"Daddy?" Diane called from the car. Tom slammed the car into park and hurried out to Michael.

Tom carefully approached him and sat down next to him against the wall. "Michael?" Tom whispered, "Michael, it's me, Tom." Michael still didn't give any indication that he knew who Tom was.

"This is my place," Michael yelled at Tom.

Tom tried to put his arm around Michael, but Michael thought somebody was trying to steal his spot.

"Leave me alone; this is my place," Michael screamed, getting upset.

Diane opened her door and rushed to Michael and Tom. She kneeled in front of her father.

"Daddy, it's me, Diane." Diane cried.

Michael looked up from the ground and recognized his daughter. He turned and saw Tom for the first time. He wanted to say something but just couldn't manage the words.

"Daddy, it's time to come home." Diane coached him. Michael looked at his daughter and nodded to her. Tom reached out and helped Michael up. Michael was so stiff from the cold and sitting beside the wall that he couldn't stand up straight. Tom practically had to carry him to the car.

Diane jumped into the back seat, holding her hand on her father's shoulders. "Daddy, everything is going to be okay," Diane assured her father.

While Tom and Diane tried to get Michael into the car, a group of homeless people gathered, staying their distance. After Tom successfully got Michael into the car, the small group started to clap. One guy yelled with joy. They were happy Michael was rescued, knowing somebody would come for them someday. Michael's spot was already taken up against the wall.

On the way home, Tom and Diane realized they had nowhere to go. Since Michael left, Diane had moved in with Charlotte and her father. When they left Paper Jack Canyon, Diane asked Tom to stop at a telephone booth so she could tell Charlotte to ask her father if Michael could stay there for a while.

"Hello, Mr. Pierce. Diane told him over the phone. "Sir, my father needs a place to stay, and I was wondering if it would be okay if he came home with us."

"Don't say another word. You bring your daddy home here. Hell, I'll sleep in the living room."

His generosity touched Diane. "Thank you, sir, and we'll be right over."

Diane jumped back in the car. "Daddy, you'll live with Charlotte, me, and Mr. Pierce for a while. You'll see, everything will be all right."

Michael was silent the entire ride to Charlotte's house. Mr. Pierce came to the car to meet with Michael when they arrived. When he saw his condition, he was eager to help Michael into the house.

"Now, you just rest right here in my home." Mr. Pierce said, setting Michael down on one of the chairs.

"We have to get him into the shower. The street grime is packed on him. Is it okay if we use yours? Tom asked.

Mr. Pierce agreed and pointed the way to the bathroom. Tom nodded and realized this one would have to be on him.

Tom entered the bathroom, turned on the hot water, let it run, and returned to get Michael. Mr. Pierce came from his room, brought in a clean pair of his pajamas, and gave them to Tom.

Tom helped Michael with his shower. After the murk was all washed away, Michael became more aware. He was clean, dressed in fresh clothes, and safe. He came out of the bathroom, overwhelmed with shame, and tried to thank Mr. Pierce, but his mind just seemed to fade in and out, not allowing Michael to focus on anything at that moment.

Diane went up to her father, took him to the bedroom, and lay him down to rest on the bed. "Now, Daddy, don't you worry about a thing; everything is going to be okay. Michael smiled at her, turned to his side, and closed his eyes.

***

1976, Houston, Texas

Spring was almost over, and nobody was looking forward to the hot summers of Houston. Michael was readjusting to his life at Pierce's house. Diane continued with her schooling and was busy pursuing her love for Tom. It was Susan who took her father's return to heart. She was faithful to her daily visits with Michael. She would arrive at 9:00 am, fix him breakfast, clean the place, and leave by 11:00 am.

The two would talk, sometimes about Michael and other times about Susan. She loved her time with her father. To her, he was like the counselor who knew all the correct answers. Besides, who else knew her as well as her father? And to Michael, it was his chance to give to somebody who gave him so much.

Michael was getting stronger and complained about being bored at home. He told Diane and Tom that he was ready to go out and get a job. "Hell, I'm strong enough to take care of myself."

Michael would complain to Tom and Diane. Besides, I must get on with my life and leave Jim and Charlotte to their own home.

Diane walked Tom to the car. "Maybe Daddy shouldn't get a job around alcohol. You know, maybe a janitor job or something."

"You know, having people around him is better for him. I think I can get him on at Stubbies. You know that bar over on 8th St. I know the manager and the clientele are his old friends. I think it would be a good thing. I'll talk to him tomorrow." Tom smiled and kissed his girl goodbye.

Diane stopped him from giving her a peck. She pushed her lips hard against his. She held him tightly, letting him know that she loved him. "Do you know how much I love you?" Diane whispered to Tom, "Yeah, almost as much as I love you." Tom kissed her again and held her in silence.

***

Michael started working at Stubbies the following week. He wasn't the primary bartender, so he had to work Monday, Tuesday, Friday, and Saturday. Tom was right; the customers were his old clientele, and they welcomed Michael back by being there for him. When word got around that Michael was at Stubbies, Mondays and Tuesdays became their most popular nights.

Unfortunately, the bottle still had hold of Michael. At first, it was a shot of courage; then, it became a salute to an old friend. Finally, it became the glue that held the bar together.

Susan, who continued to see her father daily, knew something was wrong. She could smell the alcohol seeping from his pores. And Michael was more than just tired in the morning. He was very disturbed, half the time still drunk from the night before.

"Daddy, you have to stop drinking. If your boss sees you, he will fire you, and then what? You need to get it together."
"I miss your brother so much." Michael tried to play the trump card.

"Daddy, I loved Steven, and we all know how much you loved him, but he is gone, and you are still here, and you have to let him go."

"No. You're just like your mother, another day, another time," Michael mumbled.

Susan realized she had hurt her father's feelings. "I don't want to be right. I just want my daddy to be the man he used to be." Susan lightly smiled.

"Michael stood up from the table. "You're right. I need to take hold of the horns of the bull, as your mother would say." He went over to kiss Susan on the cheek. "Thanks, sweetie," ending their private session.

Chapter 37

I Can't Move On Without My Boys

Michael continued working at Stubbies. His emotions, mixed with alcohol and a lack of sleep, caused a new depression to set in. He lived alone and didn't want anybody to save him from the darkness. He hid his pain with a smile. He avoided his children and their intervention, recognizing that something serious was wrong. In Michael's world, the pain just settled in as he drank himself to sleep at night. When he wakes up in the morning, he gathers himself together for his daily visit with Susan.

"Daddy, what can I do? I know you're in pain, but you have to pull yourself out of this depression. Daddy, please go to a doctor. Let them help you."

Michael smiled at his daughter and told her that he just needed time. Susan accepted his answer because she sensed a spark of happiness within him.

"You look different today, like things are getting better inside you," Susan said, pouring Michael a cup of coffee.

"I feel better today," Michael said. "So, stop worrying about me," Michael told her. "What's going on with you and Scott?" Michael asked.

"Same Old, same old," she said, sitting across from him with her cup of coffee.

"I think he needs to get his ass kicked, and then maybe he wouldn't feel so high and mighty."

"What do you mean?" Michael said, sipping his coffee.

"He thinks he is so clever, but I know he's screwing around," Susan said. "The funny thing is, I don't care. It just sickens me to think that he thinks he can treat me like that."

Michael listened but didn't say a word.

"Last weekend, we were at a picnic out in the woods. The people there were from his work, and suddenly, everybody was stripping off their clothes and swimming in the pond. Scott looked at me and started to take his clothes off."

"Come on, let's go skinny dipping," Scott said, removing his underwear.

"Hell no, I said. I'm not going naked in front of all these people." Susan was pissed off that Scott would suggest such a thing, especially since he was already joining in.

"Don't be such a prude." Scott barked back at her as if there was something wrong with her.

"I don't feel comfortable being naked with strangers." Susan protested.

"They're not strangers. I work with them all." Scott said, getting upset with Susan.

"You go, I'm not," Susan said. "I'm going home."

Not in my car, you're not," Scott said, giving her a stern look.

"Fine, I'll just walk," Susan said, getting up from the picnic table and heading to the parking lot.

Scott yelled at her from a distance. "Grow up, Susan, this is life."

Susan flipped him off and walked home, a distance of over two miles.

Michael was shocked by Scott's behavior. "What possessed him to do that?"

"He thinks his body is flawless, so he's doing the world a favor by exposing himself," Susan answered Michael. "Daddy, you don't think I was a prude, do you?" Susan smiled halfheartedly, feeling slightly uncomfortable discussing this with her father.

"I think there are very few things in life that we can call our own. People can take away our possessions and steal our money, but nobody can take away our minds and bodies. That is, unless we freely give it away. If we do, what do we have that is truly our own? I think you did right. Start running around naked in front of strangers; well, you may as well make some money while displaying yourself." Michael finished his coffee.

"Anyway, he hasn't talked to me since, and I don't give a shit. That's a problem, huh?" Susan gave her sad eyes to her father.

"When you and Scott were dating, he was everything, and you were nothing. I knew there would be a day when the real Susan would peek her head out and say, What about me?" Michael told her, not wanting to say, 'I told you so.' "Scott hasn't changed; you have just started to listen to yourself. And I think that is scaring the hell out of you." Michael said with a smile.

"So, what do I do?" Susan asked.

"I'm not going to tell you to leave Scott. It all depends on what you can handle. Look at all that I have been through with your mother. But if she would have me, I'd be there tomorrow."

Susan got up from the table and picked up her plate and Michael's.

She offered him more coffee, but he refused. She finished her work and went over and hugged him. "I love you. See ya tomorrow." She said as she walked out of the house.

Michael was alone, getting ready for work. He made a mental note to have Tom kick Scott's ass. A knock at the front door startled him.

Michael opened the door to find a sweet old lady with a religious pamphlet ready to give it to him.

"If you were to die tonight, do you know where you would

go?" The woman said, being bold for Christ.

Michael took a deep breath and wanted to shut the door, but he politely answered the woman. "I guess I would go to heaven."

"Do you believe that Jesus Christ died on the cross to save your soul?"

Michael didn't answer the question. "I'm catholic, and I know that I'm going to heaven," Michael said with certainty.

The old lady wouldn't allow the opportunity to pass. "We believe you have to accept Jesus Christ as your savior to be sure that you are going to heaven. The bible says there's only one way to the Father: through Christ Jesus."

"So, you're saying that if I were to die tonight, then I would go to hell?" Michael tried to make light of the woman's statement.

She looked Michael right in the eyes. "That's right, but He allows everybody to have eternal life."

Ma'am, with no disrespect to you, but I have lost two boys, and if they're not in heaven, then I don't want to be there either." Michael nodded his head and shut the door.

The voice of God haunted Michael throughout the day and night. He tried to drown out his anger toward God with a fresh bottle of whiskey.

When it was time to close, Michael had decided he had had enough of life and wanted to be with his boys. That night, after work, he felt at peace about his decision and decided to spend his last night with his wife.

It was around 2:30 in the morning when Michael arrived at Dorine's house. He went to her window and tapped until she came to see who was knocking at it.

"Michael Lore, what the hell are you doing here at my window?"

Michael looked at Dorine and smiled. "I think I need to be with you tonight."

Dorine lost her sour face and gave a smile. "You better come on in before the neighbors be a seeing you out here." She said, then left the window and went to the front door.

Michael entered the house and took Dorine in his arms. "Do you have any whiskey in the house?" Michael said with a faint smile.

Dorine clicked her tongue and went to the kitchen to fetch a bottle and two glasses. She came back and led them to her bedroom. She set the alcohol on the table, took off her robe, and lay in the bed. Michael smiled at her and poured her a glass of whiskey. He handed her the glass and sat next to her on the bed.

"Do you know you are the only girl I ever loved?" Michael started the conversation. "When I first saw you at Jimmy's funeral,

I knew right then that I wanted to be your husband for the rest of our lives," Michael said, taking a tasty sip from his glass.

"Now, why are you bringing all this up? You're already in my room." Dorine said sarcastically.

"Because no matter what happens to me, I need you to know that I love you. Always have, always will." Michael said as he took off his shoes and joined Dorine in bed.

Dorine and Michael went through all the special moments in their lives, talking about their children and grandchildren. Michael would stop and cry a couple of times through the night, allowing Dorine to hold him in her special way. Michael and Dorine finally fell asleep when the sun started peaking through the window.

Maybe the chatter of two birds outside Dorine's window or the closing of the front door as Kathy left for school woke up Michael. His head was still floating from his night of bliss with his wife. The darkness inside of him told him his time was up. Michael got up out of bed. He put on the pants that were left on the floor the previous night. Michael found his shirt at the end of the bed, tucked deep under the covers. He put on his socks and shoes and kissed Dorine on the forehead.

He heard a honk and Charlotte screaming when he stepped outside Dorine's house. "Hi, Mr. Lore!" As she streamed past him in her 1965 Ford Fairlane.

Charlotte couldn't wait to get to school and tell Diane that she caught her father grabbing a quick one in the morning from her mother.

"Diane!" Charlotte called out, using the last breath she had inside her. Her voice traveled down the hall, catching Diane before she entered her morning class.

Charlotte just had to share the news. "Guess who I saw coming from your mother's house early this morning?"

Diane put on a smile, not knowing if she wanted to know. "Who?" Diane stopped and waited for Charlotte's answer.

"Your father, Old Mr. Lore, was getting lucky last night." Charlotte squealed. Oh, he smiled from one side of his head to the other. Charlotte giggled. "I bet you he is feeling a whole lot better now." She pinched Diane's arm and told her she would meet her for lunch.

It was about a quarter to 10:00 in the morning. A guy came into the room and handed a note to Mr. Evans, Diane's English teacher. Mr. Evans read the letter, looked up, and told Diane that she needed to go home and that there was an emergency.

Diane felt slightly panicked and grabbed her books and left the school. When she got close to Mr. Pierce's house, there were at least ten police cars parked out front. She parked several houses away and started to run, thinking that her father might have had a heart attack.

When she got close, she was stopped by a policeman. She tried to explain that the note said it was an emergency. Diane saw Susan sitting on the front step outside the door. "That's my sister over there." Diane pointed. The policeman let her go, and she ran to Susan. "What happened?" Diane said, not wanting to know.

Susan looked up at Diane. Her eye makeup was all over her face. "Daddy killed himself," Susan said, not believing that she was able to get the words out. Dorine left the house, crying, trying to catch her breath.

"Mama!" Diane said to Dorine. "Is he dead?"

Dorine covered her mouth as she threw up last night's whiskey.

Diane had never seen her mother so upset. Nothing ever took so much from Dorine as Michael's death.

Diane didn't want to go inside, but she had to see that Michael was no longer alive. She walked into the room, which was filled with police and investigators. They had Michael's body covered, reminding her of Steven's death scene.

A policewoman approached Diane and turned her around. "I'm sorry you don't want to see this." The policewoman said with compassion in her voice. Diane turned again and saw the police officers on Steven's case standing over Michael. Their eyes met as he silently bowed his head.

Diane walked back outside with Susan. Susan wasn't crying; she just shook as she tried to light a cigarette.

"Our beautiful father is dead," Diane said as if nobody else knew.

Susan reached over and put her arm around Diane as Dorine stood before them, shedding tears for her husband.

The girls heard a scream from the street and saw Kathy trying to escape the police line. Diane stood up, ran to her, and told her before she got too close. Kathy sat in the middle of the walkway, refusing to hear what Diane had to say.

Somebody must have called Tom as he darted from his car, leaving it in the middle of the street.

He looked at Diane and knew it was true. Diane fell into his arms and begged him to make it all disappear. Tom was in such pain that he couldn't comfort her. His grief overcame him as Tom walked to the front of the house. He saw Dorine and Susan. He grabbed Dorine, and they both cried.

Susan stood up, and her mind was racing, blurring her vision. Tom caught her and held her up in his arms. He turned around and realized that he had left Diane alone. He sat Susan back down on the step and went back to Diane. Diane and Kathy were both sitting on a neighbor's front step when Tom sat between them and held them both.

It was Diane who called Lana first and told her. "Daddy took his life today. And we don't know what to do." Diane cried on the telephone.

Lana was so upset that she didn't respond. She just let the telephone drop to the floor as she screamed for her father. Diane hung up the telephone and tried to call Alice, but Lana's telephone blocked the line. Ten minutes had passed before Lana called back at Dorine's house.

Diane answered the telephone. "Hello," Diane's voice cracked.

"Diane, it's me, Lana. I'm sorry, sweetie, what happened?" Lana was crying on the telephone.

"Susan came to visit Daddy, and she found him in his room dead." Diane hurried the words out before she could stop and hear herself. "Please call Alice. We need you guys, hurry."

Diane didn't realize that there was no hurry. There was nothing that Lana or Alice could do. For the moment, it seemed to Diane that, if Lana and Alice were there, it would somehow bring their father back.

Alice called and talked to Dorine. She was just as upset as Lana, and they were catching the first flight out of Minnesota to Houston.

Susan went home, got her daughter, and brought her back to Dorine's house. When Scott heard the news, he insisted on coming along.

Susan didn't care one way or the other; her relationship with Scott was the last thing on her mind. She just wanted her daughter with her. By the time she returned to the house, everything was already quiet. Neighbors had brought food, and Dorine, Diane, Tom, and Kathy sat in the living room. Nobody was talking; nothing needed to be said. They only allowed each other their space. There were a few sniffs and outright cries, but everybody was under control when Susan arrived.

That evening, a car pulled up to Dorine's house. Diane looked outside the window and saw her sisters. She remembered Jimmy's funeral as she waited for them to arrive. As if everything was going to be all right once they arrived. She called out to the rest and opened the door for Lana and Alice.

Lana is dressed in black with a single strand of pearls given to her by her father. Alice was wearing dark glasses, and when she took them off, her eyes looked as though a mugger had beaten them. The sisters held each other, not crying hysterically, but comforting one another.

The funeral was held in Rutterfield. Michael would be buried next to his sons and his best friend, Jimmy. When they tried to get the same Priest who buried Jimmy and Steven, he refused because of the circumstances of the death. Dorine went to the chapel where she and Michael got married. She finds Charles and his wife and asks them to say the last words for

Michael.

Charles had long since retired and left the business to his son. When he heard it was Michael, he agreed, offering their condolence to Dorine and the family.

Lana volunteered to stay with her father all night. Each of the sisters wanted to, but they understood when Lana was persistent that she wanted the time alone with Michael.

The evening fell short as Lana prayed to God to forgive her father. Charles's son entered through the side door and approached Lana.

"Excuse me, I don't mean to intrude, and you are welcome to stay here as long as you want, but would you mind if I went home to my family? I'll lock the front door, and if you'd like to leave, simply push the lever and shut the door behind you. It will lock itself."

Lana looked up at this young man, trying to understand how this guy could stand all this pain. She smiled and thanked him for his kindness.

The front door slammed, and Lana was truly alone with her father. "Daddy?" Lana spoke out loud, as if her father was in the room with her, "Daddy, I'm sorry for not being there. It seemed you were always there for me. And when you needed me, I wasn't there for you." Lana took a long sniffle.

"I don't know if I can live without you. How am I ever going to make it without my Daddy? "I know you were not happy here, and to be with your boys, you are probably at peace, but what about us? Why couldn't you see we were in the same pain as you?" Lana started to get angry with her father. You should have thought of us, Daddy. How much will this hurt us? You should have held on for each of us. How can we not believe that we weren't enough for you, that your love for us was not enough to keep you alive?"

Lana dropped her head into her lap, crying, feeling very alone in this dark crevice. "I know, Daddy, you were sick and tired, and maybe you weren't thinking straight. Maybe you got what you wanted for a long time: a chance for rest, peace, and to be with your boys. I'm here, Daddy. I'll never leave you, as you'll never leave me. I know you'll always be there for me." Lana said, laying her head on his casket. Sleep, my daddy, and allow the angels to give you the true love you have always deserved."

The ceremony was short. The clergyman Charles took a bad situation and gave Michael peace to take to eternity. He went over and took Dorine's hand, silently offering his condolences. His wife began to sing a soft spiritual song she had chosen for the service. Her heart was torn as the girls were all crying. They went to the casket and laid a flower over the top during the song. They returned to their chairs and silently bid their father goodbye.

Chapter 38

Nothing Will Scar Their Father's Love

1976, Rutterfield, Tennessee

To each of the girls, the circumstances of Michael's death did not weigh upon them. What was important was all the wonderful ways Michael expressed his love for each of them. They missed their father. His love and wisdom are only a few things that have remained in each of their hearts. They knew their father and how he would have wanted them to carry on his love in their lives. The strength it took to overcome such a loss was a testament to Michael, who always brought his daughters closer together. The sisters had to bear the pain of Michael's death, but each of them will never forget his unconditional love for each of them.

Chapter 39

No Stopping Love

1976, Houston, Texas

Six months after Michael passed, Tom and Diane announced they would marry. Diane apologized to her sisters about the timing. She explained that they had decided to move forward with the wedding plans they had already made.

The winter cold had already struck the City of Houston. A record-breaking snowstorm hit the streets, shutting down all businesses. Diane and Tom considered postponing the ceremony due to weather *restraints, but as plans were already in force, they decided to accept whatever came their way.

On the third Saturday in November 1975, two days after Thanksgiving, a bright sunny day fell upon Houston. All airports were open, and Diane and Tom's family could attend the wedding. The church was beautiful, as Charlotte and a few friends of Diane decorated it, spreading real white rose petals down the aisle.

Tom's boys arrived, escorted by Tom's sister and her husband, Lenny. Lenny was Tom's best friend and best man. Diane was pleased and excited about meeting Tom's boys. Tom's love for them transferred to her as she hugs each boy as her own.

Several men, including Scott, Susan's husband, Mr. Pierce, and one of the guys from the bar, offered to walk Diane down the aisle. Diane gracefully refused, telling them that her father, in spirit, was taking that spot.

On the wedding day, the flower girls, being her sisters, led the parade, as Charlotte earned the position of maid of honor. Each girl is dressed in autumn colors, with Charlotte wearing a deep blue, representing the pack's leader.

Diane's gown was a long, white, lace, long-sleeved, satin, low-necked dress with a train that trailed behind her. Her bouquet was a bundle of white roses, boasting the purity of love between her and Tom. The church was filled with guests as the music stopped, and Diane appeared at the back of the church, ready to make the walk.

Diane felt her father's presence, and after a big breath, she gathered her strength to walk down the aisle. As she moved forward, she kept her eyes on Tom, who was crying over her beauty. Seeing him cry brought tears to Diane's eyes, knowing this marriage would be forever.

The ceremony was beautiful. Tom and Diane dedicated themselves to each other, and the crowd applauded when the pastor announced that they were husband and wife. The sisters gathered and posed for a photographer, one of their few pictures together.

Chapter 40

Making Changes, A Fight For Freedom

1987, Houston, Texas

It was near the end of May, almost eight years after Michael passed away. Susan gathered Haley, and the two moved to an apartment near downtown Houston. Susan got a job as a receptionist and started the divorce proceedings against Scott.

Scott tried to stop Susan by making her leave all their material possessions. He claimed everything in the house was his because he paid for it. Susan wiped her hands of their life and started new with a bed for Haley and herself. When Scott saw that his plan of keeping everything didn't work, he approached friends who knew Susan's boss and got her fired. For the betterment of their marriage, is what the boss said.

"Scott is a fine young man. Nowadays, you women think it's easy to go from one man to another. But I'll tell you, I won't be a part of it. So, pack your stuff and move along. I suggest going back to your husband." The boss said with a smile.

Susan was broken and needed the job to survive. Without work, she would lose the apartment and move back in with Scott.

Tom and Diane heard what was going on. They were living in Tennessee, and Tom drove a large truck down to Houston and pulled up in front of Susan's apartment building. Tom knocked at the front door.

"Who's there?" a slight voice came out from inside.

Tom disguised his voice. "Um, this is Acme home mover. I have instructions to move Miss Lore and all her belongings to Tennessee." Tom said, trying not to laugh.

Susan saw through the ploy and quickly opened the door. "Oh, my Lord, what in the world are you up to?"

With his big smile, Tom said, "Just showing my love to my favorite sister-in-law."

Susan held back her tears and hugged Tom. Diane and Tom's generosity touched Susan. She allowed Tom to move her and Haley to Tennessee until the divorce was final.

Scott, Susan's husband, didn't take it kindly that Susan was getting farther away from him. He constantly harassed and threatened her until she was in tears. Susan just wanted peace in her life, but with all the drama Scott caused, she couldn't enjoy her freedom. After a short while, she felt like she was intruding on Tom and Diane, as they had started their family and were blending in with Tom's boys.

"I know you all are only being nice to Haley and me. I

wouldn't want my sister hanging around my husband and me, even though I wouldn't even want to hang with us." Susan gave a pathetic laugh.

Diane spoke up, loving her sister. "We're sisters, and nobody else in this world would mean more to me than my sisters. And nobody is going to hurt a Lore without all of us fighting the fight. And if that doesn't work, we'll have Tom go down there and beat Scott up."

Susan started to laugh. She paused and remembered that her Daddy told her to have Tom kick Scott's ass. "That's right, Tom, you just go down there and beat Scott up. In fact, kick his ass." They all laughed.

The move to Tennessee didn't work. Scott started proceedings against Susan, claiming she took their child out of state without his permission. The State Court of Texas ordered Susan to return to Houston with their daughter.

Susan thought it was all over. She would have no other choice but to move back in with Scott. Diane got on the phone with Lana, and between them, they gathered enough money to rent an apartment for Susan and help her make it through until she could get a job and care for her and her daughter.

Susan's divorce was final by September 1987. She did get another job as a receptionist for a dentist's office. She loved her career, and the people at the office treated her as family.

Chapter 41

Moving on to the Other Side of the Mountain

1976, Houston, Texas

Dorine and Kathy were left in their home to grieve the loss of their family. The emptiness of the house and the loss of hope that everything would someday be normal were gone. After Diane and Tom married, Dorine decided it was time for her and Kathy to move on and start a new life.

Kathy and Alan, Kathy's boyfriend, just stopped seeing each other. After Steven died, and it seemed to hurt them both to hang together. Unfortunately, there just wasn't enough of themselves to keep their relationship going. Once again, Kathy found herself alone.

Kathy came home from community college and found Dorine drinking her coffee at the kitchen table.

"What would you say after school is out if we packed our bags and moved away from here?" Dorine simply asked Kathy.

Kathy responded."What do you mean? Move to another house?"

"No, I mean completely out of here. We can move to California." Dorine said.

Kathy, feeling that pain inside her stomach, whispered. "I don't know Mama, California, that's a long way away."

"Sweetie, we have nothing here anymore, and the more we stay, the more time will pass us by."

Kathy got up and served herself a cup of coffee. She brought the pot over to Dorine and filled her cup. "You're not afraid to leave, Houston?" Kathy asked.

"Sweetie, I've learned long ago that life goes on no matter where your mountain is." Dorine tried to show her strength to Kathy. "There's a whole lot of life out there for both of us. And if we allow all this sadness to keep us here, we may as well give it up and join those who have passed on."

Kathy tried to understand her mother, but why did they have to move so far away? In fear of questioning her mother, Kathy changed her line of questioning, "Okay, but do we have enough money to make such a move?"

Dorine smiled. "I've been saving all my birthday money, and every penny that has come my way for such a day as today." Kathy smiled, one that she hadn't seen for a long while. "Let's do it."

Dorine and Kathy sold the house and used the money to relocate to California.

They decided to sell it all: the furniture, their clothes

closet, and the haunts of yesterday. On the day they had to leave, they said their final goodbyes to the spirits of Steven and Michael and boldly headed to California.

California was refreshing because of the giant palm trees, the strength of the mountains, and the calmness of the sea. California had everything to offer, including a job for Dorine and Kathy.

The girls found an apartment on the eastern side of Los Angeles. It was a small two-bedroom apartment in the City of El Monte. Being from Texas, Dorine and Kathy weren't strangers to Latin people and found their sense of family values heartwarming and welcoming. During their family celebrations, the family next door reached out to Dorine and Kathy. The Garcias loved Dorine and felt sorry for the widow, trying to find a new meaning in her life. Kathy found it hard, as usual, to make friends, but being in California and all the good weather helped keep her spirits up.

It wasn't long before Dorine found a new man in her life. He was pleasant and invaluable to both Dorine and Kathy, but Kathy, knowing her mother's past, wasn't ready for a replacement for her father.

It was late at night, and Kathy had a late shift at the El Monte K-mart. She worked eight hours on the register, listening to people complaining that the lines were too long.

When she arrived home, Dorine waited for her, sitting in the living room.

"Mama, what are you doing still up?" Kathy asked her. "Don't you have to work in the morning?"

"We need to talk." Dorine started her well-prepared speech. "Joey asked me to marry him." Dorine sprang the news on Kathy.

Kathy felt her knees giving out and headed for the sofa. "Already?" Kathy responded.

Dorine smiled with excitement. "You'll see, sweetie, time is not a friend at my age. When somebody throws a hook at this old fish, I'd better take the bait."

"Oh, Mama, you're not that old. Besides, are we talking about marriage? Is that what you want?"

Dorine pulled herself to the edge of the chair. "Joey is nice, and yes, I want to marry him."

Kathy sat there silent, not knowing what else to say. "When is this going to happen?"

"Oh, sweetie, he only asked tonight," Dorine said kindly.

"And what did you tell him?" Kathy cautiously asked.

"I kissed him on the cheek and thanked him for asking. Then I told him I needed to talk with you and that I would give him an answer by tomorrow." Dorine said, feeling good that somebody still wanted her.

"Mama, if that's what you want to do and if this will make you happy, I'll be happy for you. Kathy tried to be sincere but was very concerned about this arrangement. "When do I need to find my own place?"

"Don't you be silly, you're going to be here right with me," Dorine said sternly. If he marries me, he must accept that you are my daughter and come way before any man in my life."

Kathy smiled. "I love you, Mama. But I don't think that's any way to start a marriage."

That night, after Dorine went to bed, Kathy made an emergency call to Diane. All the emotions of feeling abandoned haunted Kathy. She needed her sister to tell her everything was going to be okay.

"What do you mean? Mama is getting married. Oh my God, is she nuts?" Diane screamed over the telephone.

"He is a nice guy and treats Mama like a lady."

"I'm nice to my dog, too, but that doesn't mean I have to marry Pooch," Diane said, then started laughing at the example she gave.

"I'm just feeling lost in my life. I don't know where or what to do." Kathy started to share her heart.

"What do you want to do?" Diane asked.

"I would want to go to school, to a real college, and get a degree," Kathy replied. She continued. I could get a grant. I mean, my grades were always good. Maybe I could work myself through school." Kathy was thinking out loud.

"Now, that sounds like a good plan. Is there a school out there you could get into?" Diane asked.

"I would have to inquire and see what would be available for me," Kathy concluded.

"Listen, I'm here for you and will try to help you however I can. You make all the arrangements." Diane told her sister with all the sincerity in her heart.

Kathy felt 100% better and allowed herself a moment of peace after she hung up the telephone with Diane.

That same night, Diane woke up Lana and told her the news. She pleaded to Lana that Kathy needed their help, and without any hesitation, Lana committed herself to get Kathy through school. Regarding Dorine, Lana didn't even want to hear about it.

Kathy was accepted at a small private Christian school named Azusa. Pacific, just outside El Monte. It was a requirement of the school that all first-year students had to live in the dorms. Kathy moved in with four other girls and found instant friends. For once in Kathy's life, she felt at peace within herself. Through the love of her roommates, they introduced Kathy to Jesus as her personal Savior. Even though Kathy understood who Jesus was. However, raised a Catholic, she didn't understand what it meant to have a personal relationship with her true Father, Lord, and Savior. Kathy allowed Jesus to come into her life and heal her wounds. Where there was fear, she learned to trust Jesus to protect her. When she felt alone, she prayed and sensed the presence of Jesus' love, comforting her like a faithful father. Kathy was happy and found her self-worth within the Lord. She could stand firm and secure for once, allowing God to work.

Kathy met a young man not long after being at Azusa Pacific College. His name was Larry, and he was in her English class. They worked on a school project together. It was at the daily chapel that Larry sat next to Kathy, and in between worship songs, he managed to ask Kathy out.

"Would you ... would you like to go out sometime, like this Friday?" Larry asked.

Kathy took a deep breath, purposely trying to slow herself down. "That would be great." She turned, smiled, and whispered to Larry.

At one point of worship, Larry prayed for God's intervention as he reached out and held Kathy's hand. Kathy squeezed the offered hand, letting him know that she was thrilled.

After the first date, they were always together, except when Kathy would visit her mother. She didn't feel comfortable bringing Larry into Dorine's world.

She figured if this were going to be a lasting thing, then Larry would have to be introduced to her mother. If they were only going to remain friends, why torture Larry with the gospel of Dorine.

Dorine turned down Joey's proposal only with the condition that he would give it some time, and later, if the flame were still there, she would be happy to marry him. With Kathy living at Azusa Christian College, Dorine wanted Joey to play house, following all the rules of her off-and-on games, except at the end of the month when Dorine needed help with the rent. Dorine stayed with Joey for several years until she could return to Texas. She used his love and money to buy her little house on the outskirts of Houston, then sent him home, bitten by the love of Dorine. There never was a marriage between Dorine and Joey.

***

It was Kathy's 21st birthday. She had classes in the morning, but Larry told her he would take her someplace special for her birthday. Kathy and Larry had been dating for over a year. She rushed home from class and barely had enough time to shower and prepare for her birthday. When Larry arrived, Kathy opened the front door, to her surprise, and saw her sisters there, screaming, 'Surprise.' Larry was in the background, happy that he had arranged the reunion.

"Oh, my Lord! What are you all doing here? Kathy was surprised to see her sisters at her front door.

"We had to wish our baby sister a happy 21st birthday. Lana said.

"Besides, we're kidnapping you, and all of us are going to Las Vegas? Diane said.

"Lana got us reservations at the Tropicana. They even have a blackjack table in the swimming pool." Alice said with such excitement.

Kathy was overwhelmed and excited. She stepped on her tiptoes to see Larry's reaction to all this. He smiled, happy for his girlfriend.

"Las Vegas, I have to pack," Kathy said, waving the girls into the apartment.

Susan leads the sisters. "Girl!" Looking around the common space. "They don't give you all much space, do they?" Susan looked around and smiled. "Damn, I should have done this. It's like the board game Life. Initially, you decide whether to attend college or pursue a different career path. I don't know; this all looks like a lot of fun. Sure, a lot different than what we girls chose."

"I went to college and did pretty well with my grades. I was lovesick over Tom and didn't want to make school a priority." Diane said, wanting the girls to remember that she was educated, too.

"Junior College doesn't count. Hell, you may as well continue high school, especially with all the playing that you and Charlotte did," Susan said, playing with Diane.

Diane simply stuck out her tongue at her sister.

"I wanted to go to college, and the plan was that I was going, but then Junior came around, and you know what? I'm glad I had the time to spend at home with my boys. Lana said. I suppose it's different for each person. It seems perfect for Kathy. Diane looked at Larry and gave him an extra smile.

Larry excused himself and went to Kathy's bedroom to spend time with her before she had to go. Diane whispered to her sister. "I hope Kathy realizes that's a keeper."

The flight to Las Vegas was short and sweet. The girls laughed, and teased, and some of them drank miles away. By the time they got to Las Vegas, they were ready for action. The Tropicana was right on the strip, and the hotel had just built a new tower where the girls rented a suite for the weekend. The room was gorgeous, with a view of all of Las Vegas. Inside the room was an indoor spa, with fresh-cut flowers on every table. The suite came with a butler, and the girls abused him throughout the night. The sisters were happy, mainly because they were together. Even though they shared time weekly on the telephone, spending a weekend together was a real treat for all of them.

It was the last night of their vacation. The next morning, they would have to pack and return to each of their homes. The drinks and the celebration started at dinner. By the time they lost their money on the blackjack table, they were headed for the room.

"Hey! Look, a talent contest." Alice pointed to a sign.

"I bet you. It's that new thing, Karee okie." Diane said.

"$500.00 for 1st place," Alice said.

"If you think you will get up and sing, well, sister, I love you, but this isn't a pie-eating contest." Lana laughed, teasing Alice.

"Not me, beg your pardon. Susan, you could win this!" Alice turned to Susan encouraged her to join the contest.

"Me?" It's been years since I've been on stage. I wouldn't know the words." Susan protested.

"They put the words on a TV screen, and you just sing the main parts." Diane told her.

"Come on, Susan, for my birthday," Kathy begged her sister.

"Your birthday was yesterday." Susan laughed.

"You could win $ 500.00. Your odds have to be better than those blackjack tables." Diane said, trying to convince Susan to sing.

"Okay! I'll sing, but first, I'll need a couple of shots of whiskey to kick me."

The girls, all excited, entered the lounge. Diane asked if they were, too late to enter the contest. The man looked her over and told her that she was welcome anytime. Diane was drunk enough to get pissed off, but she decided to play it smart. Acting southern and sweet, she told the man it wasn't her, giving a fake giggle, but her sister, who was going to sing. The man laughed and said to her that any sister of hers was more than welcome to join. The man handed her the paperwork as Diane filled in the blanks. Lana ordered rounds of shots, and the girls toasted everything they could think of.

The sisters, all excited, entered the lounge. Diane asked if they were, too late to enter the contest. The man looked her over and told her that she was welcome anytime. Diane was drunk enough to get pissed off, but she decided to play it smart and acted southern and sweet, telling the man that it was not her but her sister who was going to sing. The man laughed and said to her that any sister of hers was more than welcome to join. The man handed her the paperwork as Diane filled in the blanks.

Not long after the drinking started, a man came to their table and escorted Susan backstage. The lights went dark, and the first singer came on stage. A full orchestra backed up the singer.

Diane turned to her sisters, "I guess it isn't Karaoke. Oh, no, what were we thinking?"

The man on stage was incredible. His voice was pure as glass, and the Righteous Brothers song brought tears to each of their eyes.

After the fourth contestant came on stage, the sisters were ready to lick their wounds and walk out. The host came out from behind the curtain and introduced Susan. "Ladies and Gentlemen, to the delight of the Tropicana Hotel. We want to present Ms. Susan Lore."

The curtains opened, and a single light searched the stage. It centered on Susan sits on a single stool with a microphone resting on her lap. The music started, and Susan came to life. She sang a country-western song, and her voice was calm, sharp as a nail. Susan posed on stage with the confidence of a pro, allowing her voice to wither when the tender parts were expressed. She stood up and approached the audience when she needed their support. By the end of the song, Susan settled back on the stool. She won the audience, and each fell in love with her. They savored her as a tender choice of beef. Susan was beautiful, and to the amazement of her sisters, she was great. After the lights came on, the audience stood up and cheered for Susan to be the winner.

The sisters jumped up and down, hugging each other as if they were the ones who performed. Susan returned to the table with a check in hand for $ 500.00.

***

It was the day that Kathy knew would come. It was time to introduce Larry to Dorine.

"Now, please, Mama, don't fuss over him. And no embarrassing stories about me. And please, Mama, like him because I think I love him." Kathy warned her mother.

The doorbell rang, and Kathy went to open the door. Larry was standing there with a bouquet for Dorine.

Kathy explained to Diane, "At first, it was going well. Larry was a gentleman and Mama were on their best behavior. I suppose the worst part was when Mama decided to say grace during dinner. The prayer was straight from the mountain. "Lord bless our home, bless our toes, may this food feed our souls. Amen!" Kathy almost cried, telling Diane what happened. She continues her conversation with Diane. "Poor Larry looked at me to see if Mama was serious or if he was supposed to laugh. I have never been more embarrassed in my life. What the hell, Diane? It would have been more acceptable if she had just kept quiet until he left and told me he was not good enough for me."

Diane screamed into the phone, "Oh my God, what did you do?"

"I just bowed my head out of embarrassment," Kathy said into the phone.

"I'm sorry, sweetie; that had to be horrible." Diane felt so sorry for her sister.

That is not the worst. Kathy continued. "Mama started a conversation about television evangelists. She pointed at Larry and proceeded to tell him."

"You know, Larry, the Lord helps those who help themselves. That's in the bible. I think all those TV preachers are all going to go to hell. It is such a crime, making people feel guilty if you don't give to their church. She turned to me and asked? What is that woman's name? She has big hair and lots of mascara running down her face. They should be ashamed of themselves for taking money from the real churches." Dorine said as she gulped down her 4th glass of wine.

Larry politely answered, "I think God uses the Bakers to reach people who are hurting and need to hear the word of God," Larry said, defending the TV ministry.

Losing focus, Dorine allowed her eyes to cross, "I think a little bit too much Jesus in your life can be harmful. Well, I just read how this lady gave all her savings to one of these TV preachers. She said the Lord told her to do it. And can you believe the preacher promised her 10 times 10 of the amount she had given, which would be returned to her."

Larry was stunned. He didn't understand where Dorine was coming from. She felt she was directing her lecture to him, but she also thought she was directing her lecture to him. Larry only smiled and excused himself early from their first meeting.

He claimed he had a lot of homework and needed to finish it before the next day's class. Kathy surely understood and walked him to the front door. Before he left, he walked into the kitchen, thanked Dorine for dinner, and told her it was a pleasure meeting her.

Dorine overindulged in alcohol and slurred, "It sure was a pleasure meeting you."

Kathy, ready to cry, hugged Larry outside the door. She whispered, "Now, do you see why I have been hiding her in the closet? Kathy was setting her head deep in Larry's chest.

"I love you, and I know who you are in Christ. That's all that matters." Larry said, lifting Kathy's head for a good night kiss.

***

The wedding was huge. Larry's parents paid for the entire wedding. It was held in Larry's parents' backyard at their Houston House, far from where Kathy and her family lived. Kathy asked Diane to be her maid of honor and for Susan to lead the other sisters to the front of the church. Kathy asked Tom if he would walk her down the aisle. Tom accepted immediately, feeling honored to take her father's place.

Kathy was nervous, not about marrying Larry; she was concerned about what Dorine might be up to while nobody was around her.

Diane consoled her sister. "Don't worry, Tom, and I will keep her occupied. However, after Larry says I do, well, it's out of our hands." Diane giggled, hugging her sister and trying to settle Kathy's nerves.

Kathy couldn't help herself from laughing. "I love you."

"I love you, too, and you're beautiful. The dress fits perfectly. I'm sorry I wasn't down here to help you more. You know, with all the arrangements." Diane said.

"Larry's mother and sister made most of the arrangements. With finals and graduation, I didn't have any time to plan the wedding. I told Larry that we should wait. Maybe until the end of summer, I would have more time, but his mother and sister were excited about putting this together. I said okay. I picked the dress out in California. Larry told me there was no limit, so I chose this dress. It cost over two thousand dollars." Kathy whispered to Diane.

Diane allowed her jaw to drop. "I think my dress cost $50.00 on sale at the budget J.C. Penney's," Diane said.

Kathy smiled and said. "It was a beautiful dress, if I remember correctly. It seems that the whole day is a blur to me. I guess that was because I was still grieving over Daddy. I mean, I was happy for you and Tom, but it was bittersweet to see you come down the aisle without our Daddy. Well, it was hard for me," Kathy confessed.

"It was hard on all of us, but I think knowing that Daddy was there in spirit made it possible for me to take the walk. He was such an important part of Tom's and my relationship that it just wouldn't have been right to have anybody take that spot." Diane smiled, remembering her wedding.

The string quartet started their warm-up music, signaling everybody to take a seat; the wedding was about to begin. Lana came into the dressing room. She had the pearls that her father gave her for her wedding. "I figure you would need something old. Kathy tried not to cry. She accepted the pearls, knowing how much they meant to her sister. She reached out to Lana.

Diane pulled out a blue silk handkerchief from her purse. "Now, both of you stop crying. This is the happiest day of your life." Diane commanded Kathy.

Lana pulled away, fanning herself. "I still can't believe that my baby sister is getting married.

Diane used the hanky to dab the tears away from Kathy. "Take a couple of deep breaths," Diane instructed Kathy.

Lana, help me get her makeup back on. It's showtime, girls."

Lana handed Diane the mascara, and Diane applied it to Kathy's eyes.

"Now listen, when all seems hard and impossible, just remember you are a Lore, and that's special because you have all of us right beside you." Diane held her sister tight.

A knock at the door brought the three sisters back to reality. Lana opened the door. Tom was there with a big smile, offering his hand and heart to Kathy, his sister-in-law.

Chapter 42

Oh No, Not Alice

1984, St. Paul, Minnesota

Alice was married for over 15 years before realizing her marriage was a sham. Her husband, Ronnie, was a poor excuse of a man, unable to keep his promise of loving his wife, but for her children's sake, she endured his abuse. It wasn't until it became physical that she had no choice but to end the marriage.

It was 3:00 in the afternoon. Alex, the oldest son of Alice, and Ronnie saw his father speed around the corner, even though Ronnie didn't see his son. The streets were slick from the cold weather. Alex bundled up, wearing his winter cap to keep his ears warm. When he arrived at his home, the front door was slightly open. Alex entered. "Mom?" Alex called out to his mother. When Alice didn't answer, he got scared, thinking about who had left the front door open. Alex went upstairs to his parents' bedroom, and next to the bed, he found his mother lying unconscious. Alex was startled with fear, hoping that his mother was still alive.

The silence of the room allowed Alex to hear his mother breathe. There was a pool of blood around her head, looking as though she had fallen on the wooden end table. Alex rushed to the kitchen, where the telephone hung on the wall.

"911, what is your emergency?" The operator asked.

Alex answered with a high, scared voice, "My Mom is on the floor. I think she is alive, but there's blood coming from her head."

"I have alerted an ambulance. What is your name?" The operator stated.

"Alex, Alex Stark. Alex answered her.

"Are you alone in the house?" asked the operator.

"Ya, I just got home, and the front door was open, and I found my mom." Alex tried not to cry.

"Okay, how old are you?" The operator tried to keep Alex on the telephone.

"Fifteen years old." Alex had to think before he answered.

"Alex, the ambulance, and the police will be there any moment." She informed Alex.

Alex heard the front door creak open. He set the telephone down and headed to the living room, where he saw his sister, Christy, and his little brother, Paul.

Alex rushed to his brother and sister and pulled them outside.

Christy started to cry, not knowing why her brother was so adamant about getting them out of the house. The sirens were heard from afar. The kids spotted vehicles approaching their house. Alex went to the sidewalk and flagged them to the house.

The firefighters were the first to arrive and approached the boy to discover the problem.

Alex cried out: "My mom is in her bedroom, and she's on the floor." Alex tried to explain.

The fireman rushed to the front door, waving the other to follow him. The paramedics arrived, and Alex only pointed to the front of the house. They rushed in with their oxygen tanks and medical bags.

The chief fireman came out to the three kids sitting on the front porch. The kids were afraid to hear the condition of their mother. "Your mother is hurt, but she is alive, and we are going to take her to the hospital. Can you call somebody over here to be with you guys?" The Chief said.

The police surrounded the house, keeping neighbors and spectators distanced from the children. Alex noticed several kids from school bundled behind the police.

"Aunt Diane?" Alex called out to his aunt over the telephone.

"Who's this?" Diane said in a cute tone, knowing it was a kid calling.

"Aunt Diane, it's me, Alex."

"Alex! What in the world are you *all* up to?"

Alex was crying. "They just took my Mom to the hospital. Somebody came into the house and hurt her."

Diane almost dropped the telephone. Not believing what she just heard.

"Where is your Dad?" Diane managed to ask Alex.

"I don't know. I saw my Dad leave the house right before I came home." Alex told his Aunt.

"Have you called your Aunt Lana?" Diane asked.

"I tried, but nobody was home. What do I do, Aunt Diane?"

"Do you have a neighbor you can call over?" Diane tried to suggest what to do.

"The police are here and won't let anybody come to the house. Please come out here. If it was my Dad, I don't want to be here with him." Alex explained, trying to stop himself from crying, but he was overwhelmed.

"I'll keep calling your Aunt Lana and head out right away. Did anybody tell you if your mom will be all right?" Diane pleaded.

"The fireman said that she was alive and that they were going to take her to the hospital," Alex told his aunt.

Okay, just stay with your sister and brother, and I'll get in touch with Lana. If they tell you anything, call me." Diane started to cry.

356

"My dad just pulled up in the driveway. He's talking to the police." Alex was describing what was happening outside. "They put handcuffs on him, and they're taking him to the police car." Alex's voice was shaking as he tried to communicate with Diane.

"Alex hangs up, just for a minute, let me try and find Lana," Diane instructed Alex. "I'll call you right back."

Diane hung up the telephone and screamed for Tom, who was outside on the patio with his best friend, Rick.

"The bastard hurt my sister." Diane cried, yelling at Tom. Tom rushed through the side door. "What?"

Diane was hysterical and tried to dial Lana's number. Her hands were shaking, causing her to hang up a couple of times, and making her fingers hit the correct numbers.

"Hello," Lana answered the telephone.

"Where have you been? You have to get over to Alice's, I think Ronnie hurt her, and the kids are all alone."

The telephone went silent. Lana was trying to make sense of what Diane was trying to convey.

"Is she all right?" Lana asked.

"I don't know they took her to the hospital. Call me when you get there. Alex said, Ronnie has just pulled up, and the police took him away in handcuffs."

"I'll head right over there," Lana said, hanging up the telephone.

Tell her that I'm on my way. Diane started to cry.

Alice was stuck in the emergency room. The doctors were concerned because she had lost a lot of blood. They placed her in intensive care, only allowing Lana in the room to sit with her. She hadn't woken up, and even though her brain waves were active, the doctors didn't know how long she would be in a comatose state.

***

Darkness surrounded Alice. It was as though she were floating, not knowing that she would fall endlessly if she just stood up. The air seemed pure, as if each breath she took purified her lungs. There was no light, no tunnel, just a sense of self.

Alice was suddenly surprised to hear her voice. Out of anger and confusion, she boldly faced the silence of God and asked Him questions that were always on her heart.

"Are you even real? Do I mean anything to you? Do you even hear me when I call you for help?"

Alice paused deliberately to see if the power around her would respond. It wasn't a massive voice, like the wizard from The Wizard of Oz. It was a sense of Peace and Love as a father who would lovingly speak to his child.

"How can you love somebody and allow such misery in their lives? Where are you, God? Look at me, my life, my marriage, there's something wrong here."

Alice realized the truth and wished she could take back

her words. Her mind was taken to the presence of Michael, her father. She started to cry, allowing her body to melt in the arms of her father.

"Daddy?" She felt his tender love as he whispered to her that everything would be all right.   When Alice opened her eyes, her father was gone, and she was floating, supported by the presence of God.

"Alice, why have you forsaken me? You have made all the decisions in your life, and when everything goes wrong, you cry to me, asking who I am and where I stand. An ominous voice filled her soul."

"The decisions you have made in your life are impetuous and ruthless, only finding room for your children in your life. When nobody wants to play with you, you blame me for all the heartaches." God continued. "Let me lead your ways. Trust me, Alice, and let my Spirit guide you. Believe in Me and have faith that I will never leave you or forsake you. I am your God, your Father, trust in Me, and let Me make you whole." The robust and gentle voice surrounded her, giving Alice peace and understanding.

Alice felt a cold, harsh push of wind scoop through her mouth. She gasped, the explosion from within popped her eyes open. She couldn't lift her head from the pillow. She opened her eyes and saw Lana asleep in a chair beside the bed.

Her memory was starting to return, along with all the pain, both emotionally and physically.

"She whispered Lana's name, but it was too soft to wake her. She moved her fingers and realized she could move her hand. She lifted her arm and touched Lana's leg. Lana woke up startled, realizing it was Alice who had woken her.

"You'll awake," Lana said, not knowing whether to be quiet or loud. She jumped to her feet and placed her face next to Alice's.

"I talked to God," Alice whispered. "I told Him that I was pissed." Alice smiled. "I saw Daddy. He held me and told me that everything would be all right." A tear formed and ran down Alice's cheek.

"I was so worried about you. That bastard is going to pay for this." Lana softly patted her sister on the shoulder.

"God said He would never leave me or forsake me." Alice interrupted her sister, not wanting to talk about Ronnie.

"Where's my kids?" Alice suddenly remembered her children.

"They're with John and the boys," Lana assured her sister. Alice lifted her hand to touch the side of her face. "I must look like a mess?"

"The bastard did a number on you this time." Lana frowned, angry and frustrated with the whole situation between

Alice and Ronnie. Being that this wasn't the first time Ronnie had beaten Alice. It was the first time Alice had to go to the hospital; therefore was forced to report the crime. The nurse came into the room and saw that Alice had come out of the coma. "Oh my gosh, how long have you been awake?" Right away, she grabbed her instruments and started taking tests on Alice. "Could you please go to the front desk and tell the head nurse that Mrs. Stark is awake." The nurse said to Lana, continuing to check Alice's vitals.

Lana left the room and passed a uniformed policeman outside her door. He asked her. "Has she come around yet?" Lana turned to him and nodded, yes. He immediately followed her to the front desk, calling his sergeant for further instructions.

Lana was happy that her sister seemed to be all right. She was glad that the police were involved this time. Her only hope was that Ronnie would be punished for inflicting such pain.

Alice told the police that Ronnie and she were arguing and that she grabbed him, trying to stop him from leaving the room. He turned fast and accidentally hit her, knocking her head on the night table.

The police released Ronnie but still cited him for leaving the accident scene.

Alice lied to the police for Ronnie, not for Ronnie's sake but for her children.

She grabbed Ronnie's shirt and tried to stop him from leaving the room. The only difference was that Ronnie turned around and punched Alice in the face, knocking her cold into the night table, leaving her to die as far as he was concerned.

After the police left, Alice felt alone. Waking from a nap, she called out to Ronnie. When her mind became clear, Alice remembered her husband had left her to face death alone. All the fears and insecurities crept into bed with Alice as she tried to shake her haunts away. Alice knew something had to be done between her and Ronnie. What would have happened to the children if she had died? Alice would have to make changes for herself and her children. Besides, she had long lost any love she felt for Ronnie. It was only a matter of trying to keep the family together. Alice was emotionally tired of trying to keep the marriage going. Ronnie treated her like dirt, and even though he claimed to love his children, they were his by name only. Ronnie had all the time in the world, but never enough time to play with the children. He drank too much, and when he wasn't drunk, he was high on marijuana or something worse.. Nothing satisfied him. Alice was too fat for him. The kids were whiners, and he blamed Alice for everything. The afternoon when he hit Alice, he had threatened her that he was going to leave them. Fifteen years were enough for him. He wanted a life, one without Alice and the kids.

Alice stared at the ceiling, "And you think my decisions are rash and ruthless. He beats me, and yet he is the one who wants out. Something's wrong here." Alice whispered to God.

Lana stayed with Alice all night; Diane and Tom arrived in Minnesota the next morning. Tom was furious and wanted to hurt Ronnie. Fortunately for Ronnie, he was in the custody of the police. He pleaded with Alice to move to Tennessee with him and Diane. Alice was so sad that she agreed with Tom, thinking she had to get her children to safety. She makes a deal with Tom when she ends her marriage to Ronnie. They would relocate to Tennessee.

When Tom went to Lana's house, Alice's children rushed to him, knowing their uncle would make it all go away. Christy was crying, knowing their lives were in trouble.

Alex looked his uncle in the eyes. "Please, Uncle Tom, help us."

Tom reached out and hugged his nephew. "Nobody will ever hurt you guys again," Tom swore to the kids. "If anybody tries, they'll answer to me."

Alex stepped back from his uncle. "Take us home with you. I don't want to live with my Dad."

Tom nodded to Alex. "You know, when I make a promise, I will always try my hardest to keep that promise. And I'm telling you, nobody will ever hurt you guys again.

It took Alice three years to complete the divorce process. She worked three jobs to make ends meet. The children and Alice were managing to survive without Ronnie. They didn't have to fear him anymore, mostly because he didn't want anything to do with them.

Alice was content with her relationship, or lack thereof, with Ronnie. She felt sad for Christy, who didn't have a father to hug, love, and conquer her fears. Even when he was around, he didn't have insight into how to be a good father.

Alex became the man of the house. He worked after school to help make ends meet. When alone at home, Alex made sure that his sister and brother were fed, their homework was done, and they were allowed a moment to share what was on their minds. He was a good brother and a caring son. Alex hated the fact that his mother had to work so much. He hated his father for being a slacker and not providing emotional or financial support. Alex appreciated his mother and always made sure to let her know that he loved her and appreciated all her hard work. Between Alex and Alice, the family was exceptional. The younger kids missed Alice, but understood she was working hard to keep them together. To Alice's eyes, the more she earned, the less chance she would have to ask Ronnie for anything.

After finishing his last year in high school, Alex and his family relocated to Tennessee. Alex was given a Job with his Uncle

Tom. Alice immediately found two jobs, and they managed to get a small house on the outskirts of Medford, Tennessee.

Diane and Tom found a man for Alice. His name was Bill, and he was a nice guy. He fell head over heels for Alice and truly understood when she told him she was too busy to think about a relationship. Frankly, if she had more time, she would have wanted to spend it with her children. Bill understood and realized it was not good to pressure her, even though her soul truly touched him.

Christy was ready to graduate, and Paul became an independent young man. Alex was living in Tennessee with a close friend from Minnesota. Everybody seemed to be happy, and nobody missed Ronnie in their life.

Alice was finding more and more peace with God. She always understood that there was a God, and she even grasped the power of God, so to Alice, there was no choice but to follow God. To realize that God wanted the best for Alice was hard for Alice to comprehend. Now, she was starting to seek God more. Asking Him for guidance and praying for the safety of her children, Alice found contentment in Tennessee and her relationship with God. She had to be willing to accept whatever God had for her. She felt all the pain and misery, and maybe this part of her life was necessary for her to understand God's love for her.

In Alice's mind, she will always remember when God personally told her, "I'll never leave you or forsake you." Alice reminded God nightly of his promise.

Bill and Alice had been casually dating for two years. They enjoyed each other's company, and when Bill asked Alice if there was any/ room in her life for him. Alice smiled, took his hand, and nodded yes. Bill almost fell off the barstool. He gave Alice a big smile, a soft hoot, and a holler that only Alice could hear.

"I didn't think this day would ever come," Bill said, looking Alice in the eyes.

Now, that doesn't mean I'm going to date you exclusively." Alice tried to keep a serious face.

Bill saw through her attempt at humor. "Oh, that's great because I wasn't ready to call it quits with, you know, all those other girls," Bill smirked.

"You better tell all those girls goodbye. It's not safe for them to come around ever again." Alice said as she bent over from her barstool to Bill's and placed her lips softly on his. Bill closed his eyes and allowed the joy to come to his heart.

"I love you," Bill whispered.

Alice kept her eyes closed and whispered back.

"I love you, too."

Chapter 43

Rock, Paper, Scissors

2004, Middleton, Tennessee

The girls were all in the living room, waiting for the right time to visit their mother. Kathy called the hospital, and the nurse said that Dorine was up and ready. She was doing so much better, taking control of her shared room. Kathy was relieved and told the nurse that they would be there within an hour.

"I think I'm going to leave tomorrow," Lana informed the others. The room went silent. Diane lit up a cigarette, and Susan came into the room, eating an apple. She sat on the floor next to Diane.

"I think we have to make a decision," Kathy announced. "Mama's doctor said she would have to stay in the hospital for a week more than she'll have to be taken care of. "I guess if nobody takes her, I'll talk to Larry and see if we can keep her with us." Kathy was disappointed with her sisters for not taking responsibility for their mother.

"What if we each take her for a month at a time," Diane suggested. I can't handle a permanent living situation now." Diane confessed, "I just don't have the patience for her."

"Listen, I'll help you guys anyway you want, but I can't imagine us together for a month," Lana spoke up to the girls.

Susan swallowed the last piece of apple. "Hell, I probably could use the company for a month at a time. She better not try to organize me." Susan laughed.

"Then that settles it. Mama will travel between the four of us. Is that okay, Alice?"

Alice smiled, "I think it will do us all good."

"I'm sorry I can't take her." Lana pleaded with her sisters.

Diane was the first to respond. "I think we all know that you and Mama haven't had any relationship for a long time. I think we'll be fine between the four of us." Diane smiled at Lana.

"Then, I'll say my goodbyes to Mom today," Lana said to the girls.

***

The hospital was busy, especially for a weekday. People were lined up in the gift shop, paying their dues, hoping that generosity would appease the god of sickness. The girls interlinked, settled into the community waiting room, Lana asked the girls if she could have a minute alone with Dorine, so that she could tell her that she was leaving for home.

Lana got up to leave and turned, smiling at her sisters as if she were in trouble, getting ready to receive her sentence. She decided to go to the gift shop and purchase a token gift to say goodbye. She bought a small teddy bear holding a small balloon, reading: 'I heart you.'

The hallway to Dorine's room seemed endless. The door to the room was open. She couldn't help trying to think when was the last time Dorine and she were in the same place together alone. All the drapes were pulled open, and each of the ladies was sitting up, talking with each other. Lana entered and bowed her head to each of them as if she were intruding.

"Hi Mom," Lana said, reaching over to kiss her, but instead stopped at her shoulder and pulled back before Dorine had a chance to reject her.

"You're looking good," Lana said, so that the other women could hear her. Dorine smiled as Lana pulled a chair up next to the bed.

"I'm thinking about leaving tomorrow." Lana blurted out. "The girls have a schedule, and they're going to take good care of you." Lana puts on a fake smile.

"I take it that you're not a part of that schedule?" Dorine said to Lana.

"Would you want me to be a part of that schedule?"

Dorine started to tear up. "Do I have to die before you forgive me?"

"Oh, Mom, do we have to do this now?" Lana became defensive.

Dorine pushed her lips together to keep the words within. She only stared at Lana, trying to figure out how she could reach her daughter.

"I'll tell you what, I hate Minnesota. I have always hated it there, but you wouldn't hear a peep out of me if you would take me home with you."

"Mom, you know we don't have much history between us."

"That's my exact point. If we don't take advantage of it now, well, who knows if we'll ever get a chance to get to know each other." Dorine said with sincerity.

Lana looked away to see if the other ladies were listening. She whispered to Dorine. "I don't think we could last two minutes with each other without killing each other."

"I sure would like to try." Dorine smiled at Lana.

Mom, I don't want to hurt you anymore. The past is the past, but to live with you, well, that's rubbing it in my face."

"I never thought any of my children would think of me as a piece of dog crap. Why'd you come, Lana? If I'm such a burden of bad memories to you, then why the hell are you here?" Dorine asked.

"I thought you were going to die. And I wanted to bury all the hurt between us."

"That's what I mean. Why do you have to wait until I die? Take me, Lana, give each of us a chance before I die." Dorine rushed the words, allowing tears to flow down her face.

Lana was placing her hand over her mouth, thinking of what to say. "Are you sure?" Lana said slowly.

"Just give us a chance. If in a month it doesn't work out well, just send me back to one of your sisters." Dorine instructed.

Lana allowed a tear to fall and nodded her head, yes. The two of them looked at each other and started to laugh. "The girls aren't going to believe this one," Lana said.

Lana stood up, "I'll go and break the news to them."

Dorine reached out and grabbed Lana's hand and squeezed it. Lana, for the first time in a long time, squeezed back her hand and smiled.

You're not planning on hurting her, are you?" Alice let it slip out, Even Lana thought Alice's statement was too blunt. Shaking her head, no, to Alice, feeling hurt that Alice would think that of her.

"You mean, you forgave her for all the wrongs she did over the years?" Diane asked.

Lana turned to Diane. "Hell no! But I think it's time to give it a try."

Alice stood up and hugged her sister. "Just when I'm convinced there is no heart in you, you pull something like this! I love you, Lana."

"She says she needs me and that I need her. I think she's right. It's time to face all that I have hated all these years." Lana announced to her sisters.

"I think it's great! She can be a handful, but there is something about her worth loving." Diane said to Lana.

"Besides, if she gives me one bit of trouble, I will not hesitate to put her away, and believe me, it won't be a quaint place. I'll make sure the nurses are mean." Lana broke out in laughter.

The girls all gave a group hug and were pleased that Lana and their Mother. All I can say is we will give it a try.

Chapter 44

Diane Reaches Out For Help

2004 Medford, Tennessee

It had been almost two years since Tom had passed away. Diane never had a chance to grieve her husband's death. Her friends and family were there to fill the loneliness, and the attention they gave her helped fill the void. When things started to settle, Dorine fell ill.

After Dorine left the hospital, the reality that Diane's husband was dead came upon her. She felt a depression that she allowed to linger. Diane didn't have the strength to answer the telephone, and most nights, as a new ritual, she would close her windows tightly and sit in the family room, crying. She was angry that she was left behind. Diane reconciled with God years ago, concerning the death of her father. Tom helped her to regain her faith. Now that Tom was gone, there was nobody to assure her that God was even there. And if He was, she really couldn't feel Him; she seemed to have lost her faith.

Kathy told her that God hadn't abandoned her, that Jesus loved her. It was hard for Diane to hear this, because if He loved her, then why did she feel so alone? It was Alice who demanded that Diane see a psychologist. Diane, having enough sense to realize she needed help, agreed to see Dr. Mark.

Dr. Mark was in his mid-forties. He worked out of his house, catering to a select clientele. He had a face that was both professional and friendly. When Diane forced herself to knock on his door, she was determined to give Dr. Mark a chance.

"I know it's going to be a waste. I'll probably end up solving all of his problems." Diane told Alice over the telephone. "Just give him a chance. He's good, and you deserve the best." Alice reassured her.

"Diane, I know that your husband has passed away, and I want to start by saying that I feel sorry for you." Dr. Mark started the conversation while Diane stepped into the examining room.

Diane was quiet and didn't want him to feel sorry for her. "Okay, that pisses me off. I'm tired of people feeling sorry for me. They don't know the pain I'm feeling, nor do I wish this pain onto anybody." Diane said, lying down on the sofa.

"I don't believe you have to be lying down to confront who you are." Dr. Mark said, not wanting to embarrass her. Diane sat up, sitting straight on the couch.

"Now you need to relax. If you want, you can lie down. Let's just start over and have a conversation. Diane, you need to pretend that you have known me for years. And in knowing me, you must believe that I would never judge you. You need to have confidence in me that I'm here because I want to help you. With these rules, you can tell me anything. Nothing would surprise me, and who gives a damn if it does? I am here for you. I'm not an individual. I am your alter ego, who will be honest with you."

Diane nodded her head, yes. Not hearing a word that Dr. Mark had said. She was thinking about the script she had decided she was going to share with him.

"Diane, let's talk about when you were a child. Tell me about the first time you felt love."

Diane closed her eyes, trying to remember that far back. "My sister Kathy and I were roller skating. Daddy bought us skates for Christmas. We were racing, and of course, I was leading. There was a big crack in the sidewalk; the winter cold caused the slab to separate. I was looking back at Kathy, teasing her that I was ahead. I hit the crack, and my whole body flew forward, scraping my face, mostly my nose, and my hands. My knees shredded as I landed flat on the sidewalk. Daddy heard my screams and rushed to me. He picked me up and carried me inside the house. He cleared the kitchen table with one free hand, and he lay me on my back.

Lana came into the kitchen and immediately grabbed a towel. Alice, my sister, went to the cupboard and pulled out a pan, filling it with water. Daddy calmly told me that I would be all right and that he was there to help me feel better. His voice and concern made the pain bearable. He took the towel from Lana and wiped my tears. He softly wiped the blood from each of the wounds. With each wipe, he told me how much he loved me. He told me that I was amazing, that I was a brave girl. When the blood cleared, he sat me up and hugged me. He kissed my cheek and blew the sting off my nose. I knew it must have been wrong because Lana and Alice were crying. But Daddy stood strong and told me that I was still beautiful."

Diane stopped to see if she had said enough to Dr. Mark.

Dr. Mark leaned forward and softly told Diane, "That was beautiful. Your father sounds like he was quite a caretaker."

"He was always there for all of us," Diane added.

"Okay, that was good, now let's talk about it. I asked you to tell me about the first time you felt love. And the incident you chose is a time when you were in pain. I think that is significant to the pain that you feel now. Where is your Daddy? Where is your husband? Who else can love you when you are in pain?"

"Diane started to cry. My Daddy is dead, and my husband is dead. And there is nobody to make the pain go away."

"Diane, think about it. What did your father really do? Did he perform surgery, or was it the magic of his love that killed the pain? It was the magic that you accepted in place of the pain. You believed in him, and when he told you that you would be all right, you listened to him. Even though your sisters were crying, which should have scared you, but you knew your father and that he was telling you the truth. His love for you bandaged the pain and fear. The most important part of this story was that you made the pain go away. It was only words, care, and love that your father could offer. It was you who accepted, believed, and made the pain go away."

Diane, you were a child then, and now, you still have the power to make the pain go away. It wasn't the words that healed. It was knowing that your father loved you. You need to draw strength from all the people you love, especially those who love you the most. And let this love be the one to make the pain go away.

"Yeah, but they're not here to love me." Diane cried.

"They are here." Mark pointed to Diane's heart. They live right here, and right here." Mark put his hands on Diane's head. It's only their physical bodies that have passed on. If you believe that they loved you, then that same love can heal you now. Just remember how precious that love was and how wonderful it felt. And find within yourself that love that makes you whole."

Diane continued to seek Dr. Mark and realized that love was not exclusive to her father and husband. That love was more than what one person could offer. There was the love of God, her children, her sisters, and, most of all, the love she had within herself.

Chapter 45

No Expeditions, No Anticipations

2004, St Paul, Minnesota

Dorine had to stay in the hospital for the entire week. By the time she was ready to leave, she was wheeling herself around the hospital in a wheelchair, making friends with patients on her floor.

Lana had gone home to Minnesota to make all the arrangements for her mother's arrival. John was just as surprised as Lana's sisters were when she told him that Dorine was coming to live with them for a while. It wasn't as though he was against the idea of Dorine residing with them. It was a shock to hear that Lana had invited her mother to live with them.

"I guess it will work. The boys are gone, and she could have either one of their bedrooms."

John paused for a moment. "Are you sure you are my wife?" John first grinned, and then he started to laugh. "I'm sorry, it's just for so many years."

Lana touched her husband's hand. "I know, and it might not work, but she is right if we don't do it now, when will we ever have a chance to see who we are?"

John reached over and hugged his wife. "I'm so proud of you. I think this is the best thing for both of you." John pulled away from Lana. "Do you think I should go hide the whiskey?" John started to laugh, hugging his wife one more time.

It was in the middle of June, and the mugginess of Minnesota had come early this year. Dorine arrived in Minnesota, escorted by two stewards, both of whom were men. Lana smiled when she saw her mother, thinking how full of life she was for a woman who was facing death a few weeks before. Dorine was laughing with the guys when they reached Lana. Dorine asked Lana for her address so she could give it to the boys. Lana, a little embarrassed, smiled, reaching into her purse for a pen.

"Oh sweetie, I'm just kidding, what would these two young men want with an old lady like me. They were just perfect gentlemen, and if I had a million dollars, I would give it to each of them." Dorine smiled and patted the young man's hand, bidding each of them goodbye.

One of the stewards smiled at Lana and told her, "She sure has a lot of fire in her. You sure are blessed to have such a mother."

Lana only smiled, thinking to herself. Fire is a good description of her.

The traffic jammed as we headed to St. Paul from the airport. Dorine just looked out the window, remembering the years she resided in Minnesota. "I know it's been years since I lived here, but it's amazing to me that nothing has really changed. I mean, yes, you have that great big 'Mall of America,' and the airport has grown enormously, but way out there, I bet you that bush over by that pond has been here since I left."

"Did you hate Minnesota that much?" Lana nicely asked.

Yeah, I think I did. My life was a complete mess in those days, and I'm truly embarrassed to admit it. It's hard to face the pains of your life, especially when they are so deep."

"Is that what this is about, Mom? Facing the pains of life."

"If it helps you to understand me more, then I'm ready to face the devil himself."

"Mom, I think that is the nicest thing I have ever heard you say to me. Thank you." Lana sincerely said.

The two of them pulled into a circular driveway lined with trees that covered the pathway.

"This is beautiful. I forgot what a lovely home you have." Dorine said, looking around at the beauty of the yard. "It's like driving into the hands of God, a good feeling," Dorine said.

"It has taken a lot of hard work to make this all, but John and I were pretty committed to providing a good home for the kids," Lana said.

Dorine was silent, thinking that it was a shot at her. "You have done a good job, Lana, and I know I made a mess of all of your lives," Dorine said quietly.

"Mom, that's not what I meant. Listen, I have a lot of skeletons in my life that don't make me proud. This is not the time to make you feel bad for your wrongs. So, each of us needs to face our past and let it die. There is no way we can change it. For me to make you feel bad, or for you to make judgments about me, is not beneficial for either of us. If I make a statement that makes you feel bad, I'm sorry, but I'm not trying to hurt your feelings. It has taken a lot of work from John and me to make our home a priority. In doing this, we have failed our children and our lives in other ways. Mom, no difference, wrong is wrong, and all the right things we do are what we need to dwell on. Like you being here right now. That's a good thing for both of us." Lana smiled at her mother. Dorine was silent and felt welcomed into Lana's world.

John was home when Lana and Dorine arrived. He welcomed them at the door, and Dorine was pleasantly surprised by how much the two of them had accomplished in their lives.

"John, you are a good man. Thank you for taking such good care of my daughter." Dorine sincerely said to John.

John put his arm around Lana, "I'm the lucky one. She is the one who has kept our family together. She's been a wonderful wife and a good mother to our boys."

"I can't believe it's been so long since we've all seen each other. This is good, and I'm glad to be here. I hope that I won't be a bother to either of you. If I had my way, I would be happy to go back to my own home and care for myself. And who knows, maybe soon that will be possible."

"Let's not talk about that now. Let's get you strong and back to your old self." Lana said to her mom. "I think you need to go to your room and rest. The boys are coming over for dinner, and they are anxious to see you." Lana reached out and placed her hand through her mother's arm. "John has fixed up Junior's room for you. I hope everything will be to your liking?" Lana nicely said.

"I've lived in rooms that had holes as big as baseballs. I'm sure it will be fine."

The telephone rang, and it was Diane on the other end of the line. "How's it going? Do I need to head to the airport to pick her up?" Diane chuckled.

Lana smiled and whispered back on the telephone that everything was going smoothly.

John led Dorine to her room. Lana waved to her mother and told her that she would wake her up when the boys got there. She continued her conversation with Diane, as Dorine followed John.

The sun was trying to set but seemed to linger, causing the sky to be a vibrant orange and red. The boys had arrived promptly, as their mother had demanded. They were laughing as they approached the door and walked in.

"Mom? Dad?" Junior called out.

Lana peeked her head from the kitchen and waved the boys over to her. They each hugged her and told her that they missed her and were glad that she was home.

"I thought Dad was going to go into a depression each night being in this big house without you. He started bringing out the old photo albums, showing us how young the two of you were." Steve giggled.

"We tried to take him out a couple of times, but he didn't want to leave the house," Junior added.

John walked in and heard his boys telling stories. "I didn't want to go because when I did, they took me to one of those disco clubs."

Steve laughed, "Dad, discos were in the seventies. The club we took you to was a lounge with two piano players."

"All I know is that it was loud, and I was afraid girls would get the wrong idea and think that I was a player." John tried not to smile, acting faithful to his wife.

"Mom, where's grandma?" Junior asked.

"Oh, I have to wake her up." Lana rushed down the hall.

Lana knocked on the door and peeked her head through the crack. "Mom, are you awake?"

Dorine smiled. "I've been sitting here for hours. What time do you people eat dinner?"

Lana made a face, forgetting that Dorine was probably on a different schedule. "Oh, I'm sorry, I should have told you that it would be a late dinner, because the boys had to get off work first. Are you starving?" Lana asked.

"No, just getting used to my new room."

"Come on. The boys are anxious to meet you." Lana opened the door wide to see that her mother was fully dressed and had applied lipstick to her lips.

"Do you think I must wear nylons?"

No, mom, you're at home, you can wear whatever you feel comfortable in," Lana reassured her mother.

The two of them headed to the dining room, where John and the boys were already seated. When they entered, the boys rose from their seats to pay their respects to their grandmother.

"Oh, my, for some reason, when I think of my grandsons, I think of them as being young boys. You both are young men, very handsome young men." Dorine was overwhelmed by their presence. Junior came around and pulled out a chair for Dorine, "And such a gentleman, too." Dorine said, accepting his polite jest.

"Grandma, I'm Junior."

"And I'm Steve." Steve cut Junior off, excited to meet his grandmother for the very first time.

Dorine closed her eyes, enjoying the moment as if she had just taken a big bite of prime steak. She tried to think of something witty to say, but no words would come to mind.

"I hope you want us to call you, Grandma." Steve broke the silence.

"Susan's child, Haley, calls me Granny, but Grandma sounds good."

Lana left the room and went to the kitchen.

"Dorine, did you get any rest?" John said.

"I just wish your father could come around and call me Mom. After all, he's been my son-in-law for over 30 years."

John blushed and felt like he had just been scolded in front of his boys.

"Mom, hum, I like that," John said.

Lana came into the room with a large roast, accompanied

by potatoes filling up the plate. She set the platter down as the boys waited for their father to say the prayer.

"Lord, we thank you for this food. We thank you for bringing Dor... Mom, to our home, we ask that you bless her with good health. In your precious name. Amen"

The boys repeated Amen and reached for the potatoes.

Dorine smiled. "I remember as a child, my father saying a prayer, and my brothers would be sitting there, hoping that it wasn't going to be a long sermon. Just as soon as he said amen, they would be reaching for the meal, making sure they got the best piece." Dorine started to laugh.

"Mama, are your parents still alive?"

"Oh sweetie, they would be way in their 90s, and everybody knows hillbillies don't live past their 60s. You know, with all their bad eating and drinking."

"Hillbillies," Steve spoke up. "Your parents were hillbillies?" He looked at Junior, trying not to laugh.

"Yep, they lived on a mountain just north of Goldenville, Kentucky." I'll bet you that they never left that hill until the day they died." Dorine reported with a sense of pride. The house they lived in belonged to my grandfather, on my Daddy's side, and when I was a baby, my parents moved us in and had four more to boot."

"Mom, you never told us these stories." Junior glared at his mother.

"Oh, I hope I haven't over spoke myself." Dorine turned to Lana.

"Well, I don't know too many of these stories, I guess I would be interested in hearing about your family." Lana pleaded that it wasn't her fault that her mother wasn't around to share these stories with her. "I mean, I knew you were from Kentucky, but your family being hillbillies, well, I never imagined," Lana looked to John to make sure this was all okay.

"I think you are giving the boys the wrong impression of their relatives," John interjected.

"No, they were all American hillbillies, and they were proud of it. That is why they never came down off the mountain."

"Do you mean like the Waltons. Steve said, looking at Junior, "Do you remember that TV show. There was John-boy and a hundred other children.

"Oh yeah, that's the show that ended each episode with "Good night John-boy, Good night Mama, Good night Daddy," Junior added.

The family all started to laugh, thinking about their experience with hillbillies.

What was it like growing up on a mountain?" Steve asked.

"Do you mean what was it like to be a hillbilly?" Dorine smiled and asked.

"Yeah." Steve seriously wanted to know.

"It was a hard way of life. You have no belongings, not even yourself, and everything is about the family, or at least the boys of the family." Dorine remembered. "It was a long time ago, I hope all has changed since the time I was home. But then again, nothing changed over the previous years." Dorine thought out loud. "It was a hard life with no rules for the boys, and no respect for being a girl in the family."

"Are there still family members there?" Junior asked.

"I don't know. When I left the mountain, I never looked back." Dorine said.

"I'm sure there's somebody still alive and living there." Dorine continued. It took all the power of God to help me escape. There was no way I was ever going to go back."

"Was our Grandpa a hillbilly?" Steve asked.

Lana spoke up. "No, his father and mother came from Germany."

"Your grandfather knew that I was a hillbilly, but during those times, there were a lot of poor folk, and Tennessee had its own hillbillies. You gotta understand, the meaning of being a hillbilly is family. Hillbillies don't have much, but they have each other, for me, a little too much.

And if they are lucky enough to have a piece of land and a still in the backyard, then they are a true family. But nowadays, who knows what these people are up to?"

"Do you know how to make 'hooch?" Steve asked.

"I'm a lady, and girls weren't allowed to be by the still. But I know good hooch from bad hooch." Dorine smiled, winking at her grandchild.

The dinner went well; the boys were interested in their Grandmother's stories and considered her quite the character. Steve seemed a little more interested in Dorine than Junior, but they both showed her respect and honor.

***

Lana and Dorine were driving back from the Mall of America. "Mom, I can't believe it's been six months. To think that we couldn't spend one hour alone without fighting. Having you with us has been a true enlightenment for me. I hope I haven't disappointed you?"

"Sweetie, this has been one of the most precious times in my life. I have gained a new respect for my daughter. I have a real relationship with my grandchildren and have fallen in love with my son-in-law." Dorine smiled. "I want to go home to my house in Tennessee. I think that I'm strong enough to take care of myself. I have my plants, animals, and memories, and besides, you and John need your space. You don't need this old lady hanging around."

Lana smiled, knowing it was best not to argue with her mother. "I'm going to miss you, and that feels good to say." Lana smiled, keeping her eyes on the road, taking small glances at her mother next to her.

"Can I impose upon you one more time?" Dorine sweetly asked, not giving Lana a chance to answer. "I want to go home to Kentucky one last time before I die. Would you come with me?" Dorine asked.

"To Kentucky, do you still remember how to get there?" Lana said.

"If you can get me to Goldenville, then I can get us home." Dorine pleaded.

"Okay, yeah, I'll go with you. But how do we know if there is still family there?"

"I don't know, but deep in my bones, I think the house and family are still a kicking."

When John got home, Lana told him that Dorine was going to be moving back to Tennessee. He was getting used to having his mother-in-law at the house. "I think I'm going to miss her," John said. "She kind of grows on you." He smiled.

"She wants me to go with her to Kentucky, to her family home on the mountain," Lana added.

"Are you going?" John asked.

"I told her I would, but frankly, I'm scared." Lana hugged her husband. "Do you want me to come with you?" John asked.

"No, I think it's one of those things again that I need to do." Lana released her husband.

"Then you better do it. Besides, I think it might be interesting for you." John concluded.

Chapter 46

Sisters Sharing the Untalkable

Dorine moved back to Tennessee. Alex, Alice's son, who was experiencing marital problems, moved in with Dorine. The two of them needed each other, even though the combination was different; they both cared for each other, keeping their independence intact. Dorine was happy being home, feeling a sense of self-worth and a responsibility to move her life forward. She was active with the senior citizens, playing cards, and going on trips. Dorine knew that staying idle would kill her; people in her life would keep her alive. Most of the time, she drove into town, but lately, Alex had been taking her to her activities and sometimes volunteering his time to move the older folks around.

It was the summer of 2005 when Lana called Dorine and asked her if she was still interested in traveling to Kentucky. Dorine got all excited and said, "Yes."

"I haven't mentioned it to you, just in case you really didn't want to go, but yeah, I would love to go," Dorine said.

"I'll fly to Tennessee and visit with Diane, then the two of us can take off on our venture," Lana said.

Dorine silently smiled, happy that she was finally on her way home.

2005 Medford, Tennessee

It was mid-April, and all the wildflowers bathed the side of the rolling hills of Tennessee. The morning breeze was soft, giving the air a freshness of spring. Lana rented a car from the airport and drove to Diane's house. It was a pleasure to visit her sister; there were no deaths, no sickness, just a time to share and receive love.

Diane was outside running to the car when Lana rolled up in the driveway. Her smile was wide, her heart bursting out to her sister as they hugged each other.

"This is so nice. I couldn't believe it when I got your message that you were coming out. Look at you! You look like a fresh peach ready to be picked." Diane complimented her sister.

"You look good too!" I know it's been a tough road, but you really do look good. And look at your hair. You have always looked so beautiful with your hair long."

"Come on, let's go in. I want to hear all about you, John, and the boys." Diane took Lana's arm and led her into the house.

"You changed the house all around. It looks beautiful." Lana said, setting her purse on the kitchen table. Okay, what have you been up to? Are your boys doing okay?" Lana asked.

Ronnie has finally settled down in college, and I think Paul is going to be a minister. He graduates from Tennessee State in a couple of months, and now he's telling me that he wants to get a Master's degree in theology. I guess he wants to learn more and more about God." Diane smiled.

"How have the boys recovered from Tom's death?" Lana asked.

"I think at times it's tough, but we talk a lot about it, and I think that helps. It's kind of funny, but when Daddy died, nobody talked about it. Of course, I got married and moved away from Houston, but I think for me, if I didn't mention it, then maybe it didn't happen." Diane said. "Hey, how about something to drink? It's only 10:00 in the morning, but I could make a killer Bloody Mary."

"You know me, if it's not whiskey, it's not liquor. Besides, I was hoping we could do some shopping. Mom and I are going to Kentucky, and I don't have a thing to wear. How do you dress to meet hillbillies?" Lana started to laugh.

"Mama told me, I can't believe you two. Most people go to Hawaii or Las Vegas, and you and Mama go to Kentucky. Whose idea was this?" Diane chuckled.

"It was mom's idea, and I think it's important to her, so what the hell." Lana quickly said.

"I'm so proud of you, how you have given yourself and Mama a chance. I know it's all still right there, the hurt and the feeling she caused, but she is our mother. Good for you, girl." Diane expressed, reaching out for a hug.

"How's your boys doing?" Diane asked.

"I think my grandson is coming from California for the summer. Junior is excited; he misses his boy so much. Steve is dating a new girl. He tells me, "Isn't she hot?" God, I wish he would find a good girl, not one who is so "Hot." Both girls giggled.

"I remember when we were hot," Diane said.

"That's funny because I only remember being pregnant." Lana lifted her head high, laughing at the thought of being so young.

"These girls these days. No way did we ever look so slutty. Here, my son, who wants to be a priest or a minister, brings home this Jezebel and dares to ask me if they can share the same room. I told him no. Go get a hotel, but in my home, there will be no sharing of rooms." Diane was lifting her hand in the air, nonverbally saying, "No way." "She ended up staying. Who do they think they're fooling? I saw her early in the morning, running from Paul's bedroom right to Ronnie's room. I think they don't even realize that we were young, too. Both girls started to laugh.

"So, how is it going with Dr. Mark? Lana reluctantly asked. I'm not sure if this is a suitable subject option.

"God, I wish I had gone to him years ago. I mean, it's not all heavy sessions, but when I leave there, I really feel good, and if I don't, it's because there are deep pits within me that need to be dealt with." Diane smiled. "Anyway, it's going well. Someday, I would like to talk to you about Daddy. But it doesn't have to be now."

"What about Daddy?" Lana softly asked.

"Just the fact that we never talk about him, I mean, it seems like when we buried him, everybody was so upset that we never discussed his death." Diane started to get teary-eyed. She lifted her head and continued. "I had a hard time over the years because I loved him so much, and yet he chose death over my love," Diane admitted to her sister.

"Daddy was sick, you and Susan did your best to keep him alive."

"We should have forced him to get help. What were we thinking?" Diane now started to cry.

"He didn't want help," Lana said. He wanted to be with his boys."

"But what about us? Didn't he find us worthy enough to keep his life going?" Diane pleaded with her sister.

"I think he was so depressed, tired, and disturbed that it wasn't a question of how much each of us loved him; he was through." Lana tried to comfort her sister. "I don't know about you, but I always try to keep the good things about him in my mind. All the years he gave himself to each of us. His total love, his sacrifices, and his ability to be both mother and father to us. That's what I remember of my father." Lana allowed a tear to rise and fall.

"I know, it just seemed he was doing fine. He was working again and had lots of friends who loved him. Daddy and Mama were getting along better than ever, and for him to suddenly decide to take his life. It just baffles me." Diane said. "You know, before he died, we used to spend every Tuesday together." Diane started to lose control. "It made me feel so special to have a day with him. God, if I only knew, I was so young. At the time, all I could talk about was Tom, and he would sit there, smile, and encourage me. He loved Tom, too. Tom would have done anything for Daddy. Hell, most of all, our dates were either spent with Daddy or Mama. At first, I thought it was just a ploy for Tom to get closer to me. After a while, when he had already won me over, his love for them continued. He wanted to see Mama and Daddy get back together. Sometimes, when I was at school, Tom would be over at Daddy's drinking and having a good time. Daddy's death had always been brutal on him. It's so hard when you give all of yourself to a person, and they die.

Lana shook her head, letting Diane know she understood. "I have always felt guilty that I didn't spend enough time with him. I loved him so much, and it always amazed me that he could make me feel as though he was only moments away, but it was always my problems, my life, that I needed him to repair. But just as you and Susan showed him, I think he knew that I loved him too." Lana started to cry. I wish he were still alive. Sometimes, living in Minnesota, I forget that he's dead, and even still, I think he is only a few states away. One time, Alice moved out. John and I were just having a few problems, mostly because I was utterly lost, having a husband and a baby. One night, I was sitting alone at home. John and Junior were at his mother's house, and I was just spending the time alone, trying to get myself together.

I called Daddy and told him that I was sad when I shouldn't have been feeling sad. The next day, he drove out just to hold me. He wanted to be that something familiar in a world that seemed so strange to me. Daddy held me, and I lay my head into his chest and allowed myself to explode inside, draining myself of all tears. Lana paused, gathering her thoughts and emotions. "At first it was sad, but when I realized that I was in my daddy's arms, my sadness went away, and I even started to laugh, because it all seemed so serious, and at that moment in his arms I completely understood that I was still alive."

I guess I just needed somebody to show me love. I knew that John loved me, and of course, my baby needed me, but I felt empty. When Daddy died, I was afraid I would never feel his love again. John told me how lucky I was to have a father who loved me. Some people don't have either parent who loves them as much as Daddy loved us. Lana reached out to Diane's hand. His love was unique, and that's why each of us loved him so much. If we didn't love him, or he didn't show his love, then it wouldn't have hurt so much." Lana explained to Diane.

Diane realized her sister was right, and as much as it hurt to talk about it, it felt enlightening being able to share with somebody who truly understood. "I think I always hid my feelings of Daddy's death with Tom. But now that Tom has died, there's nobody to take away the pain when it all comes up. So, I'm dealing with it. Diane said, covering her mouth with her hands. "Sometimes I don't know if anybody is going to love me again, or if I really want to allow somebody to love me. I'm afraid that I would always be measuring the love of the person compared to Daddy's and Tom's love. I realize that it was best in my life to experience love, rather than never experiencing it. But when that love is gone, it's like a knife being slowly inserted into my gut." Diane looked up to see if Lana understood.

"I don't know, sweetie, but I do know it will drive us crazy if we keep trying to make sense of it. I'll tell you right now; it was real love."

It was close to 6:00 a.m. Diane was still asleep in her bedroom, and Lana was upstairs in Ronnie's room. There was a loud knock, and the familiar voice of their mother filtering through the front door, "Diane! Get up, child." Dorine yelled to her daughter.

Diane dragged herself out of bed, feeling the previous night's drinks she had had with Lana. When she reached the front door, Dorine was still pounding hard as if she were late for something.

"Mama, what are you doing? You're going to wake up the whole neighborhood."

Alex, Alice's son, was there even though he looked as though he was still asleep. "I told her it was too early, but she said that they had to get a move on if they were going to make it to Kentucky."

"Mama, are your nuts. I think you only have a three-hour drive to get to Goldenville."

Dorine, still in her curlers, hurried her way into the house. "Is Lana ready to go?" Dorine asked.

"No, she's still asleep," Diane complained.

"Lana, sweetie, let's get a move on," Dorine screamed at the top of her voice.

Lana groggily came to the landing of the stairs. "Mom, what in hell are you doing here so early?"

"Early, hell, half the day has already passed. Those mountain folks they rise early, and they go to bed early. We really need to get a move on." Dorine said, as sweet as pie.

Diane went into the kitchen to fix them all some coffee. "Do you all want me to make you some breakfast before you leave?" Diane asked, hoping they would say no.

No, thank you, sweetie. There just isn't the time. Maybe Lana and I can get something on the way over there. You know a driving break." Dorine tried to explain to Diane.

"Oh, Mama, you are going too far. It's not going to take long at all

to get there." Diane was annoyed, telling her mother for the second time. Dorin just pushed her lips together and stayed silent. In her mind, it had to be longer, or why else hadn't she made this trip before?

"Lana came down the stairs, ready to go. "Mom, you still have curlers in your hair." Lana didn't even say good morning first.

"Are you kidding, in this weather, if I take out my curlers now, my hair would be as straight as a board before we got out of this city," Dorine said, pouring herself a small cup of coffee. She had already made up her mind; it was only a matter of brushing out her hair for her to be ready.

Diane turned to Dorine and asked, "Where's Alex?" Dorine made a gesture with her face, saying she didn't know, being very careful not to leave too much lipstick on her cup. Diane walked out of the kitchen to the living room and found Alex curled up asleep on the front sofa. Diane went back into the kitchen.

Mama, you just better be careful, don't you be a running Alex out of your house, with your pestering, thinking he has to take you here and there. Alice will be right on you if you take advantage of her son." Diane warned Dorine.

He's fine, and I asked him very nicely last night before we went tobed," Dorine replied.

"Right, like what time was that?" Lana asked.

"Well, it was nearly eight o'clock," Dorine said, feeling as though she was on trial.

Diane chuckled, "Yeah, like a boy his age went to bed at 8:00 p.m."

"He said he didn't mind, and I offered to pay for the gas. we have to get on the road." Dorine smiled at her daughters.

***

Chapter 47

Homeward Bound

The drive to Kentucky was a little less than three hours. When Lana and Dorine reached the center of Goldenville, they decided to stop and eat breakfast.

"My grandfather lived somewhere down here. Dorine told Lana. He came to the house a few times, but I never recall visiting him. Probably couldn't afford the extra time to get us all down here."

Goldenville was a small city in comparison to Houston, St Paul, or any other place Dorine lived in her life. The people there were one step civilized than the mountain people themselves. Everyone was waving and talking to one another. Dorine and Lana had to explain why they were there at least three times, Dorine insisting that she do all the talking. Most people in town had a drawl that made them sound as though they were visiting a foreign country. Dorine almost got teary-eyed, just listening to folk making general conversation.

"So, where are you all visiting from?" A sweet girl with golden blonde hair politely asked Lana and Dorine.

"We're from Tennessee. Oh, I guess I am, but my daughter here is from Minnesota." Dorine rattled on.

The young girl just stared at them, not quite getting all that Dorine said.

After breakfast, Lana and Dorine figured they better get moving on with their mission. Dorine asked the waitress, Sally Sue, if she could point them in the direction of how to get to Middleton. Sally Sue thought for a moment, trying to comprehend all that Dorine said.

Middleton! That's where my family is from. What business do you have in Middleton?" Sally Sue is being a little cautious not to lead a stranger home.

Oh, my gracious," Dorine said a little too loudly. "Are you a Honeycutt?"

Yes, Mam," Well, my Mama was a Honeycutt, now she is a Smith after she married my Papa. The two of them almost spent an hour talking mountain talk. Dorine, a squealing like a happy pig, was talking to one of her own. Lana, a little embarrassed, since they were standing at the cash register, holding up a small line of people who wanted to pay and leave. Lana rushed Dorine out of the restaurant before she had an opportunity to ask Sally Sue all the questions she wanted to ask.

"My god, Lana, why are you in such a hurry?" Dorine said, stepping into the passenger side of the car.

"You were giving that poor girl your whole life story." Lana gave her the eyes.

"I was just trying to find out if we were family or not." Dorine muffled her voice, trying not to ruin the trip. I think she said to turn left at the stop sign and follow that road until you get out of town. Then she said there was a wooden sign with an arrow saying, Middleton.

Lana, agitated, said. "I know, I was standing right there and heard her directions."

Dorine just folded her arms, not wanting to fight with Lana.

Lana realized she had hurt her mother's feelings and was too hard on her. After all, she was just excited about being home. When they reached the edge of town, they saw the wooden sign indicating which way to go. Lana took a deep breath before allowing the car to enter the dirt road.

"Are you trying to tell me nobody ever paved this road since you left?" Lana cheerfully said, trying to make up.

Dorine was way too busy looking and remembering to even respond to Lana's comments.

"That's the creek where I stayed the first night from home," Dorine pointed, not too far from the main intersection. Lana slowed down, looking at a clump of trees and a small pond that settled over the rocks.

"How much further do you think?" Lana felt bad that she hadn't disclosed to the car rental agency that she would be off-roading.

"Well, when I walked, it took me pretty close to four hours to get to this place." Dorine tried to remember. Even Dorine was quiet as they continued up the hill, winding back and forth, dodging rivets in the road, keeping them under five miles an hour. When they got to the top of the mountain, the way ended in the Honeycutts' driveway. Lana turned in and was ready to proceed. Dorine stopped her, thinking that if things hadn't changed, it could be a dangerous thing to approach the house.

"I think we'd best wait here a moment to see if they want to come to us to meet us, or if we should go to them," Dorine said, looking up at the old house. "Oh my god, that's the house."

Sure enough, moments passed by, and a group of guys with rifles came up to the car. They surrounded Dorine and Lana, not knowing who they were.

"Excuse me, fellows," Dorine yelled out her window. "My name is Dorine Honeycutt, and this is my Daddy's place. Dorine looked up at the house and saw the woman coming out to the porch, wondering if it was a friend or foe coming to visit.

Dorine whispered to Lana, "Oh my god, it's just like the old days. The men are down here investigating, while the women and children stay in the safety of the house.

"How do you know about the Honeycutts?" one of the older boys said.

"My Mama and Daddy were Honeycutt's, and we lived right there in that house."

The boys all got talking, and a man about sixty-five years old, looking a hundred years old, came up to the car. He pushed his face right up to Lana and then quietly walked over to Dorine's side of the vehicle. He stared at her, and suddenly a smile broke out. "Well, I'll be a blowing over, if it's not my sister Dorine. I'm your little brother, Adam. It's been since I was a little boy that I last saw you, but you a looking like my mama, of course, having a lot of extra skin on you." Adam said. He turned to the other boys and announced that his sister had come home. The boys all got wild, yelling for the women to come on down here. Adam opened Dorine's door, and she got out, giving her brother a big hug.

Lana was afraid to get out, but even more afraid to stay in the car, so she allowed the boys to help her out. They were all talking at one time, excited to have visitors, especially family. The woman and children joined the men, each of them explaining who these people were. They gathered around Dorine as if she were a celebrity. Dorine really couldn't answer any direct questions. They all asked her things at one time.

"Oh, my Goodness, child." The younger girl folk were holding up this woman by her arms. "Dorine, I'm Lana, your cousin."

All fear left Dorine, and her heart settled on Lana, her cousin. Dorine wanted to reach out to her, but the surprise that she was still there was too overwhelming.

"When my Daddy was mean, dirty, spiteful, this woman, my cousin, gave me a helping hand. She wiggled away from the younger girls and moved up to Dorine."

Dorine moved to tears, grabbed hold of her cousin. "It's so good to see you. I never thought in a million years that I would ever get to see you again." Dorine cried.

Lana moved next to her mother, feeling the eyes of all her cousins on her.

"You all, this is your cousin, my daughter Lana. I named her after my dear cousin. I wanted her to be strong-minded and gentle."

Adam approached his sister and told the rest of the group to give them all some room. They all started up to the house, and Lana followed close to her mother.

The younger kids brought chairs from inside and set up on the porch. A couple of the girls brought out a large pitcher of lemonade with strawberries painted on the side.

"I can't tell you how many years I've waited for you to come home. Just to tell me of your adventures, all that it seems that I have missed."

"I can't believe you are still here. Did you ever leave?" Dorine asked.

"No, after you left, about a year later, I married your brother Henry. We had all these kids, and they all had kids. Some of them left, and a lot of us stayed. Lana tried to fit it all in. Pretty much we are still the same, just some of the older ones have passed on, and now the younger ones are pushing us older ones in that direction." Lana tried to chuckle but turned a laugh into a mean hack.

"My Henry died about five years ago, and it seems that I'm ready to meet my maker soon." Lana smiled.

"I can't believe that nothing has really changed. It's as though I left yesterday. The house, all the family." Dorine had to put her hands to her eyes to hide the tears she was shedding.

A woman, maybe in her sixties, came out of the house with a fresh-baked pie. "Hello, Aunt Dorine, my name is Dorine."

Lana smiled. "Dorine was my first child, and I named her after you."

Dorine put out her hand to shake the woman's hand. The woman smiled, lacking all her teeth. Mama has always told us so much about you." Dorine, Lana's daughter, said.

Dorine smiled. All my children know their Aunt Lana. They all know the story of how she helped me gather the strength to leave this mountain."

"Daddy said we weren't good enough for you," Adam seriously said, thinking about his sister. I was just a youngum when you left. I remember a crying on the porch here, waving goodbye.

Her brother touched Dorine. "I just couldn't live on the mountain when there was a valley below me." Dorine tried to explain to her brother.

"So many questions; what about Peggy? My sister."

"A young preacher man came to visit and asked your father for Peggy's hand. They married and moved to California together. I get a letter from her every Christmas. But since her wedding, she has never come home."

Dorine reached out to Lana's hand. "How long ago did my Daddy and Mama pass on?"

"Oh, your mother died a couple of years after you left. A bad flu came here and took her away. Your daddy lasted until 1982 and was the oldest man in these all parts. Until he went to meet the Lord, he would get up each morning and go to the still and taste the hooch throughout the day."

Dorine and Lana talked, cried, and shared their lives throughout the day. Lana Lore was giving a tour of the house by her cousin Dorine. They had extended the house since Dorine left, adding a new kitchen, bathroom, and three bedrooms to the south side of the house. Next to the side of the house was still the old outhouse that Dorine used when she was a child.

Lana was pleased to meet Dorine, her cousin, and asked if she would show her the still. The two of them excused themselves and left Dorine and Lana alone on the porch.

At the still, Adam oversaw the operation. In Lana's mind, she always imagined the still to be a few pots and pans hooked together with a garden hose. But it was nothing like that. There's a building and large vats that brew the mixture. All the research and years of experimenting make their hooch one of a kind. The boys were all sitting on the side of the building, gazing out over the mountain.

Lana realized that was how they knew that somebody was coming up the mountain.

"This is the original still?" Lana asked her cousin.

Dorine laughed. "No, my cousin Garret went off to school, and when he came back, he designed and made all this for our grandpa." Dorine handed Lana a jar filled with a sample of the alcohol.

Lana sat on the edge of the mountain and drank her drink. Lana was impressed. "Have you ever lived off the mountain?" Lana asked Dorine.

"I think sooner or later, all of us, one time or another, leave. We think we are going to find our way, but it always seems to lead us back home. These people are my family and my friends; for me, everybody else was a stranger in my life. I just didn't like feeling so alone." Dorine tried to explain.

You know us mountain folk; we all seem to marry early, but maybe it was the name and all the stories about my aunt that made me set out to be sure I wanted to marry. I was away for about a year, and my grandpa sent me money and letters. He kept saying, 'Now you better be sure of who you are.' And always know we love you the most right here at home. He never wrote it because he didn't know how to write, but he would tell my Mama, and she would write it for him.

"What was he like?" Lana had to ask.

"He was how anybody would picture their grandpa. He was big and burly, and always wanted to hug you. And if you were on the same porch as him, you had better be on his lap. He loved us all. He was very special."

Lana and Dorine finished their drinks and headed back to the house. Dorine and Lana were still on the porch, hugging and crying.

The ladies finished their lemonade and were sampling the hooch. Dorine, Lana's mother, was feeling nostalgic as she remembered it from her childhood. Just the different smell, the sweetness of the wildflowers, made Dorine sad that it had taken her so long to come home.

"You know all these years I have been searching and searching for my own personal mountain. When my husband tried to give me a good resting place, I was so afraid that it would take away all my freedom, so I would run until I felt safe. I was so certain that nothing was going to tie me down." Dorine looked at Lana, her daughter, "not even my own children could keep me in one place." Dorine felt a shame come over her. "I had the best of a husband, the finest kids, and blamed them all for trying to make me settle for who I was. And now that I'm home, I finally realize that this mountain has always been inside of me. That it's not this place that held me down, it's all the choices in my life and how I dealt with them that made me who I am. To think of all that fear I felt over the years, causing me not to settle my grief, was only my own mountain within me. It was just home all along. A place special for me, and I always thought all the bad had to come with it. How foolish can one person be?" Dorine looked at her daughter for forgiveness.

Lana reached over and took her mother's hand. She smiled at her mother, and a look of enlightenment came over her. Lana has never known her mother to admit to any wrongdoing in her life. She always believed that life has its direction. Whether it was life or death, Dorine didn't realize that life was surrounding her.

This day was totally unexpected to Lana. She had understood when she left Tennessee that it would be different, but the sharing of love and watching this family help each other was overwhelming. It was hard for Lana not to think about who really had the better life. Of course, her life was different, and to be confined to a mountain would probably never satisfy her. Throughout the day, she had to chuckle a couple of times, thinking of John living on this mountain, but this family made her miss her sisters, her grandchild, the happiness of her boys, as they strive to make their lives more successful. Maybe their mountains are within themselves, and they are blinding what is right, as Dorine did for so many years. Perhaps their failed marriages, their separation from their children, and the longing for truth are just right inside each of them.

The sun was falling in the west. The family wanted Lana and Dorine to stay for supper, but Lana was afraid of the road conditions at night. After embracing everybody, Dorine saved her last hug for her cousin, Lana. Tears came upon both as they held each other for the last time in this life.

Adam, her brother, hugged her tightly. "I remember the last time you left. I tried hard not to cry. I ran to the peak, watching you disappear around the mountain. That was the last time I saw you until today. Please don't make it a lifetime before you come back again. You'll always have family here. And this mountain will always welcome you and your family to our home."

Dorine released her brother and hurried into the car. As they started down the driveway, the whole family waved to them. Lana honked the horn of the rental car as they made their way onto the dirt road. When they got out of eyesight, Dorine and Lana could hear a couple of gunshots in the air, signifying that family had just left the mountain.

THE END